FEDERAL MULTIDISTRICT LITIGATION

IN A NUTSHELL®

ROBERT H. KLONOFF
Jordan D. Schnitzer Professor of Law
Dean of the Law School, 2007–2014
Lewis & Clark Law School

WEST ACADEMIC PUBLISHING

444 Cedar Street, Suite 700
St. Paul, MN 55101
1-877-888-1330

Printed in the United States of America

ISBN: 978-1-64020-254-2

To the many members of the federal bench who have served with distinction as federal multidistrict litigation judges or as members of the Judicial Panel on Multidistrict Litigation

PREFACE

This text is for students taking courses in complex litigation, advanced civil procedure, or mass torts. It is also designed as a concise book for members of the bench and bar who are handling multidistrict litigation cases. Its focus is on all aspects of federal multidistrict litigation (MDL), including statistics on MDL cases; comparisons with other aggregation devices (such as class actions); the decision of the Judicial Panel on Multidistrict Litigation (the Panel) to centralize cases (including the standards for centralization and the selection of the MDL district court and judge); appellate review of Panel decisions; tag-along cases; the role of the MDL transferee judge (including case management, designating lead lawyers and committees, deciding motions, conducting bellwether trials, overseeing settlements, and awarding attorneys' fees); choice-of-law issues in MDLs; personal jurisdiction and venue issues; remand of transferred cases; federal/state coordination (including state MDL statutes); and proposals for reform of MDL practice.

In addition to covering the topics listed above, I have included, as appendices, the MDL statute, the Panel's rules, and a case study of orders from the *Volkswagen "Clean Diesel"* MDL.

I have been immersed in the subject of multidistrict litigation for many years. In addition to my scholarship and teaching in complex litigation, I have served as an attorney in a number of MDL cases. I have also served as an expert in several high-profile MDL cases (some of which are discussed in this text), including: *BP Deepwater Horizon*, *Chinese-Manufactured Drywall*, *Equifax Data Breach*, *National Football League Concussion*, *National Prescription Opiate*, *Syngenta Corn*, and *Volkswagen "Clean Diesel."* In addition, I served as the academic member of the Federal Civil Rules Advisory Committee from 2011–2017, and was an Associate Reporter for the American Law Institute's project, *Principles of the Law of Aggregate Litigation*.

This Nutshell uses a number of conventions. Most importantly, because it cites numerous secondary sources, it uses an abbreviated cite form, with full citations in the table of secondary sources. For example, a law review article or book by Professor Robert Klonoff will be cited as Klonoff at ___. If Klonoff has two publications that are cited, they are further identified—*e.g.*, Klonoff (Wash. U.) at ___. The full list of citations in the table of secondary sources (*see* Appendix D) provides a treasure trove of additional resources on the various topics covered in this Nutshell. Another convention is that the Nutshell does not include references to citations omitted or footnotes omitted. With respect to italicized quotes, the Nutshell notes when emphasis is added but not when emphasis is in the original. At times, the Nutshell uses short form citations to save space (for instance, *Vioxx MDL* instead of *Vioxx Products Liability Litigation MDL*). The Nutshell also minimizes the use of signals, such as *See*. For instance, it omits the signal *See* when the citation is to a single secondary source. Finally, each of the many MDLs discussed in the text involves numerous important players: the Panel members who transferred the cases, the transferee judges, and the appointed leadership teams. The Nutshell omits the names of those various individuals in discussing specific cases. Based on the citations in the book, the reader can easily find the names of the key players. Ultimately, including so many names would have made the text read less like a Nutshell and more like a Russian novel.

I wish to express my appreciation to my research assistants. Jacob Abbott and Zach Nelson deserve special recognition for their major roles in all aspects of this Nutshell. Other research assistants who provided able assistance include Annie Barber, Hannah Clements, Sara Densmore, Anna Fugate, Meggie Kirchner, Gracey Nagle, Elizabeth Stowe, and Aaron Trukositz.

I also wish to thank Professors Elizabeth Chamblee Burch, Brian Fitzpatrick, Samuel Issacharoff, Alexandra Lahav, Arthur Miller, John Parry, and D. Theodore Rave; Judges Robert Dow, Jr., Paul Grimm, Lee Rosenthal, Michael Simon, and Amy St. Eve; senior research associate Margaret Williams; and attorneys Elizabeth Cabraser, Richard Clary, Stephen Herman, David Herr, Ben Pepper, and Christopher Seeger for their thoughtful comments on an earlier draft of this text.

Finally, Lisa Frenz of Lewis & Clark Law School deserves recognition for her assistance in the preparation of this text.

Of course, the statements and conclusions in this text are mine alone.

ROBERT H. KLONOFF

October 2019

OUTLINE

TABLE OF CASES

References are to Pages

FEDERAL MULTIDISTRICT LITIGATION

IN A NUTSHELL®

CHAPTER 1

INTRODUCTION TO FEDERAL MULTIDISTRICT LITIGATION

This Chapter introduces the basic concept of federal multidistrict litigation (MDL). It first provides an overview of the enabling statute. It then discusses the history leading to the statute's enactment. Next, it presents various statistics regarding the prevalence and types of multidistrict litigation cases. Following the statistical discussion, the Chapter provides an overview of the special procedural rules that govern multidistrict litigation practice. The Chapter then describes the MDL Panel's website, a useful resource for anyone involved in MDL practice. Finally, the Chapter compares and contrasts multidistrict litigation with several other devices for aggregating cases.

§ 1.1 OVERVIEW OF THE MULTIDISTRICT LITIGATION STATUTE

The multidistrict litigation (MDL) statute, 28 U.S.C. § 1407 (reproduced in Appendix A), was enacted in 1968. It provides, in relevant part, that "[w]hen civil actions involving one or more common questions of fact are pending in different [federal] districts, such actions may be transferred to any district for coordinated or consolidated pretrial proceedings." Such transfers are ordered by a special panel, established under section 1407, known as the Judicial Panel on Multidistrict Litigation (the "Panel" or "JPML"). The Panel consists of seven federal circuit and district court judges designated by the Chief Justice of the United States. The stated purpose of section 1407 is to achieve judicial efficiency in *pretrial* proceedings. (As discussed below, section 1407 requires that each case be sent back from the transferee court to its original district court, the transferor court, at the conclusion of pretrial proceedings.) In ordering transfer, the Panel must find that the actions involve "one or more common questions of fact . . . pending in different districts" and that transfer "will be for the convenience of parties and witnesses and will promote the just and efficient conduct of [the transferred] actions." 28 U.S.C. § 1407(a).

In essence, the Panel is free to centralize related federal cases (but not state cases) by transferring such cases to any district judge in the United States, even a judge who does not already have one or more of the cases to be centralized. And this is true even though some or all of the defendants may not be amenable to personal jurisdiction or venue in the transferee district. Once the Panel enters a transfer order, it has no role in overseeing the litigation (other than replacing an MDL judge who becomes unable to serve for any reason). It becomes involved again only if it must decide whether to transfer additional ("tag-along") cases (*see* §§ 6.1–6.3) or if it must decide whether to remand some or all of the cases to the transferor courts (*see* §§ 15.1–15.2).

The importance of MDL cannot be overstated. As discussed below (*see* § 1.4), MDL cases make up a significant percentage of the federal civil docket.

Since the statute's enactment in 1969, the MDL Panel has transferred hundreds of thousands of complicated, high-value cases for coordinated proceedings. These cases have included antitrust, data breach, employment, intellectual property, mass tort, and securities cases. Many of the most highly publicized civil cases in U.S. history have been MDLs, including *BP Deepwater Horizon*, *Volkswagen "Clean Diesel," National Football League Concussion*, numerous medical device and pharmaceutical cases, asbestos cases, cases involving major financial misconduct (such as the Bernie Madoff Ponzi scheme, litigation involving the collapse of Lehman Brothers, and litigation involving the 2006 home mortgage crisis), and many others. *See* Williams & George at 427–28 (providing numerous examples of high-profile MDL cases). Moreover, "the largest class action settlements of late . . . all emerged from MDL consolidation[s] . . . ." Cabraser & Issacharoff at 850–51.

A recent example of a prominent MDL is the opiate litigation, in which the Panel assigned numerous federal cases pending around the country to a federal judge in Cleveland. *In re Nat'l Prescription Opiate Litig.*, 290 F. Supp. 3d 1375 (J.P.M.L. 2017). The cases involve lawsuits by various governmental entities and other plaintiffs against major pharmaceutical manufacturers and distributors. The *Opiate* MDL has been widely covered in the popular press, and many billions of dollars are at stake. As one commentator notes, "the opioid-addiction crisis . . . has thrust MDL into the public consciousness." Bradt (Fordham) at 88. The MDL judge has appointed three special masters to oversee global settlement discussions, an approach that would be almost inconceivable without centralization of the cases.

At times, the litigation is so complicated and diverse that more than one MDL must be established. For instance, in the *BP Deepwater Horizon* litigation, the Panel selected a federal judge in New Orleans as transferee judge to handle the economic, property, and personal-injury claims, *In re Oil Spill by the Oil Rig "Deepwater Horizon" in the Gulf of Mexico, on Apr. 20, 2010*, 731 F. Supp. 2d 1352, 1356 (J.P.M.L. 2010), but selected a federal judge in Houston to handle the securities, pension, and shareholder-derivative suits, *In re BP p.l.c. Secs. Litig.*, 734 F. Supp. 2d 1376, 1378–79 (J.P.M.L. 2010). As another example, from 2010 to 2014, the Panel assigned seven separate MDLs involving different but related pelvic mesh products to "a single cross-cutting MDL coordinated proceeding within one court." *In re Cook Medical, Inc., Pelvic Repair Sys. Prods. Liab. Litig.*, 365 F. Supp. 3d 685, 692 (S.D.W.Va. 2019). In explaining the complicated nature of the litigation, the MDL judge noted that "[w]hat began as 36 plaintiffs suing one company for one allegedly defective pelvic mesh product transformed into over 104,000 individual plaintiffs suing numerous defendants who manufactured many different pelvic mesh products." *Id.* at 690.

One commentator states that more than 75 percent of MDLs involve class actions. Gluck at 1695. But some of the largest MDLs are product liability suits that frequently are not suitable for class action treatment because of individual issues of causation. *See* § 1.4.

Although section 1407 provides that centralization is for pretrial proceedings, it is "the worst kept secret in civil procedure" that transferred cases almost never return to their transferor courts. Gluck at 1673; *see also* MDL Standards at ix. Instead, virtually all of them are settled or otherwise disposed of by the transferee court. It is highly unlikely that the MDL statute's drafters contemplated that almost none of the cases would be remanded. *See* Bradt (Penn.) at 871. To the contrary, the drafters likely expected that "most cases" would be remanded at the conclusion of pretrial proceedings. Marcus (Tulane) at 2264–65.

MDL aggregation can empower plaintiffs and place pressure on defendants. But it can also benefit defendants by offering coordinated discovery (*e.g.*, minimizing the burdens on high-level corporate executives) and providing a mechanism to achieve global peace. Gluck at 1698.

The impact of the MDL process on the federal judiciary's caseload has been enormous. As the Panel Chair noted in 2015, "[i]n the 53 mass tort MDLs since 1968, the judges terminated 354,535 cases[.]" Vance Speech at 26. Because many (if not most) of those cases would not have been suitable for class certification, *see* § 1.4, the existence of the MDL process clearly avoided what could have been judicial paralysis. Of course, a counterargument is that the MDL process itself encourages the filing of cases. As one commentator has noted, in the multidistrict litigation world, "as in the *Field of Dreams*, '[i]f you build it, they will come.' " Herrmann (Litigation) at 45.

Curiously, despite the importance and sheer volume of MDL cases, the subject is rarely discussed in basic civil procedure courses. Indeed, the most widely used civil procedure casebooks devote, on average, only two pages to MDL. Gluck at 1672. As a result, most law school graduates have little or no exposure to the subject. Even the U.S. Supreme Court has rarely addressed MDL; it has decided only two cases raising MDL issues: *Gelboim v. Bank of America Corp.*, 135 S. Ct. 897 (2015), and *Lexecon, Inc. v. Milberg Weiss Bershad Hynes & Lerach*, 523 U.S. 26 (1998); *cf. Merck Sharp & Dohme Corp. v. Albrecht*, 139 S. Ct. 1668 (2019) (ruling on federal preemption issue in the context of the *Fosamax* pharmaceutical MDL). Those cases are discussed in §§ 8.7, 14.2, and 15.2.

A note on terminology: "The Panel uses the terms transfer and centralize somewhat interchangeably," Heyburn at 2227 n.12, as does this Nutshell. However, the term "centralize" is more encompassing; an MDL may include not only cases transferred from another district but also cases that were originally filed in the MDL court and do not need to be transferred.

The statute also refers to "coordinated or consolidated pretrial proceedings," but in practice, the Panel has not differentiated between "coordinated" and "consolidated" proceedings.

Heyburn at 2227 n. 12. The term "consolidated" proceedings suggests that the cases are joined "for the purpose literally of litigating identical issues on common evidence," whereas "coordinated" cases may be more loosely bound, while sharing a "common core" of fact. *Lexecon Inc. v. Milberg Weiss Bershad Hynes & Lerach*, 523 U.S. at 34.

§ 1.2 SCOPE OF CIVIL ACTIONS COVERED

The vast majority of civil actions are potentially eligible for transfer under the MDL statute, assuming that they meet the requirements of section 1407(a). Excluded from the statute, however, are antitrust actions filed by the United States (28 U.S.C. § 1407(g)) and injunctive suits brought by the Securities and Exchange Commission (SEC), absent SEC consent (15 U.S.C. § 78u(g)). Also, the statute does not apply to related *criminal* cases.

Strictly speaking, there is no legal impediment to centralizing cases that can be characterized as "public law" cases. For instance, myriad related suits have been filed against President Trump or other officials contesting executive actions such as the "travel ban." MDL treatment has not been used in these cases, and two commentators argue that such treatment would "risk[ ] politicizing the Panel[.]" Bradt & Clopton at 106–07.

The MDL statute "authorizes the Panel to transfer only 'civil actions,' not claims . . . ." Manual § 20.131. Despite that limitation, section 1407(a) enables the MDL Panel "to accomplish 'partial' transfer by (1) transferring an action in its entirety to the transferee district, and (2) simultaneously remanding to the transferor district any claims for which transfer was not deemed appropriate, such as cross-claims, counter-claims, or third-party claims." *Id. See* § 15.1.

It should be noted that, in certain cases, bankruptcy can be a significant limitation on the MDL judge's authority. Herr (Annotated Manual) § 20.14 (noting that "[t]he filing, and automatic stay of proceedings imposed by 11 U.S.C. § 362(a), can be quite disruptive of the proceedings in the transferee court," and citing authority discussing that issue).

§ 1.3 HISTORY OF THE MDL STATUTE

A. GENESIS: THE SPRAWLING ELECTRICAL EQUIPMENT ANTITRUST LITIGATION

The MDL statute was created based on the federal judiciary's experience in coordinating (without a statute) massive federal antitrust litigation in the early 1960s. In 1960, 20 indictments were issued against 29 electrical equipment manufacturers for antitrust violations. All of the cases were assigned to the Chief Judge of the Eastern District of Pennsylvania. Those cases were ultimately resolved through guilty pleas and fines.

In addition to the criminal litigation in Philadelphia, civil electrical equipment antitrust cases were filed across the country. In total, 25,632 claims were filed in 35 federal districts. To deal efficiently with those cases, the Judicial Conference of the United States created a subcommittee, the

Coordinating Committee on Multiple Litigation (Coordinating Committee), consisting of seven federal judges. The Coordinating Committee was tasked with helping to manage the litigation, including the coordination of depositions and other discovery in all of the civil cases. The Coordinating Committee had no authority to act, but instead relied on the "voluntary cooperation" of the various district judges assigned to the cases. Bradt (Penn.) at 857.

Through the work of the Coordinating Committee, great efficiencies were achieved. The plaintiffs' lawyers appointed a steering committee to assign the work. A depository was established in Chicago to store defendants' documents, and another depository was established in New York for plaintiffs' documents. Counsel for each side decided who would conduct the depositions—to be used by all parties—with other lawyers being permitted to ask additional questions. Uniform interrogatories were issued to defendants. Bradt (Penn.) at 857–58.

Settlement discussions subsequently ensued. In 1964, the largest defendant agreed to settle all claims against it for about $300 million. Numerous other cases settled as well. The judges assigned to the various cases decided to consolidate the remaining cases by designating a district for each product line. One defendant had approximately 365 remaining claims against it. The judges decided, over that defendant's objection, that those cases should all be consolidated in the Northern District of Illinois. The defendant sought mandamus, but the appellate court refused to grant relief, praising the efficiency of the transfer to achieve a resolution. After the transfer, the parties quickly reached settlements in various cases. Chief Justice Earl Warren praised the actions of the Coordinating Committee, saying that without the cooperation and efforts of the numerous judges involved, the workload consequences for the judiciary would have been disastrous. Bradt (Penn.) at 859–61; Williams & George at 430–32.

B. THE ENACTMENT OF SECTION 1407

The Coordinating Committee predicted that the electrical equipment antitrust cases would not be the last collection of related cases to burden the federal courts. Thus, the Committee undertook to identify what was successful in the electrical equipment litigation and to make those features permanent and broadly applicable. The Committee wanted its mechanism to apply in a wide variety of cases. Bradt (Penn.) at 869.

In 1964, members of the Coordinating Committee met in Chicago to begin drafting the MDL statute. In 1965, the Judicial Conference of the United States proposed a draft statute to Congress. The bill faced opposition from the American Bar Association, as defense lawyers were concerned that this litigation mechanism could adversely affect their clients. In 1968, the American Bar Association changed its position and voiced support for the legislation. Congress subsequently passed the bill, and President Johnson signed it into law. Bradt (Penn.) at 871, 883, 887, 902, 906.

The two principal drafters of the statute were Judge William Becker of the Western District of Missouri and Dean Phil Neal of the University of Chicago Law School. Becker was the chairman of the Coordinating Committee; Neal was the executive secretary. *See* Bradt (Penn.) at 871–907 (recounting the statute's history).

The history of MDL is informed by the Manual for Complex Litigation and the 1983 amendments to Federal Rule of Civil Procedure 16. The Manual was originally published in 1968, the same year that the MDL statute was enacted. "A number of the Manual's general principles regarding judicial control, the scheduling of the pretrial process, the pretrial elimination of extraneous matters, and the promotion of settlement and alternative dispute resolution were encapsulated in an extensive revision of Federal Rule 16" that took place in 1983. A. Miller at 294. That revision added detailed provisions on pretrial case management, reflecting the changing landscape of civil litigation and the judge's role as a case manager. In short, "the story of MDL is a microcosm of the story of modern [civil] procedure[.]" Bradt (Penn.) at 908.

§ 1.4 MDL STATISTICS

A. OVERALL STATISTICS

From its inception in 1968 through September 30, 2018, the Judicial Panel on Multidistrict Litigation has centralized 673,104 civil actions for pretrial proceedings. According to the 2018 statistics, 16,728 of these civil actions have been remanded for trial and 499,865 have been terminated (by settlement or dismissal) in the transferee courts. This leaves a total of 156,511 actions pending in front of the 48 transferee district courts as of September 30, 2018. 2018 Fiscal Year Statistics at 3.

MDL cases constitute 51.9 percent of the civil caseload in the federal district courts, according to a study released in March 2019. That number is up from 46.7 percent in 2017, and from only 16 percent in 2002. *See* LCJ, Rules 4 MDLs at 1; Fed. Civil Caseload at 1. (These numbers exclude Social Security cases and cases brought by prisoners, other than death penalty cases, although the rationale for excluding those cases is unclear.)

Focusing on the percentage of MDL cases in the total federal civil caseload is controversial because the average MDL case "lasts about twice as long" as the average non-MDL case. M.S. Williams at 1271. Thus, some commentators focus instead on the percentage of civil cases filed each year that are included in MDL proceedings. That number has been as high as 21 percent in recent years, but never close to the 51.9 percent figure noted above. *Id.* at 1272.

Whether the relevant figure is 21 percent or 51.9 percent, there has clearly been an explosion in MDL cases. The reason is not difficult to discern. As reflected in JPML statistics, mass tort personal injury cases make up more than 90 percent of all MDL cases. *See* Bradt (Penn.) at 843. Beginning in the 1990s, the federal courts—including the United States Supreme Court—made it very difficult for plaintiffs to obtain class certification in mass tort cases. *See* Mullenix (Emory) at 403. Seminal cases included *Amchem Products, Inc. v. Windsor*, 521 U.S. 591 (1997), and *Ortiz v. Fibreboard Corp.*, 527 U.S. 815 (1999), both of which overturned massive asbestos settlements on the ground that they did not meet the class certification requirements of Federal Rule of Civil Procedure 23. *See also, e.g., Castano v. Am. Tobacco Co.*, 84 F.3d 734 (5th Cir. 1996) (overturning class certification in tobacco class action); *In re Am. Med. Sys., Inc.*, 75 F.3d 1069 (6th Cir. 1996) (overturning class certification in case involving penile implants).

Without the availability of the class action device to aggregate thousands of mass tort claims in the federal courts, MDL became a logical method to achieve the efficiencies of aggregation. As a result, there are numerous mass tort MDLs, and they tend to contain large numbers of cases, making them much larger than most other kinds of MDLs. *See* M.S. Williams at 1273 (listing average MDL proceeding by size, type, and decade).

The difficulty in certifying mass tort class actions is not the only explanation for the explosion of mass tort MDLs. The Supreme Court's legalization of lawyer advertising in 1977 has led plaintiffs' lawyers to "develop[ ] massive advertising campaigns[.]" Vance Speech at 4. Also, "[t]he plaintiffs' bar has . . . become more sophisticated in its ability to finance large scale litigation" and in using large amounts made in one MDL to finance others. *Id.* In addition, the enactment of the Class Action Fairness Act of

2005 "made access to state court class certification much more difficult in the mass torts context." *Id.* at 6. As a result, federal court "MDL centralization has become one of the few options left for parties who seek aggregation of mass tort personal injury claims in a single forum." *Id. See generally* Willging & Lee at 806 (discussing the trend away from class certification and toward MDL in mass tort cases).

As noted, mass tort MDLs tend to be very large. In 2015 there were 21 mass tort MDLs, yet they "ma[d]e up 90% of the cases pending in all 268 MDL dockets . . . ." Vance Speech at 1. Focusing on the years 2008 to 2017, for example, the average product liability MDL encompassed 2,256.9 cases; in contrast, the average employment MDL encompassed 10.2 cases. Other categories include air crash MDLs (28.4 cases), antitrust MDLs (38.1 cases), common disaster MDLs (1,544 cases), contract MDLs (19.1 cases), intellectual property MDLs (16.3 cases) and securities MDLs (26.2 cases). M.S. Williams at 1273–74.

Most mass tort MDL cases have involved "widely used products, usually prescription drugs or medical devices." Vance Speech at 8. One prominent example is the pelvic mesh litigation discussed above. This was "the largest mass tort MDL phenomenon since asbestos." *Id.* at 9.

Given the high volume of mass tort cases within a relatively small number of MDLs, it follows that most of the remaining MDLs have far fewer cases. Thus, 22 MDLs (mostly mass torts) have 1,000 or more pending cases; 33 MDLs have between 101 and 999 pending cases; 87 MDLs have between 11 and 100 pending cases; and 57 MDLs have 10 or fewer pending cases. MDL Statistics Report, July 16, 2019 at 4. Over 90 percent of MDLs involve only "a few dozen plaintiffs," but a small number of MDLs have "hundreds or thousands of plaintiffs[.]" MDL Standards at ix. *See also* M.S. Williams at 1273–74 (listing MDL proceedings by size, decade, and type).

In terms of the overall number of MDL cases, as of July 16, 2019, there were 199 MDL dockets in 46 transferee districts before 158 judges (13 chief judges, 97 other active judges, and 48 senior judges). MDL Statistics Report, July 16, 2019 at 4.

B. CATEGORIES OF MDL MOTIONS AND GRANT RATES

Between 1968 and 2017, the largest category of motions for centralization was "miscellaneous" (654), which includes cases such as data breach, environmental contamination, and sports injuries. The largest remaining categories (with more than 100 motions for centralization) were securities (436), antitrust (404), product liability (340), sales practices (221), intellectual property (216), air crash (189), employment (164), and contract (154). M.S. Williams at 1262. The composition has changed over time. For example, centralization motions in product liability cases and sales practices cases have become much more common in recent years, with those two categories representing 37 percent of the total number of motions during 2008–2017, but only 19 percent of motions during the prior ten years. M.S. Williams at 1264.

Between 1968 and 2017, the Panel established 1,707 proceedings. From the enactment of the MDL statute in 1968 until 2013, 74 percent of the motions for centralization were granted. Lee, Borden, Williams & Scott at 219–20. For whatever reason, starting in 2015, the Panel has consistently denied more motions for centralization each year than it has granted. In 2015, the numbers were 33 grants versus 36 denials; in 2016 those numbers were 28 versus 29; in 2017 the numbers were 19 versus 20, and in 2018 those numbers were 28 versus 33. 2018 Calendar Statistics at 7. *See also* Herr (Annotated Manual) § 20.14 ("In recent years, the Panel ha[s] shown a greater willingness to deny motions to centralize.").

Of the 1,707 MDLs created between 1968 and 2017, 3.6 percent were so-called mega cases, involving 1,000 or more cases. M.S. Williams at 1274. For reasons explained above, more than 92 percent of all mega MDLs are product liability cases. *Id.* at 1275. For figures current as of July 16, 2019, 22 MDLs accounted for 88.24 percent of all cases in MDLs. Those 22 MDLs each contained at least 1,000 civil actions. Collectively, those 22 MDLs consisted of 123,681 actions. MDL Statistics Report, July 16, 2019, at 5.

Mass torts have long been the focus of MDLs. In recent years, a "growth area" has been data breach and privacy litigation. *See* Rothman at 1. Some of the most prominent data breach MDLs include *In re Marriott Int'l, Inc. Customer Data Sec. Breach Litig.*, 363 F. Supp. 3d 1372 (J.P.M.L. 2019); *In re Equifax, Inc., Customer Data Sec. Breach Litig.*, 289 F. Supp.

3d 1322 (J.P.M.L. 2017); *In re Anthem, Inc., Customer Data Sec. Breach Litig.*, 109 F. Supp. 3d 1364 (J.P.M.L. 2015); *In re Home Depot, Inc., Customer Data Sec. Breach Litig.*, 65 F. Supp. 3d 1398 (J.P.M.L. 2014); and *In re Target Corp. Customer Data Sec. Breach Litig.*, 11 F. Supp. 3d 1338 (J.P.M.L. 2014). As of July 16, 2019, there were 16 pending MDLs involving data breaches.

C. DISTRICT ASSIGNMENT STATISTICS

Although most districts receive MDL assignments, major urban centers, including Boston, Chicago, New York, and Philadelphia receive the most MDLs. The Southern District of New York has received the most MDLs of any district (primarily securities and antitrust cases). Of course, districts that receive MDL cases also lose cases to other MDLs. Focusing on net changes during the period 1997–2017, the greatest net transferee court was the Eastern District of Pennsylvania (encompassing Philadelphia), while the greatest net transferor court was the Northern District of Ohio. M.S. Williams at 1276–78. Put another way, MDL has resulted in heavier workloads in the Eastern District of Pennsylvania and lighter workloads in the Northern District of Ohio. *Id.*

Between 1968 and 2017, most MDL assignments (53 percent) went to judges without other MDL cases. Yet there were also repeat players, with seven judges handling at least 10 MDL proceedings each. The average MDL judge's tenure was 11 years on the federal bench (7 years if the focus is solely on the first

MDL assignment to each judge). Not surprisingly, initial assignments to MDL judges involve smaller numbers of cases (average of 169), versus a higher number for subsequent assignments to the same judge (average of 582 actions). M.S. Williams at 1282–83.

In recent years, the Panel has assigned a higher percentage of cases to judges who have not had prior MDL experience (for instance, 60 percent of MDLs were assigned to new judges in 2015 versus about 25 percent assigned to new judges in 2010), although the number dropped to under 40 percent in 2016. M.S. Williams at 1284.

The percentage of MDLs assigned to non-white and female judges has increased significantly from the late 1960s and early 1970s (0–5 percent) to recent times (*e.g.*, more than 30 percent in 2016). This increase corresponds to the increased diversity of the federal bench as a whole. M.S. Williams at 1284–86. *See* § 17.6. To some extent, however, the repeat player effect dampens the number of MDL cases assigned to newer and more diverse judges.

D. FREQUENCY OF CENTRALIZATION MOTIONS

During the initial years after its enactment, the MDL statute was used infrequently. In the 1970s and 1980s, the Panel averaged only about 40 motions for centralization per year. But in the early 2000s, the Panel averaged 60 motions per year. By 2010, the Panel was averaging almost 100 motions per year. Since 2010, however, there has been a decline in motions for centralization. The Panel received 109 motions for centralization in 2011, 94 in 2012, 91 in 2013, 89 in 2014, 82 in 2015, 74 in 2016, 60 in 2017, and 56 in 2018. 2018 Calendar Statistics at 6.

Following this trend, the Panel has granted fewer motions for centralization in recent years. In 2011, the Panel granted 55 motions for centralization. The Panel granted 57 in 2012, 46 in 2013, 48 in 2014, 33 in 2015, 26 in 2016, 19 in 2017, and 28 in 2018. 2018 Calendar Statistics at 7.

The Panel is much more likely to grant centralization in some kinds of cases than in others. From 2008 to 2017, the Panel granted centralization in 76 percent of antitrust cases, 66 percent of product liability cases, 63 percent of air crash cases, 61 percent of securities cases, 51 percent of intellectual property cases, 47 percent of cases involving contractual disputes, and just 24 percent of employment cases. M.S. Williams at 1268.

Motions are granted more frequently in cases involving class actions. Williams & George at 442. Although empirical studies on this point are sparse, the Panel has stated that it has a preference for centralizing cases involving class allegations because centralization helps to prevent conflicting and overlapping class actions. Willging & Lee at 794. In 2017, 184 of the 256 MDLs on the docket (72 percent) contained class allegations. According to one source, more than 75 percent of MDLs have involved class actions. Gluck at 1695.

§ 1.5 OVERVIEW OF MDL RULES

Although the Federal Rules of Civil Procedure are technically applicable to MDL transfer proceedings, "most of the rules have no relevance for Panel proceedings," because the Panel does not manage cases, oversee discovery, rule on dispositive motions, or conduct trials. Herr (MDL) § 1:1. Instead, most of the Panel's work is governed by special rules applicable to the Panel (reprinted in Appendix B). After transfer, of course, the Federal Rules of Civil Procedure clearly apply.

The Panel promulgates the Rules of Procedure of the United States Judicial Panel on Multidistrict Litigation ("JPML Rules") pursuant to its statutory authority. *See* 28 U.S.C. § 1407(f). The rules were first promulgated in 1968 and have been amended several times. The most recent version of the rules became effective in October 2016. The rules cover basic procedure in multidistrict litigation proceedings. The Panel retains the power to amend its rules as it deems necessary. The Panel's rules are cited throughout this Nutshell, but for convenience, this section describes the overall structure and content of the JPML Rules. It highlights particularly important rules, but does not purport to be an exhaustive overview.

A. DEFINITIONS AND BAR ADMISSION

Rule 1.1 defines commonly used words in the rules. These include such terms as "Panel," "Chair," "Tag-along action," "Transferee-district," and "Transferor-district."

B. RULES AND PRACTICE

Rule 2.1 contains various rules of practice. For instance, Rule 2.1(c) states that "[e]very member in good standing of the Bar of any district court of the United States is entitled to practice before the Panel, provided, however, that he or she has established and maintains an [Electronic Case Filing (ECF)] account with any United States federal court." This rule further states that attorneys who have had their cases transferred under section 1407 may continue to represent their clients without obtaining or associating with local counsel in the district where the case is transferred. Rule 2.1(c).

Rule 2.1(d) makes clear that a motion to transfer or a conditional transfer order does not affect or suspend orders in the transferor court. Rule 2.1(e) authorizes the Panel to reassign the MDL cases if the original transferee judge can no longer serve.

C. ELECTRONIC RECORDS AND FILING REQUIREMENTS

Rule 3.1 addresses electronic records. Rule 3.1(a) states that the official record of an action is the electronic file that is maintained on the Panel servers, along with any documents or exhibits that are impractical to scan, which are kept in the Panel offices in Washington, D.C.

Rule 3.2(a) prescribes the required form of the pleadings for ECF users, including font size and spacing. Rule 3.2(a)(iv). Briefs and responses may not exceed 20 pages, and replies may not exceed 10 pages. Rule 3.2(a)(iii). The pleadings must be identified as follows: "Before the United States Panel on Multidistrict Litigation," with the identification "MDL No. ___," and the descriptive title designated by the Panel (*e.g.*, "*In re National Prescription Opiate Litigation*" or "*In re Disposable Contact Lens Antitrust Litigation*"). Rule 3.2(a)(i).

Rule 3.2(a)(ii) provides that "[a] pleading filed electronically constitutes a written document . . . and is deemed the electronically signed original thereof." The pleadings must be submitted online through the attorney's ECF account and may not be transmitted directly to a Panel member. Rule 3.2(b)(i). For certain types of pleadings, attorneys must also fax or mail a courtesy copy to the Clerk of the Panel. *See* Rule 3.2(d).

Rule 3.3 applies to all pro se individuals (non-ECF users), unless the Panel orders otherwise. Those parties must send written or typed originals plus one copy of the pleadings to the Clerk of the Panel, or they may fax pleadings that are less than 10 pages. Rule 3.2(c)(i). Rule 3.2(b)(i) specifies the font, spacing, and other requirements for pro se filings.

D. SERVICE OF PLEADINGS

Rule 4.1 applies to service of pleadings. By registering and possessing an ECF account, counsel consents to receiving electronic service for all pleadings. Rule 4.1(a). The Panel's notice of electronic filing after submission of the pleadings is considered service of the pleadings. *Id.*

Within 14 days of the issuance of a motion to transfer, an opposition to a conditional transfer order, a show cause order, or a motion to remand, one designated attorney for each party must provide contact information to the Clerk of the Panel. Rule 4.1(c). Rule 4.1(d) provides that "if the transferee district court appoints liaison counsel, this Rule shall be satisfied by serving each party in each affected action and all liaison counsel."

E. CORPORATE DISCLOSURE STATEMENTS

Rule 5.1 requires nongovernmental corporate parties to disclose any parent corporations or publicly held corporations that own ten percent or more of their stock, or to state that there is no such corporation. Rule 5.1(a). This disclosure must be filed within 14 days of the notice of filing of a motion to transfer or remand, an order to show cause, or a motion to vacate a conditional transfer order or conditional remand order. Rule 5.1(b). If the required information changes, the corporation must notify the Panel. Rule 5.1(c).

F. MOTION PRACTICE

Under Rule 6.1, motions must describe the action or relief sought and include a brief stating the background of the litigation, the legal and factual contentions, the name of each party, the district court where the action is pending, the civil action number, the name of the judge assigned, proof of service, a copy of all complaints and docket sheets for actions listed on the schedule, and any exhibits. Rule 6.1(b).

Any party may file a response to a motion within 21 days; if no response is received, the motion is treated as unopposed. Rule 6.1(c). Reply briefs may be filed within seven days of the deadline for filing a response brief. Rule 6.1(d).

G. MOTIONS TO TRANSFER

Under Rule 6.2, any party may initiate transfer proceedings by filing a motion. Rule 6.2(a). Within 14 days of that filing, each party must file a notice of appearance. Rule 6.2(c). Any party in any potential tag-along action, and any amicus curiae, may file a response to the motion in a pleading called an Interested Party Response. Rule 6.2(e). The rule further specifies that if oral argument is needed, the Panel will schedule it. Rule 6.2(h).

H. MOTIONS FOR MISCELLANEOUS RELIEF

Rule 6.3 allows parties to move for miscellaneous relief, such as "requests for extensions of time, exemption from ECF requirements, page limit extensions, or expedited consideration of any motion." Rule 6.3(a). The Panel, through its clerk, has discretion to act on these motions at any time, without waiting for a response. Rule 6.3(b). If a party disagrees with the action of the Panel's Clerk, that party may file an objection to the decision asking for reconsideration. *Id.*

I. CONDITIONAL TRANSFER ORDERS FOR TAG-ALONG ORDERS

A tag-along action is "a civil action pending in a district court which involves common questions of fact with either (1) actions on a pending motion to transfer to create an MDL or (2) actions previously transferred to an existing MDL, and which the Panel would consider transferring under Section 1407." Rule 1.1(h). Rule 7.1(a) states that parties to actions previously transferred under section 1407 must notify the Clerk of the Panel of any potential tag-along actions. Rule 7.1(a). The Clerk of the Panel will decide whether to enter a conditional transfer order. Rule 7.1(b). If the Clerk decides not to enter the order, any party may move for transfer under Rule 6.1. Rule 7.1(b)(i). A party who opposes a motion for conditional transfer must file a notice within seven days, in which case the Clerk of the Panel will not transfer the action, but will instead issue a briefing schedule. Rule 7.1(c). The party that gave notice of its opposition to the order must file a motion to vacate the conditional transfer order within 14 days, or it will be treated as having withdrawn its motion, and the Clerk of the Panel will transmit the order. Rule 7.1(f).

Rule 7.2 states that failing to serve a defendant in a potential tag-along action does not preclude transfer, but it may be a reason to deny transfer if prejudice can be shown. Rule 7.2(b). Any failure of the Clerk of the Panel to serve the parties may be grounds for the Clerk to reinstate the conditional transfer order or for a party to seek remand. Rule 7.2(b).

J. SHOW CAUSE ORDERS

When the Panel is considering transfer on its own initiative, a party may be ordered to "show cause why a certain civil action or actions should not be transferred for coordinated or consolidated pretrial proceedings." Rule 8.1(a). Any party may file a response within 21 days, or that party will be treated as acquiescing to the Panel's decision. Rule 8.1(c). Any party may reply to the response within seven days after the deadline to file a response. Rule 8.1(d).

K. TRANSFER, TERMINATION, AND REMAND

(1) Transfer of an Action

Rule 9.1 addresses transfer of files and notification requirements. The Clerk of the Panel will notify the clerk of the transferee district when a transfer order should be filed in the transferee court. Upon receipt of an electronically certified copy of a Panel transfer order from the transferee court clerk, the transferor court clerk shall transmit the record of each transferred action to the transferee clerk and, unless JPML Rule 9(b) applies, shall close the transferred action in the transferor district. Rule 9.1(a). However, under Rule 9.1(b), if the transfer order provides for separate and simultaneous remand of any claim, cross-claim, counterclaim, or third-party claim, then the clerk of the transferee district shall retain jurisdiction over that claim and shall not close the case. Rule 9.1(b).

(2) Termination and Remand

When the transferee district court terminates an action, including by a grant of summary judgment, the transferee court retains the records and transmits a copy of the order to the Clerk of the Panel. Rule 10.1(a). The transferee court may also recommend remand of all or part of an action. Rule 10.1(b). The Panel retains the power to remand any action or any separable claim, cross-claim, counterclaim, or third-party claim, either on its own initiative or on the motion of any party. Rule 10.1(b)(i)–(iii). Remand is not common unless the transferee judge requests it. *See* Burch (Louisiana) at 402 (noting that the Panel's practice is to "wait[ ] for the transferee judge to admit defeat and suggest remand[.]").

Upon the suggestion of the transferor judge, the Panel's own initiative, or motion of a party, the Clerk of the Panel shall enter a conditional remand order. Rule 10.2(a). Any party opposing the conditional remand order must file notice within seven days, and file a motion to vacate the order within 14 days of that notice. Rule 10.2(b), 10.2(e). If no notice or motion to vacate is filed, that inaction is treated as the party's acquiescence to the Panel's decision. Rule 10.2(c), 10.2(e).

Rule 10.3 notes that the Panel is reluctant to order remand without the transferee judge's suggestion. Consequently, the parties must include any final pretrial order of the transferee court. They must also include "[a]n affidavit reciting whether the movant has requested a suggestion of remand and the judge's response, whether the parties have completed common discovery and other pretrial proceedings, and whether the parties have complied with all transferee court orders." Rule 10.3(a)(i).

Rule 10.4 states that on remand, the record will be transferred from the transferee district back to the transferor district. Rule 10.4(b).

L. HEARINGS AND ORAL ARGUMENT

Rule 11.1 addresses hearing sessions and oral argument. The Panel schedules oral argument as it deems desirable or necessary. Rule 11.1(a). The Chair of the Panel determines the time, place, and agenda for any hearing. The Clerk of the Panel gives notice to the parties of the scheduled hearing or argument. If a party affected by a motion wants (or does not want) oral argument, the party may file a brief limited to two pages on why oral argument should (or need not) be heard. Rule 11.1(b). The Panel will generally not consider an opposed transfer or remand motion without first holding oral argument. Rule 11.1(c). Nonetheless, Rule 11.1(c) provides that the Panel may dispense with oral argument if the dispositive issues have already been decided or if oral argument will not "significantly aid the decisional process." Rule 11.1(c)(i)–(ii). If a party does not attend oral argument, its position is submitted on its briefs. Rule 11.1(d). Absent exceptional circumstances, the Panel schedules a maximum of 20 minutes for oral argument in each matter. Rule 11.1(f).

§ 1.6 COMPARISON WITH OTHER AGGREGATION DEVICES

This section compares MDL with other aggregation devices, including class actions, permissive joinder, interpleader, consolidation, and transfer of venue under 28 U.S.C. § 1404(a).

A. CLASS ACTIONS

(1) Link Between Class Actions and MDLs

Modern class actions and MDLs are closely linked in time. The federal class action rule, Federal Rule of Civil Procedure 23, was substantially revised in 1966, only two years before the adoption of the MDL statute in 1968.

In the years immediately following the adoption of Rule 23 and the MDL statute, most scholarly and judicial attention was focused on class actions. However, starting in the 1990s, the Supreme Court and the federal circuits made it more difficult to certify class actions. *See* Klonoff (Wash. U.) at 745–55. As class certification became more difficult to establish, MDLs filled the void. MDLs have less stringent requirements than class actions (*see* § 1.4), but nonetheless allow the aggregation of multiple claims (and thus can facilitate a global settlement). As a result, MDLs have rapidly taken the place of class actions in many kinds of cases—particularly mass tort personal injury cases. Fallon at 372–73; Bradt & Rave at 1261–71; Willging & Lee at 806.

When a class action is potentially viable, it frequently happens that competing class actions are filed in multiple districts. That occurred, for example, in the *Volkswagen "Clean Diesel"* case, in which "hundreds of lawsuits against VW, most of them class actions, [were] filed in or removed to over sixty federal district courts." *In re Volkswagen "Clean Diesel" Mktg., Sales Practices, & Prods. Liab. Litig.*, 895 F.3d 597, 603 (9th Cir. 2018). MDL allows for competing and overlapping class actions to be managed by a single judge. This consolidation also helps to avoid the "reverse auction" problem that can occur with competing class actions, *i.e.*, when the defendants play one set of class counsel against another to obtain the lowest settlement amount.

(2) Different Purposes

Both class actions and MDLs are aggregation devices that are designed to achieve efficiency. However, these devices operate very differently from each other.

Class actions authorize litigation for claimants who, in many instances, have claims that are too small to justify individual lawsuits. Such cases are referred to as "negative value" claims. As the Supreme Court has stated:

> The policy at the very core of the class action mechanism is to overcome the problem that small recoveries do not provide the incentive for any individual to bring a solo action prosecuting his or her rights. A class action solves this problem by aggregating the relatively paltry

> potential recoveries into something worth someone's (usually an attorney's) labor.

Amchem Prods., Inc. v. Windsor, 521 U.S. 591, 617 (1997). In contrast, the individual claims in MDLs are often relatively high-value claims, and individual plaintiffs (unlike most unnamed class members) have their own attorneys.

By including absentee class members, class actions empower aggrieved parties to secure collective relief. MDLs, by contrast, aggregate *existing* federal court lawsuits to expedite their resolution and to achieve efficiencies in discovery and pretrial rulings. Of course, new cases can be added to MDLs as tag-along cases or directly filed cases. *See* §§ 6.1–6.3.

(3) Structural Differences

Class actions are representative suits. One or more named representatives stand in place of numerous other claimants who are similarly situated. The litigation of the representative's claim largely determines the resolution of the absent class members' claims. Except for those who opt out of the class, this resolution applies to all representative and absentee class members equally.

By contrast, non-class MDLs function as a collection of individual cases that, unlike class actions, maintain their individual identities throughout the MDL process. MDLs are structured by statute to limit the aggregation of cases to pretrial matters, with claimants able to return to the transferor courts at the conclusion of the pretrial proceedings. Bradt & Rave at 1269–71. As noted, this distinction may be more theoretical than real, because most cases are disposed of in the transferee court. *See* § 1.1.

These distinctions break down when an MDL includes class actions and is resolved on a classwide basis. A classwide settlement within an MDL has all of the features of a non-MDL class settlement. Similarly, in a litigated class action, various features of class actions (such as opt-out rights) exist even if the class action is part of an MDL.

Several structural differences between class actions and non-class MDLs are discussed in more detail below.

(a) The Presence of Absentee Plaintiffs

Because non-class MDLs do not involve representative or absentee plaintiffs, the legal standards required to certify a class action do not apply. In a class action, the plaintiffs must establish numerosity of class members, common issues of law or fact, typicality of the class representative's claim, and adequacy of the class representative and class counsel. *See* Fed. R. Civ. P 23(a)(1)–(4). Moreover, a class action must satisfy the requirements of one of the four categories of Rule 23(b). *See* Klonoff (Class Action Nutshell) §§ 3.1–4.4. By contrast, the creation of an MDL requires only a common question of fact, along with a showing that such a procedure will: (1) foster convenience for the parties and witnesses; and (2) "promote the just and efficient conduct of [the individual] actions." 28 U.S.C. § 1407(a).

(b) Right of Exclusion

Most class actions for money damages are brought under Rule 23(b)(3). That subsection permits class members to opt out of the class and litigate individually. By contrast, a plaintiff in a filed case that has been transferred to an MDL judge has no right to opt out and return to the transferor court. (Of course, if a class is brought under Rule 23(b)(1) or (b)(2), there is no opt out right either.) In short, claimants in a (b)(3) class action who are unhappy with class counsel, the venue of the case, or the decision to aggregate into a class in the first place can opt out and pursue litigation separately, in their forum of choice and with their choice of counsel. By contrast, individual litigants in an MDL (other than unnamed class members) are given no choice about whether to participate or where. And even their choice of counsel for their individually filed case may be undercut because the MDL judge invariably appoints a leadership team, leaving other counsel to take a back seat (or have virtually no role at all in the MDL). *See* §§ 7.1–7.5.

(c) Judicial Approval of Plaintiffs' Counsel

In a class action, the court must determine that counsel for the class is adequate, Fed. R. Civ. P. 23(a)(4). *See also* Fed. R. Civ. P. 23(g) (court is responsible for appointing class counsel). In an MDL, although the court appoints a leadership team, there are no specified criteria to ensure that those appointments satisfy a threshold adequacy requirement, and no remedy for the plaintiff under the Federal Rules of Civil Procedure if those appointed to leadership positions end up being grossly inadequate. (Some transferee judges invoke standards for MDL leadership that are arguably analogous to those in Rule 23, but those standards are not set out in the MDL statute, the JPML Rules, or the Federal Rules of Civil Procedure.)

(d) Settlement

As with the determination of adequacy of counsel, a court in a class action is intimately involved in the settlement process, and by rule must ensure that any settlement agreed to is "fair, reasonable, and adequate." Fed. R. Civ. P. 23(e). Similarly, under Rule 23(h), any attorneys' fees awarded to class counsel must first be approved by the court. By contrast, nothing in the MDL statute, JPML Rules, or Federal Rules of Civil Procedure gives the MDL judge authority to review and disapprove a privately negotiated settlement. Nor does the court have statutory or rule-based authority to pass on the reasonableness of attorneys' fees. Although some MDL judges have asserted their inherent authority to review settlements and attorneys' fees, using an analogy to class actions (so-called quasi-class actions, *see* §§ 10.2, 11.2), there are no standards for quasi-class actions and no clear path for appellate review by plaintiffs who object to a settlement's terms or to an attorneys' fee award. An MDL plaintiff can choose not to participate in a settlement, but as discussed (*see* § 10.2), there is pressure on plaintiffs to go along with a broad settlement, and a potentially high price to pay (such as withdrawal of a plaintiff's attorney) for refusing to do so.

(e) Choice-of-Law

Choice-of-law issues also play out differently in class actions than in non-class MDLs. In class actions, especially those under Rule 23(b)(3)—in which common questions of law or fact must *predominate* over individual questions—the application of the laws of multiple states may be fatal to class certification. *See* Klonoff (Class Action Nutshell) § 7.1. By contrast, MDL centralization can readily occur even if the constituent cases are brought under the laws of multiple states. For example, in *In re Vioxx Products Liability Litigation*, 239 F.R.D. 450 (E.D. La. 2006), in which 20,000 plaintiffs from around the country sought damages against a single defendant, the myriad differences in applicable state laws and the facts of individual plaintiff cases precluded class certification, *id.* at 461–63, but presented no barrier to centralization as an MDL. *Id.* at 452.

B. PERMISSIVE JOINDER

Joinder under Federal Rule of Civil Procedure 20 is broader than MDL in that it applies to all proceedings (trial and pretrial), not just pretrial proceedings. But joinder is also much narrower in that it allows only limited aggregation, *i.e.*, it allows multiple plaintiffs to sue in the *same lawsuit*. Joinder does not allow for cases in multiple federal districts to be combined. Moreover, the test for joinder is far more difficult to satisfy than for centralization under the MDL statute. The basic MDL test is whether the cases share a common question of fact. For joinder, however, the plaintiffs must establish not only a common question (which can be either one of fact or law) but also that the claims involve the "same transaction or occurrence." That is a much narrower test than the "common questions of fact" test under the MDL statute. For instance, "courts have held that the 'transaction or occurrence' test is not satisfied if plaintiffs all complain about the same allegedly defective product, such as an automobile, but the plaintiffs used the product in different ways, at different times, and in different locations." Klonoff (Class Action Nutshell) § 15.1.

C. INTERPLEADER ACTIONS

Interpleader, like permissive joinder, is broader than MDL in the sense that it applies for both pretrial and trial proceedings. Yet it is much narrower than MDL in other respects. It allows aggregation only when the parties are all fighting over a single fund or piece of property. Klonoff (Class Action Nutshell) § 15.4. Few cases in MDL proceedings would satisfy the strict requirements under Fed. R. Civ. P. 22 (or statutory interpleader, 28 U.S.C. § 1335). The fact that multiple plaintiffs have similar lawsuits against a defendant (for example, for producing a dangerous drug) would not establish that the various plaintiffs are fighting over the same fund or piece of property.

D. CONSOLIDATION

Like joinder and interpleader, consolidation under Fed. R. Civ. P. 42 is broader than MDL consolidation in the sense that the former applies to both pretrial and trial proceedings, and because it is allowed with either a common question of fact *or* law. It is much narrower, however, in that it allows cases to be consolidated only if they are in the same federal district. Unlike section 1407, Rule 42 does not allow consolidation of cases in multiple federal districts.

E. TRANSFER UNDER 28 U.S.C. § 1404(a)

Under 28 U.S.C. § 1404(a), a court may transfer a case to a district "where [the case] might have been brought" (where there would be personal jurisdiction and venue). The transfer is for all purposes and, unlike transfer to an MDL, is not limited to pretrial proceedings. On the other hand, with cases filed in myriad federal districts, it would be difficult to orchestrate a scenario under section 1404(a) in which all of the judges independently choose to transfer their cases to the same district. And unlike MDL, in which transfer can be made to any judge in the United States (whether or not personal jurisdiction or venue can be established), *see* §§ 13.1–13.4, under section 1404(a), transfer is not appropriate if the transferee court would lack personal jurisdiction or venue. Thus, absent the consent of all parties, lack of personal jurisdiction or venue is fatal under section 1404(a). *See* Venue Clarification Act of 2011, § 202, 125 Stat. 763; *Hoffman v. Blaski,* 363 U.S. 335 (1960). With multiple defendants, it might be hard to find any district in which all of them are subject to personal jurisdiction and venue.

§ 1.7 JPML WEBSITE AND ADDITIONAL RESOURCES

The JPML website is located at https://www.jpml.uscourts.gov/. It is an invaluable resource. It includes information on the Panel judges; links to the JPML Rules; statistics on MDL cases; information on hearings; recent Panel orders; forms, tutorials, and other information for attorneys; information for parties proceeding pro se; and general news and announcements about the Panel.

Additional resources exist for both judges and attorneys involved in MDL practice. There is an annual conference for MDL judges. And there are multiple conferences each year for MDL attorneys. *See, e.g.,* https://harrismartin.com/conference/ (listing upcoming MDL attorney conferences). Other resources include the Manual for Complex Litigation, which is cited frequently in this text, and various other publications of the Federal Judicial Center. There are also MDL-specific websites. *See* § 8.11.

CHAPTER 2

MDL PANEL: COMPOSITION, AUTHORITY, AND PROCEDURES

This Chapter discusses the Panel's composition, authority, and basic procedures for centralizing cases. Chapter 3 addresses the criteria the Panel uses in deciding whether to centralize cases.

§ 2.1 COMPOSITION

The Panel consists of seven federal judges appointed by the Chief Justice of the United States, with no two judges being from the same circuit. 28 U.S.C. § 1407(d). The judges appointed typically have experience with complex litigation. Williams & George at 434. The Panel usually has had "at least one circuit judge and at least five district judges," *id.* at 433, although at times it has consisted entirely of seven district judges. Judges appointed to the Panel maintain their own caseloads; they undertake the responsibilities of the Panel (including oral argument sessions every other month) in addition to their normal tasks. *Id.*

The statute specifies no term of service for Panel members. Chief Justice Warren, who selected the first panel, envisioned three-year terms, but his choices remained, on average, for 10 years. In 2000, then-Chief Justice Rehnquist adopted a policy of seven-year terms, which Chief Justice Roberts has applied as well. Williams & George at 434. The current list of judges on the MDL Panel can be found at https://www.jpml.uscourts.gov/content/panel-judges.

The Panel's main function is to decide whether to centralize cases under the MDL statute and to designate which MDL district and judge will receive the cases that it chooses to centralize. That function is the focus of this Nutshell. The Panel does, however, have another function (not discussed further in the text): It has authority to consolidate, in one federal circuit, cases pending in more than one circuit in which parties are appealing a ruling of an administrative agency. *See* 28 U.S.C. § 2112(a)(3).

§ 2.2 AUTHORITY OF THE PANEL

This section discusses the scope of, and limits on, the Panel's authority.

A. PRETRIAL ONLY

The Panel's authority is limited to transferring cases for *pretrial* proceedings. *See, e.g., Lexecon Inc. v. Milberg Weiss Bershad Hynes & Lerach,* 523 U.S. 26 (1998), discussed in §§ 9.2 and 15.2. The Panel may initiate transfer proceedings or wait until a party does so. The Panel also has authority to decide when, if at all, transferred cases should be remanded to the transferor courts.

The Panel cannot transfer isolated factual or legal issues but instead must transfer the cases in their entirety. Herr (MDL) § 3:9. *But see* § 15.1 (Panel can remand particular claims). In addition, the Panel has no transfer authority with respect to lawsuits pending in state court.

B. NO SUBSTANTIVE OR ONGOING ROLE IN THE CASES

When the Panel centralizes a case and designates a federal district court, its order attaches no conditions and provides no rulings—advisory or otherwise—on any aspect of the cases. Once the Panel has ordered centralization, it takes no role in the cases other than: (1) designating a new transferee judge if the one designated is no longer able to serve; (2) ruling on whether to transfer tag-along cases; and (3) deciding whether or when to remand cases to the transferor court. *See* §§ 2.2, 6.1–6.3, and 15.1–15.2. The Panel has no power over the selection of lead attorneys to run the MDL, no power over how discovery is conducted, no power over the disposition of motions, and no power over whether cases that were removed to federal court and transferred to the MDL should be remanded to state court. In short, the Panel has no power over any of the myriad decisions facing the transferee judge.

On the other hand, only the Panel can transfer cases under section 1407. And once the cases have been transferred, only the Panel can re-transfer cases to another judge. The transferee judge is not authorized to re-transfer the cases, although an unauthorized re-transfer does not affect the court's subject matter jurisdiction. In *In re IKO Roofing Shingle Products Liability Litigation*, 757 F.3d 599 (7th Cir. 2014), the Panel transferred cases to the

Central District of Illinois for pretrial proceedings. The transferee judge, who was also the chief judge of the district, then reassigned the cases to another judge in that same district. Eventually, the Panel entered an order reassigning the cases to the second judge, but by that point, the second judge had ruled on plaintiffs' motion for class certification. In the Seventh Circuit, a threshold issue (before the court addressed class certification) was whether the second judge lacked subject matter jurisdiction in ruling on class certification. The Seventh Circuit held that the chief judge's violation of section 1407 did not implicate subject matter jurisdiction. The MDL statute, the appellate court said, was "a case-processing rule rather than a jurisdictional one." *Id.* at 600. Although section 1407(b) "gives the Panel exclusive authority to select the transferee judge," the district court's error in complying with that statute did not deprive the second judge of jurisdiction. Because no one had objected to the re-assignment as a violation of section 1407, any argument that the second judge lacked authority to rule on class certification had been waived.

C. CONDUCTING A HEARING AND RENDERING A DECISION

Hearings before the Panel are en banc. "Four panelists must agree for consolidation, or any other action, to occur." Williams & George at 435 (citing 28 U.S.C. § 1407(d)).

The Panel has "unusually broad discretion to carry out its functions, including substantial authority . . .

to decide how the cases under its jurisdiction should be coordinated." *In re Wilson,* 451 F.3d 161, 173 (3d Cir. 2006). According to one study, no transfer decision of the Panel has ever been overturned on appeal. Williams & George at 435. Indeed, the Panel has authority to centralize cases "even if all parties are opposed[.]" *Id.*

The Panel has authority to centralize cases *sua sponte*, and in the early years following the statute's enactment, it looked for suitable cases to do so. Williams & George at 435. That practice has changed. From 1980 to 2011, the Panel acted on its own to centralize cases on only two occasions (both asbestos cases). MDL Overview at 1.

Today, transfer is invariably initiated by one or more parties. The Panel generally relies on the parties to determine whether particular cases may be suitable for MDL treatment. MDL Overview at 1. The Panel also encourages district court clerks to notify it of cases that may be appropriate for MDL treatment. Herr (MDL) § 4:4.

D. ONLY FEDERAL CASES

The Panel is authorized to centralize only *federal* cases. This is a significant limitation. It is not uncommon for cases involving a particular issue to be filed and litigated in both federal and state courts. For example, the *Vioxx* litigation involved "thousands of individual suits and numerous class actions . . . in state and federal courts throughout the country . . . ." 478 F. Supp. 2d 897, 901 (E.D. La. 2007). Similarly, *In re Syngenta AG MIR 162 Corn*

Litig., 357 F. Supp. 3d 1094 (D. Kan. 2018), *appeal docketed*, No. 19-3009 (10th Cir. Jan. 8, 2019), included hundreds of suits consolidated into an MDL, as well as "thousands of similar suits" filed and litigated in state courts. *Id.* at 1099–1101.

Coordination would work best if the transferee court could control both the federal and state cases, ensuring orderly discovery, consistent rulings on dispositive motions, and coordination in settlement. Proposals to expand MDLs to include related state court cases have been made, *see* § 17.8, but they have not made headway in Congress. Many MDL transferee federal judges, however, have achieved substantial efficiencies through informal coordination with state courts, a point addressed in detail below. *See* § 16.1. MDL makes this coordination far easier, because the state judges need to coordinate with only one federal judge.

§ 2.3 PANEL PROCEDURES

A. COMMENCEMENT OF PROCEEDINGS

The Panel's process in deciding whether to centralize is highly compressed, compared with most other federal court proceedings. The briefing is usually done within 30 days after a motion to transfer is filed, and the Panel normally enters its order "within about two weeks of the argument." Heyburn & McGovern at 27. As a result, the Panel usually decides whether to transfer within two to four months after the filing of the motion to transfer. *Id.*

A potential MDL action may be initiated by any party in any action, or by the Panel on its own motion. 28 U.S.C. § 1407(c). The Panel decides whether centralization is warranted after considering the statutory criteria, *i.e.*, looking at whether there is a common question of fact, 28 U.S.C. § 1407(a), and whether an MDL would be convenient for the parties and witnesses and would promote justice and efficiency. As noted below, oral argument is common. The Panel usually explains its decision in a brief written order. If the Panel chooses to centralize the cases for pretrial proceedings, it will identify the district court and judge that it has selected.

As noted, the Panel rarely initiates a transfer proceeding. The typical procedure is for a party to initiate a potential MDL proceeding by filing a Motion to Transfer for Coordinated or Consolidated Pretrial Proceedings. JPML Rule 6.2. Under the Panel's general rules on motions, the motion to transfer must list all of the actions involved, the name of each party, the courts where the actions are pending (and the civil numbers of each action), and the name of the judge assigned to each action. JPML Rule 6.1(b)(ii). The motion must also be accompanied by a brief (discussed below). All parties on the docket sheets of the cases must be served. JPML Rule 6.1(b)(iii).

Upon receipt of that motion, the Clerk of the Panel will issue a notice of filing of motion to transfer to the list of service recipients. The notice will specify, among other things, the filing date of the motion, the

MDL docket number, and the briefing schedule. JPML Rule 6.2(b). Each party or designated attorney must file a notice of appearance within 14 days after the notice issues. JPML Rule 6.2(c). Responses to the motion (along with briefs) are due 21 days after the motion is filed, JPML Rule 6.1(c), and replies are due within seven days after the deadline to file a response. JPML Rule 6.1(d). (These periods may be "shorten[ed] or enlarge[d]" by the Clerk of the Panel "as necessary." JPML Rule 6.1(e).) Parties (or their counsel) in actions under consideration for MDL transfer are required to "promptly notify the Clerk of the Panel of any potential tag-along actions in which that party is also named or in which that counsel appears." JPML Rule 6.2(d).

B. BRIEFS

Briefs in support of transfer are limited to 20 pages, exclusive of exhibits. Responsive briefs are also limited to 20 pages. Replies are normally limited to 10 pages, but may be 20 pages when responding to more than one response in opposition. JPML Rules 3.2(a), 6.1(d). Amicus briefs are allowed under the JPML's rules, JPML Rule 6.2(e), and the 20-page limit applies to submissions by amici. *See* JPML Rule 6.2(e) ("amicus curiae may file a response to a pending motion to transfer"); Rule 3.2(a)(iii) ("any response to" a brief or motion filed with the Panel "shall not exceed 20 pages"). Amicus briefs, however, are rare in MDL practice. Herr (MDL) § 4:25.

The purpose of the briefs is to argue whether the Panel should order centralization and, if so, to which district court and judge. The briefs should focus on the statutory criteria (common question of fact, convenience to parties and witnesses, and promotion of justice and efficiency), and on other compelling facts relevant to the transfer decision. As discussed in detail in §§ 3.1–3.5 and 4.1–4.3, the Panel has considered numerous factors in its transfer decisions. Counsel should be familiar with those factors and should decide which ones may be important, recognizing that the Panel has broad discretion in ordering transfer when there are common questions of fact and efficiencies to be gained. In some instances, centralization is a foregone conclusion, and it is futile to waste valuable space arguing against transfer. In those circumstances, the advocate is best advised to focus on the selection of the transferee district and judge.

In arguing for a particular district court or judge, advocates should be careful not to disparage particular judges. Arguments attacking particular judges have generally not been well received. Also, advocates should not appear to be seeking a judge who may be predisposed to rule in the advocate's favor.

Because the time allotted for oral argument is so limited (*see* below), the brief is the critical place to spell out the major arguments for or against centralization, and for or against particular districts and judges.

The bottom line of MDL advocacy is that facts are generally more important than legal precedent. The Panel has broad discretion in transfer decisions, and basing an argument on prior Panel orders or other judicial precedent is likely to be ineffective. As one authority has noted, arguments should be "very pragmatic and fact-oriented in tone"; thus, "[a] compendium of airline schedules" could—in a particular case—be more persuasive than a judicial opinion. Herr (MDL) § 1:1. Nonetheless, a prior Panel opinion will sometimes be helpful authority for an advocate. Indeed, the Panel frequently cites its prior decisions in ruling on transfer motions. *Id.*

After the briefs are filed, the Panel sets oral argument to decide: (1) whether to transfer the cases into an MDL; and (2) if so, to which district and judge. DeGaris at 184.

C. ORAL ARGUMENT

The Panel's general practice in deciding petitions for MDL centralization is to hold oral argument. *See* Heyburn at 2235–36. The Panel typically meets six times a year in various cities around the country. DeGaris at 184.

Since a single proposed centralization may involve many attorneys with various perspectives, and since numerous proposed MDLs will be calendared for a single Panel sitting, the Panel may need to hear argument from as many as 50 to 70 attorneys during a 2½ hour court session. Heyburn at 2236. That practice has led to criticism. As one critic has noted, attorneys end up devoting substantial time and expense "to present two to three minutes of oral argument," a presentation that is unlikely to change the outcome. Varner at 230. Despite such criticism, the Panel values oral argument and continues to require it in most situations before ruling on centralization.

Advocates before the Panel should use common sense, focusing on the facts that matter: the common factual issues (or lack thereof), the conveniences and efficiencies to be gained (or not), the status and progress of the various cases, and the pros and cons of particular districts and judges for transfer. DeGaris at 185.

D. PANEL OPINIONS

When the Panel decides against centralization, it will usually issue an opinion explaining its reasoning. Similarly, when the Panel decides to centralize cases in an MDL, it will typically issue an opinion explaining why transfer is appropriate. The opinion will also name the transferee district and judge, designate the official title and case number for the MDL, and list the actions that will be transferred. Fallon at 372. The Panel's opinions are generally short (sometimes just a couple of pages), even in high-profile cases. Brevity is common even when there is substantial disagreement among the parties about the need for transfer or where the cases should be transferred. For instance, in *In re National Football League Players' Concussion Injury Litigation,* 842 F. Supp. 2d 1378 (J.P.M.L. 2012), the Panel's ruling was only three pages long, even though the parties disagreed on the need to transfer and on which district and judge should be designated.

Sometimes the Panel will provide details supporting its choice of district and judge. *See, e.g.*, *In re Proton-Pump Inhibitor Prods. Liab. Litig. (No. II)*, 261 F. Supp. 3d 1351, 1355 (J.P.M.L. 2017) (explaining the Panel's selection of district and judge in terms of party support, pending actions, convenience, and fact that the transferee judge was already managing some of the actions); *In re Toyota Motor Corp. Unintended Acceleration Mktg., Sales Practices, & Prods. Liab. Litig.*, 704 F. Supp. 2d 1379, 1382 (J.P.M.L. 2010) (listing numerous factors supporting the Panel's choice of district and judge, including the number of pending actions, the location of the defendant's headquarters, docket conditions in the transferee district, and the transferee judge's experience with complex cases).

Sometimes, however, the Panel will merely name the district and judge, offering little or no support for the selection other than conclusory comments. *See, e.g., In re 3M Combat Arms Earplug Prods. Liab. Litig.*, 366 F. Supp. 3d 1368, 1369–70 (J.P.M.L. 2019) (noting that the transferee district had "the necessary judicial resources and expertise to manage this litigation efficiently and in a manner convenient for the parties and witnesses," and that the transferee judge "is an able jurist with experience in presiding over a large products liability MDL"); *In re Anheuser-Busch Beer Labeling Mktg. & Sales Practices Litig.*, 949 F. Supp. 2d 1371, 1372 (J.P.M.L. 2013) ("[T]he Northern District of Ohio . . . provides a geographically central forum for this nationwide litigation, and is equally convenient to plaintiffs and defendant"; the transferee judge, "who is presiding over one of the actions, is an experienced transferee judge").

Panel opinions are normally unanimous, although on occasion there has been a concurrence or dissent. Herr (MDL) § 2:5 (citing rare examples of concurring or dissenting opinions). Panel opinions are typically signed by the Panel Chair on behalf of the Panel, although for many years most Panel opinions were per curiam. Herr (MDL) § 4:27. Four Panel members must join an order for it to be binding. *See* § 2.2.

E. RECUSAL

Recusals of Panel members are rare, even when potential conflicts of interest exist. Because there is no procedure in the statute or rules for designating substitute Panel judges, the designated Panel judges must rule under the Rule of Necessity. For example, in *In re Tribune Co. Fraudulent Conveyance Litigation,* 831 F. Supp. 2d 1371 (J.P.M.L. 2011), the Panel announced that three of the seven members had conflicts in connection with the case that would "normally disqualify them under 28 U.S.C. § 455 from participating in the decision in this matter." *Id.* at 1371 n.*. Nonetheless, the Panel "invoked the Rule of Necessity rejecting recusal where neutral, qualified judges are not available." *Id.* As a result, "all Panel members participated in the decision . . . in order to provide the forum created by the governing statute." *Id.*

In addition to the Rule of Necessity, in some cases, Panel members have renounced their participation in claims brought on behalf of classes when they might be class members. *See, e.g.*, *In re iPhone/iPad Application Consumer Privacy Litig.*, 802 F. Supp. 2d 1363, 1363 n.* (J.P.M.L. 2011). Also, Panel judges might recuse themselves if they are being considered as the transferee judge in a case. *See, e.g.*, *In re Volkswagen "Clean Diesel" Mktg., Sales Practices, & Prods. Liab. Litig.*, 148 F. Supp. 3d 1367, 1367 n.* (J.P.M.L. 2015) (Judge Breyer, to whom the Panel assigned the MDL, did not participate in the Panel's decision).

F. TRANSFEROR COURT'S AUTHORITY TO RULE WHILE TRANSFER ORDER IS PENDING

Between the time when a motion to transfer is filed and the time when the Panel issues its ruling, the transferor court continues to have jurisdiction over the cases originally assigned to it. The fact that the Panel is considering whether to centralize cases under section 1407 does not deprive the transferor court of the ability to act. As provided in JPML Rule 2.1(d), "[t]he pendency of a motion, order to show cause, conditional transfer order or conditional remand order [under section 1407] does not affect or suspend orders and pretrial proceedings in any pending federal district court action and does not limit the pretrial jurisdiction of that court." Unless and until the Panel issues a transfer order, the transferor court may continue to rule on motions, oversee discovery, and do anything else within its power to oversee the litigation. For instance, the transferor judge might rule if an issue has been fully briefed and argued. Of course, many judges find it prudent to defer ruling on motions while awaiting the

Panel's decision. Herr (Annotated Manual) § 20.133 (citing cases staying discovery while the Panel's decision whether to transfer is pending).

A transfer order becomes effective "only upon its filing with the clerk of the transferee district court." JPML Rule 2.1(d). Nonetheless, transferor courts will sometimes stay discovery, defer ruling on motions, or otherwise suspend the proceedings until the transfer issue has been resolved. Whether to continue full steam ahead or halt the proceedings is within the discretion of the transferor courts. *See, e.g.*, *Bartolucci v. 1-800 Contacts, Inc.*, 245 F. Supp. 3d 38, 44 (D.D.C. 2017) ("A court is not deprived of its discretion to transfer cases [under 28 U.S.C. § 1404(a)] during the pendency of a section 1407 motion for pretrial consolidation.").

G. TAG-ALONG ACTIONS

Tag-along actions are "those filed after the initial hearing on transfer and actions that were then pending but were not brought to the attention of the Panel." Herr (MDL) § 8:1. Also included as tag-alongs are cases filed after centralization. The decision whether to transfer tag-along cases rests with the Panel. Tag-along cases are discussed in detail in §§ 6.1–6.3.

H. REMAND

As noted (*see* § 1.2), the Panel is responsible for deciding whether and when cases (or certain claims, cross-claims, counter-claims, and third-party claims within cases) should be remanded to the transferor court. Because the vast majority of cases are resolved in the transferee court, either through settlement or pretrial disposition, *see* § 1.1, the function of considering and ordering remand has not been a major task of the Panel. Nonetheless, remand can be important in particular cases. The issue of remand is addressed in §§ 15.1–15.2.

CHAPTER 3

MDL PANEL'S TRANSFER DECISION

§ 3.1 OVERVIEW OF TRANSFER CRITERIA

This Chapter examines the criteria the Panel uses in deciding whether to transfer cases under the MDL statute. The Panel looks only at pending federal cases. It does not take into account cases that the transferor court has remanded to state court or that have been resolved or otherwise dismissed. Herr (MDL) § 3:8. Also, the Panel does not consider cases in which trial is underway. *Id.*

The statute specifies three criteria for the Panel to consider: (1) whether "one or more common questions of fact are pending in different districts"; (2) whether transfer "will be for the convenience of parties and witnesses"; and (3) whether transfer "will promote the just and efficient conduct of such actions." 28 U.S.C. § 1407(a).

As discussed below, the first criterion is regularly considered and is always important. In some instances, the Panel finds the commonality of fact requirement to be a minimal one. In other cases, the Panel applies a standard more akin to the "predominance" test for class actions under Federal Rule of Civil Procedure 23(b)(3)—whether common questions *predominate* over individual questions.

The second and third criteria are somewhat of a mystery. Although research has uncovered no empirical studies directly on point, a review of many

Panel opinions suggests that the Panel rarely applies these two requirements as free-standing tests. Nonetheless, as discussed in this Chapter, the Panel regularly considers numerous factors, such as the location of the parties and evidence, that relate to convenience and efficiency.

§ 3.2 TRANSFER IS A LAST RESORT

Even though the Panel transfers a large percentage of matters that it considers (*see* § 1.4), it operates under the principle that "centralization under Section 1407 should be the last solution after considered review of all other options." *In re Gerber Probiotics Prods. Mktg. & Sales Practices Litig.*, 899 F. Supp. 2d 1378, 1379 (J.P.M.L. 2012). "These options include: Section 1404 transfer; dismissal or stay under the first-to-file doctrine; agreement by plaintiffs to voluntarily dismiss their actions in favor of one district; and cooperation and coordination among the parties and the various transferor courts." *Id.* at 1379–80. In short, the Panel starts with a stated presumption against transfer. The Panel routinely asks whether substantial efficiencies can be achieved in some other manner, without the need to transfer cases under the MDL statute. (That said, because so many Panel members have served as MDL judges, it is likely that they are inclined to appreciate the benefits of transfer from the outset.)

§ 3.3 BASIC TEST: COMMON QUESTION(S) OF FACT

Under 28 U.S.C. § 1407(a), the Panel may centralize civil actions pending in multiple federal districts for pretrial purposes only when "one or more common questions of fact" exist. Since the enactment of section 1407, the Panel has viewed this commonality test as a critical inquiry, and has treated it rigorously and explicitly. Common facts are the glue that justifies transferring cases to a single judge. Without commonality, it is difficult to imagine how transferring myriad cases to a potentially distant forum would promote efficiency or fairness. Advocates proposing or opposing transfer must be familiar with the nuances of the particular litigation and must be able to explain why common factual issues do or do not exist. That requires the advocate to have a solid understanding of the Panel's approach to the subject.

A. DISSECTING THE TEST

The wording of section 1407(a) reveals two important points.

First, the language "one or more" makes clear that only *one* common question of fact needs to be present. The language indicates that this is not the "predominance" test used in Federal Rule of Civil Procedure 23(b)(3). The court need not weigh the common questions against the individual questions and figure out whether common questions predominate. Yet, as discussed below, the Panel has not been clear in this area. At times, it applies the test under section 1407(a) literally, finding transfer appropriate after isolating one or more common factual issues. At other times, however, the Panel has applied a more rigorous test, asking whether the common factual issues *predominate* over the individual factual issues, a test that is much harder for a proponent of transfer to satisfy. *But cf. Wal-Mart Stores, Inc. v. Dukes,* 564 U.S. 338, 350 (2011) (under Rule 23(a)(2), the commonality requirement is not satisfied unless the "determination of its truth or falsity will resolve an issue that is central to the validity of each one of the claims in one stroke"); *id.* at 375–77 (Ginsburg, J., concurring in part and dissenting in part) (accusing the Court of conflating commonality and predominance).

Second, the language of section 1407(a) states that the commonality test is one of *fact*, not of law. As discussed (§ 1.6), this test differs from the commonality test applied to some other aggregation devices, such as class certification, joinder, and consolidation, in which a common question of law can satisfy the test, even in the absence of common questions of fact. Under the MDL statute, even if myriad common questions of law exist, transfer is not permitted unless there is at least one common question of fact.

B. THE PANEL'S APPLICATION OF THE "COMMON QUESTIONS OF FACT" TEST

(1) Commonality Test Satisfied

This section discusses several cases, in a variety of contexts, in which the Panel found that the common questions of fact test was satisfied.

Antitrust. In *In re Railway Industry Employee No-Poach Antitrust Litigation*, 326 F. Supp. 3d 1381 (J.P.M.L. 2018), the Panel held that three civil antitrust actions, as well as 14 potential tag-along actions, involved common questions of fact justifying the creation of an MDL. The issue involved the hiring practices of several defendants, alleged to be "a conspiracy not to recruit, solicit, or hire each other's personnel without prior approval," thereby "suppressing the compensation of defendants' personnel[.]" *Id.* at 1382. Because the facts underlying the alleged conspiracy were common to all of the claimants, the Panel held that MDL transfer was appropriate.

In *In re Chicago Board Options Exchange Volatility Index Manipulation Antitrust Litigation*, 325 F. Supp. 3d 1374 (J.P.M.L. 2018), the Panel also found common questions of fact. At issue was whether the defendants—including various John Doe financial institutions—exploited weaknesses in a complex stock-auction system, resulting in artificial price-setting. The plaintiff in one of the actions argued against MDL transfer on the ground that the involvement of John Doe defendants made it "difficult to assess" whether centralization by transfer would make sense. *Id.* at 1376. The Panel disagreed, finding that centralization was justified because all the actions "share[d] complex factual issues," were "on behalf of overlapping putative nationwide classes," and asserted claims under federal antitrust and securities laws. *Id.* at 1375–76.

Environmental Litigation. In *In re Aqueous Film-Forming Foams Products Liability Litigation*, 357 F. Supp. 3d 1391 (J.P.M.L. 2018), the Panel centralized cases alleging that aqueous film-forming foams used for extinguishing liquid fuel fires were released into the groundwater in numerous areas, contaminating the drinking water. Opponents of transfer pointed to the fact that there were numerous separate contamination locations. The types of plaintiffs also varied, from those suing for personal injuries, to those seeking medical monitoring, to those suing for property damage, to water authorities and other governmental entities seeking costs for remediation or upgrades to water treatment systems. The Panel found commonality. It noted that, with only minor variations, "the same group of [alleged contaminants] manufacturer defendants is named in each action," and the actions "share factual questions concerning the toxicity of [the alleged contaminants] and their effects on human health; the chemical knowledge of the . . . manufacturers regarding the dangers . . .; their warnings, if any, regarding proper use and storage of [the alleged contaminants]; and to what extent, if any, defendants conspired or cooperated to conceal the dangers of [the alleged contaminants] in their products." *Id.* at 1394.

Mass Torts. In *In re Zostavax (Zoster Vaccine Live) Products Liability Litigation*, 330 F. Supp. 3d 1378 (J.P.M.L. 2018), the Panel held that 98 civil actions based on alleged injuries from a shingles vaccine involved common questions of fact and warranted transfer to MDL proceedings. Although each plaintiff had individualized injuries, the Panel found that these variations were "not an obstacle" because the claims "share[d] a common factual core." *Id.* at 1379. Issues relating to "the design, testing, manufacture, regulatory approval, labeling, and marketing" of the vaccine were "common to all actions." *Id.*

Similarly, in *In re Davol, Inc./C.R. Bard, Inc., Polypropylene Hernia Mesh Products Liability Litigation*, 316 F. Supp. 3d 1380 (J.P.M.L. 2018), the Panel held that 53 civil actions (and 69 potential tag-along actions) alleging defects in the defendants' hernia mesh product involved common questions of fact despite the plaintiffs' claims of individualized injuries. The Panel explained that "[a]ll of the actions share common factual questions arising out of allegations that defects in defendants' polypropylene hernia mesh products can lead to complications when implanted in patients, including adhesions, damage to organs, inflammatory and allergic responses, foreign body rejection, migration of the mesh, and infections." *Id.* at 1380–81.

In *In re Wright Med. Tech. Inc., Conserve Hip Implant Products Liability Litigation*, 844 F. Supp. 2d 1371 (J.P.M.L. 2012), the plaintiff moved to centralize five actions pending in five districts alleging defects in the defendant's hip implant products. The defects involved high levels of metal debris, causing metallosis in the surrounding tissue or early failure of the product. The defendants, two manufacturer entities, opposed centralization, arguing "that the multiple intervening causation issues—such as a given plaintiff's health, medical issues and lifestyle—are prominent in all actions," making the actions "dissimilar." *Id.* at 1372. In rejecting that argument, the Panel noted that "almost all injury litigation involves questions of causation that are case- and plaintiff-specific," and that "[s]uch differences have not been an impediment to centralization in the past." *Id. See also, e.g.*, *In re Asbestos Prods. Liab. Litig. (No. VI)*, 771 F. Supp. 415, 416–17 (J.P.M.L. 1991) (centralizing 26,639 actions pending in 87 federal districts in mass tort asbestos litigation where the actions "involve[d] common questions of fact relating to injuries or wrongful death allegedly caused by exposure to asbestos or asbestos-containing products"); *In re Temporomandibular Joint (TMJ) Implants Prods. Liab. Litig.*, 844 F. Supp. 1553, 1554 (J.P.M.L. 1994) (finding common questions of fact in personal injury actions alleging that defendants' joint implants were defective and unreasonably dangerous).

These mass tort cases illustrate why the MDL procedure can facilitate aggregation even when the cases are not suitable for class certification. The Panel acknowledged individual issues that, under Rule 23(b)(3), might defeat class certification, but nonetheless satisfied the more flexible standard for MDL treatment.

Patent Cases. The Panel held that a collection of 12 civil patent actions shared common questions of fact sufficient for transfer to MDL proceedings because each action arose from the "alleged infringement, validity, and enforceability" of two patents. *In re Iron Oak Techs., LLC*, 325 F. Supp. 3d 1371, 1373 (J.P.M.L. 2018). Because the actions primarily involved the same plaintiff suing different alleged infringers, each action turned on the common question of whether the patent went as far as the plaintiff claimed in each lawsuit.

Similarly, in *In re Personalweb Technologies, LLC, and Level 3 Communications., LLC, Patent Litigation*, 340 F. Supp. 3d 1373 (J.P.M.L. 2018), the Panel held that 48 civil actions centering on alleged patent infringement merited transfer because they shared common questions of fact. A single patent holder had launched 47 infringement actions against various internet-based companies, and each suit involved the scope and enforceability of the identical patent. *Id.* at 1374.

It should be noted that the parties sought centralization of these patent cases as a result of the Supreme Court's decision in *TC Heartland LLC v. Kraft Foods Group Brands LLC*, 137 S. Ct. 1514 (2017). Prior to *TC Heartland*, the Federal Circuit had interpreted the patent venue statute, 28 U.S.C. § 1400(b), broadly, so that litigants in patent cases could file suit in virtually any federal district. The Eastern District of Texas was a particularly popular forum, with nearly 44 percent of patent cases filed there in 2015. Wee at 982. In *TC Heartland*, the

Court held that for purposes of the patent venue statute, a domestic corporation "resides" only in its state of incorporation. 137 S. Ct. at 1517. In light of that decision, patent litigants are more restricted in their choice of forum, leading the parties in the above cases to seek MDL treatment.

(2) Commonality Test Not Satisfied

In many instances, the Panel has denied transfer because the common questions of fact test was not satisfied. In some cases, the Panel has found that even a liberal application of that test was not satisfied. In other cases, the Panel has essentially applied a more demanding "predominance" test in finding a lack of commonality. Those two variations of cases are discussed below.

(a) Application of a Liberal Commonality Test

In several cases, the Panel has found that, even construed liberally, the "common questions of fact" test was not satisfied.

For example, in *In re Starbucks Corp. Access for Individuals With Disabilities Litigation*, 326 F. Supp. 3d 1370 (J.P.M.L. 2018), defendant Starbucks moved to centralize 21 actions alleging violations of the Americans with Disabilities Act in its stores. In each action, the plaintiff, who was quadriplegic, alleged that he visited a Starbucks and "encountered one or more illegal barriers to access that caused him difficulty and frustration" and deterred him from returning. The Panel denied centralization, finding that the "actions are only facially similar." *Id.* at

1371. It explained: "[E]ach action involves a different Starbucks ... and the unique circumstances in existence at that Starbucks at the time of plaintiff's visits." *Id.* Although one specific alleged barrier was common to all 21 actions, a number of actions involved other alleged barriers.

Similarly, in *In re Uber Technologies, Inc., Wage & Hour Employment Practices Litigation (No. II)*, 254 F. Supp. 3d 1376 (J.P.M.L. 2017), which involved whether the defendant misclassified its employees as independent contractors to avoid paying required overtime compensation, the Panel emphasized the need to show common *factual*, as opposed to legal issues. The transfer proponents had urged centralization based on "common questions of law," not "common questions of fact." *Id.* at 1378. As a consequence, the Panel denied transfer.

In *In re Brown*, 158 F. Supp. 3d 1374 (J.P.M.L. 2016), a pro se plaintiff moved to transfer two civil rights actions along with 27 potential tag-alongs. The Panel denied transfer because the plaintiff "failed to demonstrate any common factual issues" between the two primary actions. *Id.* at 1375. The first action centered on an allegedly unlawful denial of temporary housing; the second action centered on alleged police brutality. Although both actions named the City of New York as a defendant, that was the only factual overlap. The 27 potential tag-alongs similarly represented "a broad range of civil rights violations by many different defendants" without a nexus of common factual issues. *Id.*

And in foreclosure litigation consisting of two civil actions and seven tag-along actions, the Panel held that transfer was inappropriate because common questions of fact were "simply . . . not present[.]" *In re Mortg. Indus. Foreclosure Litig.*, 996 F. Supp. 2d 1379, 1379 (J.P.M.L. 2014). Each action shared a theory of contract interpretation, but each contract was subject to different state laws, and each action involved different defendants, plaintiffs, and mortgage loan companies. *Id.* at 1379–80.

(b) Application of a Predominance Test

At times, the Panel has denied transfer, even when there were common questions of fact, on the ground that individualized factual questions *predominated* over the common questions. In those cases, the Panel has applied a more exacting test (akin to Rule 23(b)(3)) than the language of 28 U.S.C. § 1407(a) requires.

For instance, in *In re Table Saw Products Liability Litigation*, 641 F. Supp. 2d 1384 (J.P.M.L. 2009), plaintiffs sought centralization of 42 actions pending in 11 federal districts involving injuries from allegedly defective table saws. The Panel recognized the existence of common questions, but denied centralization because the "common issues [were] overshadowed by the non-common ones." *Id.* at 1384. The Panel explained that "[e]ach action arises from an individual accident that occurred under necessarily unique circumstances." *Id.* Moreover, "[m]ultiple different saws made by multiple different manufacturers were involved in the various accidents," "[n]o defendant is sued in all actions, and several entities . . . are named in, at most, two or three of them." *Id.*

As another example, in *In re National Credit Union Administration Board Mortgage-Backed Securities Litigation*, 996 F. Supp. 2d 1374 (J.P.M.L. 2014), the plaintiffs alleged that defendants had made misstatements of fact in their offering documents for mortgage-backed securities. Although 120 securities offerings were implicated, only 14 of those offerings were common across the civil actions. Although the actions shared "some general common factual questions," the Panel found that different offerings purchased by different plaintiffs from different defendants presented factual variations. *Id.* at 1375–76. Each civil action necessarily dealt with different representations made to different plaintiffs, and thus required individualized discovery. As a result, the Panel held that the plaintiffs "failed to convince [it] that any common questions of fact [were] sufficiently complex and/or numerous" to make transfer appropriate. *Id.* at 1376. *Accord, e.g.*, *In re Ambulatory Pain Pump-Chondrolysis Prods. Liab. Litig.*, 709 F. Supp. 2d 1375, 1377 (J.P.M.L. 2010) (rejecting centralization of mass tort personal injury cases in part because "individual issues of causation and liability . . . *predominate*, and are likely to overwhelm any efficiencies that might be gained by centralization" (emphasis added)); *In re Mortg. Lender Force-Placed Ins. Litig.*, 895 F. Supp. 2d 1352, 1353 (J.P.M.L. 2012) (denying centralization of 31 actions (pending in 14 districts) involving alleged abusive practices in the banking and insurance industry, finding that "[c]ommon questions of fact . . . do not *predominate*") (emphasis added).

§ 3.4 CONVENIENCE AND EFFICIENCY FACTORS

As noted, in addition to the "common questions of fact" criterion, the MDL statute requires the Panel to determine whether centralization "[1] will be for the convenience of parties and witnesses and [2] will promote the just and efficient conduct of such actions."

While the Panel repeatedly examines the commonality factor as critical, it rarely discusses convenience and justice/efficiency as freestanding criteria. Indeed, the Panel does not appear to have identified any core definition for either requirement. Instead, the Panel often uses boilerplate language that encompasses these concepts.

For instance, the Panel often notes that "[c]entralization will eliminate duplicative discovery; prevent inconsistent pretrial rulings . . .; and conserve the resources of the parties, their counsel, and the judiciary." *In re Uber Techs., Inc., Data Sec. Breach Litig.*, 304 F. Supp. 3d 1351, 1353 (J.P.M.L. 2018); *In re Local TV Adver. Antitrust Litig.*, 338 F. Supp. 3d 1341, 1343 (J.P.M.L. 2018) (using same language). The Panel frequently considers whether transfer "prevent[s] duplicative discovery, motion practice, and *Daubert* hearings, avoid[s] inconsistent rulings on pretrial issues, and avoid[s] scheduling conflicts in proceedings before multiple courts." Vance Speech at 10–11.

The Panel has also referred to party support for transfer as "critical[ ]" for the "just and efficient" standard, *In re Sorin 3T Heater-Cooler Sys. Prods. Liab. Litig.,* 273 F. Supp. 3d 1357, 1358 (J.P.M.L. 2017), and it has referred to party preferences and agreements in determining convenience. *See, e.g., In re Facebook, Inc., Consumer Privacy User Profile Litig.*, 325 F. Supp. 3d 1362, 1363–64 (J.P.M.L. 2018) (centralization was supported by the plaintiffs in 15 actions and potential tag-along actions, as well as by the responding defendants); *In re Opana ER Antitrust Litig.*, 65 F. Supp. 3d 1408, 1409 (J.P.M.L. 2014) (centralizing actions when "[a]ll plaintiffs and defendants in the actions support centralization"); *In re Gen. Motors LLC Ignition Switch Litig.*, 26 F. Supp. 3d 1390, 1390 (J.P.M.L. 2014) (same). The Panel, however, has not clarified which factors are important (or necessary) in evaluating convenience and which are important (or necessary) in evaluating justice/efficiency.

Early on, the Panel's failure to apply the convenience and efficiency tests in a clear and rigorous manner created controversy. In *In re Equity Funding Corp. of America Securities Litigation,* 375 F. Supp. 1378 (J.P.M.L. 1973), the Panel stated in conclusory terms that its choice of a district for transfer was "for the convenience of the parties and witnesses and the just and efficient conduct of the litigation." *Id.* at 1381. One Panel member dissented, offering a detailed analysis of why many of the parties would be inconvenienced by the choice of district. He concluded that "the 'convenience of the parties and witnesses' is a statutory criterion for transfer that cannot be treated as cavalierly as the majority of the Panel seems to treat it." *Id.* at 1393. Yet decades later, the Panel does not treat the convenience and efficiency factors as strict, independent requirements.

In fact, the Panel often selects districts that are not convenient for some (or even many) of the parties and witnesses. And some plaintiffs may not find it just or convenient that their chosen attorneys have essentially been displaced by attorneys selected for leadership positions by the MDL judge. *See* §§ 7.1–7.5. As one commentator has pointed out, the convenience and efficiency criteria are "functionally meaningless when the litigants are scattered throughout the country." Bradt (William & Mary) at 1174. Nonetheless, while the Panel does not always articulate all of the competing concerns in its typically brief opinions, it is engaged in "a constant balancing act to advance the goals of efficiency and economy without jeopardizing the fairness to the parties." Vance Speech at 22. Ultimately, the most important consideration appears to be convenience to the federal judicial system, rather than convenience to particular litigants.

§ 3.5 OTHER PANEL CONSIDERATIONS IN DECIDING WHETHER TO TRANSFER

In addition to relying heavily on the common questions of fact test (and referring, in a conclusory fashion, to the convenience and efficiency tests), the Panel has discussed many other factors in deciding whether to centralize cases. Williams & George at

442. Without purporting to be exhaustive, the discussion below focuses on some of the factors that the Panel often discusses.

A. MULTIPLE DEFENDANTS AND/OR PRODUCTS

In some cases, the presence of multiple defendants or products weighs heavily against centralization, or in favor of multiple MDLs as opposed to just one. In other cases, these factors are not given substantial weight.

For instance, in *In re 100% Grated Parmesan Cheese Marketing and Sales Practices Litigation*, 201 F. Supp. 3d 1375 (J.P.M.L. 2016), the Panel addressed cases involving the allegedly false and misleading labeling of various cheese products as "100 percent" grated parmesan cheese, even though the products allegedly contained cellulose filler. Many brands and companies were involved. Several parties proposed multiple MDLs, arguing that each defendant had different labeling, marketing, manufacturing and distribution practices, and that such differences could be better managed in separate MDLs. *Id.* at 1376–77.

The Panel rejected that approach, noting: "In many situations, we are hesitant to bring together actions involving separate defendants and products, but when, as here, there is a significant overlap in the central factual issues, parties, and claims, we find that creation of a single MDL is warranted." *Id.* at 1378. The Panel pointed out that "Section 1407 does not require a complete identity of factual issues or parties as a prerequisite to transfer." *Id.* The Panel expressed its "confiden[ce] that the transferee judge can accommodate any issues involving the different products and defendants, including confidentiality and defendant-specific resolutions, in a manner that guarantees the just and efficient resolution of all cases." *Id.*

In *In re AndroGel Products Liability Litigation*, 24 F. Supp. 3d 1378 (J.P.M.L. 2014), the Panel noted that while it is "typically hesitant to centralize litigation on an industry-wide basis," *id.* at 1379, centralization was appropriate in cases against a number of different defendants alleging injuries from the use of testosterone replacement therapies. Centralization, the Panel found, "will reduce potentially costly expert discovery, facilitate the establishment of a uniform pretrial approach to these cases, reduce the potential for inconsistent rulings on such matters as *Daubert* rulings, and conserve the resources of the parties, their counsel, and the judiciary." *Id.*

Similarly, in *In re National Prescription Opiate Litigation*, 290 F. Supp. 3d 1375 (J.P.M.L. 2017), the Panel centralized numerous claims against multiple defendants in an MDL involving "the alleged improper marketing of and inappropriate distribution of various prescription opiate medications into cities, states and towns across the country." *Id.* at 1377. Some parties argued that "centralization of so many diverse claims against manufacturers and distributors will lead to inefficiencies that could slow the progress of all cases." *Id.* at 1378. The Panel disagreed, finding that "[a]ll of the actions can be expected to implicate common fact questions as to the allegedly improper marketing and widespread diversion of prescription opiates . . . and discovery likely will be voluminous." *Id.* at 1378–79. *See also, e.g., In re Humana, Inc., Managed Care Litig.*, Nos. MDL-1334, MDL-1364, MDL-1367, MDL-1366, 2000 WL 1925080, at *2 (J.P.M.L. Oct. 23, 2000) (centralizing actions involving multiple managed care companies because of "common questions of fact concerning whether defendants . . . unlawfully deprived health care plan subscribers of the health care for which they contracted and/or unlawfully interfered with health care providers' delivery of that care").

By contrast, in *In re Power Morcellator Products Liability Litigation,* 140 F. Supp. 3d 1351 (J.P.M.L. 2015), the Panel decided not to create an industry-wide MDL against multiple defendants that manufactured allegedly defective power morcellators used for surgical procedures. In creating an MDL limited to cases against a single defendant, the Panel noted that "we are 'typically hesitant to centralize litigation against multiple, competing defendants which marketed, manufactured and sold [allegedly] similar products.' " *Id.* at 1354.

Similarly, in *In re Yellow Brass Plumbing Component Products Liability Litigation,* 844 F. Supp. 2d 1377 (J.P.M.L. 2012), the plaintiffs sued multiple unrelated defendants alleging that certain plumbing components contained high zinc-content brass. Various homeowners and property owners sought to centralize the actions pending in three districts. The Panel denied centralization, noting that "[t]hough the Panel has in the past centralized litigation involving market-wide conduct, we are typically hesitant to centralize litigation against multiple, competing defendants which marketed, manufactured and sold similar products." *Id.* at 1378. The Panel noted that "[a]t least three industry manufacturing standards [were] involved in [the] litigation." *Id.* at 1379. Even though "the actions share[d] some basic questions of fact," *id.* at 1378, the Panel ruled that centralization was inappropriate.

B. POSSIBILITY OF INFORMAL COORDINATION AND COOPERATION

A crucial issue in a number of Panel opinions is whether informal coordination can achieve efficiencies without the need for formal MDL centralization. The Panel sometimes rejects the argument that informal cooperation will be sufficient, but it sometimes agrees with an informal approach over centralization. Although it can be difficult to predict how the Panel will come out in any given case, the fact that attorneys or judges in the pending cases have been informally cooperating (for example, by cross-noticing depositions, holding joint hearings, or appointing a joint master) may be a forceful argument against centralization. Then again, such an argument depends on whether the record supports the effectiveness of informal cooperation.

For instance, in *In re Generic Pharmaceuticals Pricing Antitrust Litigation*, MDL No. 2724, 2017 WL 4582710 (J.P.M.L. Aug. 3, 2017), the Panel addressed the possible transfer—to a previously created MDL (involving private plaintiffs)—of an antitrust action by 40 states against six pharmaceutical manufacturers targeting two products. The Panel held that transfer was appropriate and that informal coordination and cooperation among the parties and courts would be insufficient to eliminate the potential for duplicative discovery and inconsistent pretrial rulings. *Id.* at *2.

In *In re Viagra (Sildenafil Citrate) Products Liability Litigation,* 224 F. Supp. 3d 1330 (J.P.M.L. 2016), the Panel addressed whether lawsuits alleging that an oral erectile-dysfunction drug, Cialis, caused or increased the risk of melanoma should be transferred to an existing MDL involving similar claims relating to the drug Viagra. The manufacturer of Cialis argued that informal cooperation was preferable to transferring all of the Cialis cases into the Viagra MDL. The Panel disagreed. It noted that "Cialis-only actions are pending in nine districts," and that "the general causation questions presented by the Viagra and Cialis actions are complex, and involve many of the same studies." *Id.* at 1331. The Panel rejected the argument "that informal coordination is an appropriate alternative [to MDL]," pointing out that "[t]he number of involved districts and the complexity of the factual issues pose significant obstacles to informal coordination." *Id.*

In *In re Yosemite National Park Hantavirus Litigation*, 24 F. Supp. 3d 1370 (J.P.M.L. 2014), the Panel granted centralization despite the plaintiffs' contention "that they [had] agreed among themselves to cooperate and coordinate discovery to avoid unnecessary duplication and [to promote] convenience." *Id.* at 1370. The Panel was "not convinced . . . that plaintiffs' proposed discovery plan is a workable substitute for centralization." *Id.* at 1370–71.

And in *In re Uber Techs., Inc. Data Security Breach Litigation*, 304 F. Supp. 3d 1351 (J.P.M.L. 2018), Uber urged the Panel to deny centralization because the various courts could coordinate informally. In analyzing that argument, the Panel noted that "[t]here are ten actions on the motion and seven potential tag-along actions, which are pending in nine districts. Fourteen distinct groups of plaintiffs' counsel represent plaintiffs in these actions." *Id.* at 1354. Based on those facts, the Panel concluded that "the number of actions, districts, and involved counsel, and the complexity of the litigation, make effective coordination on an informal basis impracticable." *Id.*

But informal cooperation is sometimes found to be an adequate substitute for formal centralization. For example, in *In re Uponor, Inc., F1960 Plumbing Fittings Products Liability Litigation,* 895 F. Supp. 2d 1346 (J.P.M.L. 2012), which involved allegedly defective plumbing products, the Panel noted that the actions involved were "in distinct procedural postures, and most of the advanced actions seem[ed] to be progressing well" before the district judge. *Id.* at 1349. As a result, "voluntary coordination and cooperation among the parties . . . and the involved judges [was] a preferable alternative to centralization." *Id.* The Panel "encourage[d] . . . the parties to pursue such cooperative measures and minimize the potential for duplicative discovery and inconsistent pretrial rulings." *Id.*

Similarly, in *In re Dry Bean Revenue Protection Crop Insurance Litigation*, 350 F. Supp. 3d 1381 (J.P.M.L. 2018), the Panel denied centralization because "it appear[ed] feasible for the involved parties and courts to cooperate informally to coordinate any overlap in pretrial proceedings and minimize the potential for inconsistent rulings." *Id.* at 1382.

The Panel has sometimes found less need for centralization when cases involve common plaintiffs' counsel, thereby facilitating coordination. For example, in *In re Lloyds Bank PLC International Mortgage Service Loan Litigation*, 997 F. Supp. 2d 1352 (J.P.M.L. 2014), the Panel denied centralization of three actions from two federal districts. While it "acknowledge[d] that the subject actions d[id] share, to some extent, factual issues," the Panel denied transfer because "[i]nformal coordination seem[ed] practicable," given that the same counsel represented the plaintiffs in two of the actions and the same law firm represented the defendant in all the actions. *Id.* at 1353.

Likewise, in *In re Ocala Funding, LLC, Commercial Litigation*, 867 F. Supp. 2d 1332

(J.P.M.L. 2012), the Panel denied transfer of four actions filed by the same counsel. *Id.* at 1332. Noting that there had already been "extensive coordination" among three of the actions, the Panel concluded that "informal cooperation among the involved attorneys and courts is both practicable and preferable." *Id. See also In re Lipitor (Atorvastatin Calcium) Mktg., Sales Practices & Products Liability Litigation*, 959 F. Supp. 2d 1375, 1376 (J.P.M.L. 2013) (denying centralization of five actions and 23 potential tag-along actions in part because "many of the actions involve common plaintiffs' counsel.")

C. POTENTIAL FOR TRANSFER UNDER 28 U.S.C. § 1404

When faced with a choice between transfer under 28 U.S.C. § 1407 for pretrial proceedings or a change of venue under 28 U.S.C. § 1404(a), the Panel frequently opts to deny centralization under section 1407 so that the transferor court can decide whether to transfer the cases under section 1404(a). Unlike section 1407, section 1404(a) applies to both pretrial proceedings and trial.

For example, in *In re Best Buy Co., California Song-Beverly Credit Card Act Litigation*, 804 F. Supp. 2d 1376 (J.P.M.L. 2011), the Panel denied centralization because of the possibility of a section 1404(a) transfer. All of the constituent actions "involve[d] either California plaintiffs or transactions within California," and thus the Panel reasoned that the cases could be transferred under section 1404(a). *Id.* at 1378. In the Panel's view, section 1407 centralization "should be the last solution after considered review of all other options." *Id.* The advantage of section 1404 was that it is a transfer "for all purposes," not merely for pretrial proceedings. *Id.*

Similarly, in *In re Gerber Probiotic Products, Marketing & Sales Practices Litigation*, 899 F. Supp. 2d 1378 (J.P.M.L. 2012), the Panel denied section 1407 transfer because "transfer under Section 1404 may moot the multidistrict character of a litigation and allow a consolidated proceeding in one court with jurisdiction over the pretrial, trial, and post-trial aspects of the litigation." *Id.* at 1380. The Panel concluded that, "where a reasonable prospect exists that resolution of Section 1404 motions could eliminate the multidistrict character of a litigation, transfer under Section 1404 is preferable to centralization." *Id.*

And in *In re Truvia Natural Sweetener Marketing & Sales Practices Litigation,* 996 F. Supp. 2d 1377 (J.P.M.L. 2014), the Panel denied centralization based on pending section 1404(a) motions. It noted that while it "does not judge the merits of [the section 1404 motions], it seems quite possible that this litigation ultimately will proceed in either the District of Hawaii or the District of Minnesota without Panel intervention." *Id.* at 1378.

A possible transfer under section 1404(a), however, will not always foreclose transfer under section 1407. In *In re Natrol, Inc. Glucosamine/Chondroitin Marketing & Sales Practices Litigation*, 26 F. Supp. 3d 1392 (J.P.M.L. 2014), the Panel noted that "we previously have denied centralization when there is a 'reasonable prospect' that Section 1404 transfer will eliminate the multidistrict character of the litigation." *Id.* at 1393. Yet, in *Glucosamine*, the Panel granted transfer under section 1407 because rulings on section 1404(a) motions "[did] not appear imminent," and because the "nationwide sales of an allegedly widely used dietary supplement . . . suggest[ed] that additional actions also are possible." *Id.*

Similarly, in *In re Oxycontin Antitrust Litigation*, 314 F. Supp. 2d 1388 (J.P.M.L. 2004), the Panel granted centralization despite the defendants' argument that section 1404(a) transfer was preferable to section 1407 transfer. The Panel found section 1407 transfer to be warranted, given the large number of actions pending in 11 districts. *Id.* at 1390.

And *In re Schnuck Markets, Inc., Customer Data Security Breach Litigation*, 978 F. Supp. 2d 1379 (J.P.M.L. 2013), the Panel denied a defendant's request to defer ruling on section 1407 centralization to await rulings on pending section 1404(a) transfer motions. Although the Panel found it to be "a close call," it held that "[o]n balance . . . there is not a sufficiently reasonable prospect that the Section 1404 motions will moot the multidistrict character of this litigation." *Id.* at 1380. The Panel distinguished other decisions denying MDL transfer in favor of section 1404(a) motions, explaining that those cases "involved fewer districts than here and/or indications from counsel that they were amenable to Section 1404 transfer." *Id.* at 1381.

D. PRESENCE OF JURISDICTIONAL ISSUES

"The panel often has held that jurisdictional issues do not present an impediment to transfer, as plaintiffs can present these arguments to the transferee judge." *In re Cook Med., Inc., IVC Filters Mktg., Sales Practices & Prods. Liab. Litig.*, MDL No. 2570 (Doc. 318) (J.P.M.L. Aug. 1, 2017), at 1–2. *Accord, e.g., In re New England Compounding Pharmacy, Inc. Prods. Liab. Litig.*, 38 F. Supp. 3d 1384, 1385 (J.P.M.L. 2014).

Thus, the pendency of a motion to remand to state court will not prevent transfer because the transferee judge can decide the issue. *See, e.g., In re Vioxx Prods. Liab. Litig.*, 360 F. Supp. 2d 1352, 1354 (J.P.M.L. 2005) (so holding); *In re Ford Motor Co. Speed Control Deactivation Switch Prods. Liab. Litig.*, 560 F. Supp. 2d 1365, 1366 (J.P.M.L. 2008) (same). Similarly, the argument that the transferor court lacks personal jurisdiction or venue will not prevent transfer because the transferee judge can decide the issue. *See, e.g., In re RAH Color Techs. LLC Patent Litig.*, 347 F. Supp. 3d 1359, 1360 n.5 (J.P.M.L. 2018) (centralizing patent litigation over the defendant's objection based on lack of personal jurisdiction).

On the other hand, the Panel has recognized that the lack of service of process on defendants may weigh against transfer. The Panel has identified several factors to consider in determining whether to centralize in the absence of service, including:

> (1) the strength of the showing that transfer is desirable, (2) the presence or absence of

> plaintiff's good faith in naming the unserved defendants, (3) the extent of plaintiff's effort to serve each defendant with process, (4) the degree to which the unserved defendant's interests appear to be the same as those of the defendants coming before the Panel, (5) the number of unserved defendants, and (6) the importance of their presence before the Panel in aiding its decision.

In re Library Editions of Children's Books, 299 F. Supp. 1139, 1143 (J.P.M.L. 1969). Even without explicitly applying these factors, the Panel will occasionally deny transfer in the face of unserved or ineffectively served defendants. *See, e.g., In re Brandywine Commc'ns. Techs., LLC, Patent Litig.*, 959 F. Supp. 2d 1377, 1378 n.5 (J.P.M.L. 2013) (denying centralization of patent cases where, *inter alia*, defendants had not been served with process in several of the actions).

E. DIFFERENT KINDS OF PLAINTIFFS

When cases involve different kinds of plaintiffs (*e.g.*, private plaintiffs and government entities), the question arises whether centralization is appropriate. The Panel has ruled both ways, depending on the facts and circumstances.

In *In re Generic Pharmaceuticals Pricing Antitrust Litigation*, MDL No. 2724, 2017 WL 4582710 (J.P.M.L. Aug. 3, 2017), a case alleging antitrust violations by six pharmaceutical manufacturers, the Panel addressed possible transfer of antitrust cases brought by 40 states to a previously created MDL that involved private plaintiffs (but the same defendants). In finding that the actions brought by the states could be handled as part of the existing MDL, the Panel noted that "[i]n similar circumstances, the Panel has transferred state enforcement actions to MDLs involving cases brought by private litigants[.]" *Id.* at *2.

In *In re Volkswagen "Clean Diesel" Mktg., Sales Practices, & Products Liability Litigation*, No. 2:16-cv-00979 (Doc. 11) (J.P.M.L. Aug. 5, 2016), the Panel rejected a state plaintiff's argument against transfer to an existing MDL involving "clean diesel" claims by private plaintiffs, noting that "[t]he Panel often has transferred claims brought by a State so long as the action involves facts common to the MDL proceeding . . . ." *Id.* at 2. *See also In re Fresenius Granuflo/Naturalyte Dialysate Prods. Liab. Litig.*, MDL No. 2428 (Doc. 993) (J.P.M.L. Dec. 11, 2014) (rejecting a state attorney general's argument that its action should not be transferred to an existing MDL involving private plaintiffs; the Panel noted that, "while plaintiff . . . may seek different relief, its claims are based on the same underlying facts" as the actions already centralized).

The Panel has applied similar reasoning in the face of arguments that the differing characteristics of individual private plaintiffs warranted separate treatment. In *In re Power Morcellator Products Liability Litigation*, 140 F. Supp. 3d 1351 (J.P.M.L. 2015), a plaintiff sought exclusion from a product liability MDL because, unlike the other plaintiffs, she faced a dire medical condition (recurrence of cancer) and feared that transfer would "delay her action." *Id.* at 1354. The Panel rejected the argument, noting that "[w]hile we are sympathetic to [plaintiff's] arguments . . . [they] are best addressed to the transferee judge," who [could] decide whether remand to the transferor judge was appropriate. *Id.* *See also In re Infants Born Opioid-Dependent Prods. Liab. Litig.*, 350 F. Supp. 3d 1377, 1378–79 (J.P.M.L. 2018) (rejecting request to create a new MDL for cases that "substantial[l]y overlap[ped]" with an existing MDL; the Panel found that "[f]ew efficiencies [would] be gained" because "[t]he substantial duplication of activity would be costly, and it would likely slow the pace of" the existing MDL).

By contrast, the Panel has sometimes refused to centralize cases involving different kinds of plaintiffs. For example, in *In re Mirena IUS Levonorgestrel-Related Products Liability Litigation*, 38 F. Supp. 3d 1380 (J.P.M.L. 2014), the plaintiffs sought to centralize nine actions alleging that the synthetic hormone released by the defendants' IUDs caused abnormal elevation of cerebrospinal fluid in the skull, resulting in neurological injuries. The Panel had previously centralized litigation involving the IUD at issue, which focused on a different type of injury (uterine perforation and migration). Nonetheless, the Panel denied centralization of the nine actions at issue. It explained that the alleged injuries in the instant litigation, "principally headaches and vision problems," were "nonspecific," leading to "individualized causation issues." *Id.* at 1381 & n.3. Notably, three years later the Panel granted centralization of claims raising the same allegations after finding that the circumstances had changed. *In re Mirena IUS Levonorgestrel-Related Prods. Liab. Litig. (No. II)*, 249 F. Supp. 3d 1357 (J.P.M.L. 2017). Among other things, the Panel found that the record of the litigation demonstrated that plaintiff-specific causation issues did not "appear to be an obstacle to centralization[.]" *Id.* at 1359.

F. MULTIPLE KINDS OF CLAIMS

The fact that various lawsuits raise different kinds of claims is usually not a basis for denying transfer.

For instance, in *In re Toyota Motor Corp. Unintended Acceleration Marketing Sales Practices & Products Liability Litigation*, 704 F. Supp. 2d 1379 (J.P.M.L. 2010), the Panel centralized automobile-defect class action claims seeking economic loss damages as well as individual personal injury and wrongful death claims. The Panel noted that even though "the personal injury and wrongful death claims will require considerable individual discovery in addition to the common discovery in each case," the transferee judge would be able to "design the kind of distinct discovery tracks often employed to address these concerns." *Id.* at 1382.

In the pharmaceutical context, the Panel "has frequently combined actions involving claims relating to sales and the marketing of medications with actions involving personal injury claims from use of the same pharmaceutical products." *In re Yasmin & Yaz (Drospirenone) Mktg., Sales Practices & Prods. Liab. Litig.*, 655 F. Supp. 2d 1343, 1344 (J.P.M.L. 2009). *Accord, e.g., In re Avandia Mktg.,*

Sales Practices & Prods. Liab. Litig., 528 F. Supp. 2d 1339 (J.P.M.L. 2007) (centralizing marketing, sales practices, and product liability claims in a single MDL); *In re Vytorin/Zetia Marketing, Sales Practices & Prods. Liab. Litig.*, 543 F. Supp. 2d 1378 (J.P.M.L. 2008) (same).

G. NUMBER OF PENDING ACTIONS

Unlike the "numerosity" requirement applicable to class actions, *see* Fed. R. Civ. P. 23(a)(1), there is no strict "numerosity" requirement under the MDL statute. Nonetheless, the number of cases that would be transferred is certainly relevant to the Panel's decision on whether to order transfer. A former chair of the Panel suggested that, in general, the minimum number of cases needed for centralization is between three and seven. Hodges Interview at 2.

In *In re Power Morcellator Products Liability Litigation*, 140 F. Supp. 3d 1351 (J.P.M.L. 2015), the Panel found that 28 actions naming a particular defendant were "a sufficient number . . . to warrant centralization, given the complexity of anticipated overlapping fact and expert discovery." *Id.* at 1353.

Similarly, in *In re Stryker Orthopaedics LFIT V40 Femoral Head Products Liability Litigation*, 249 F. Supp. 3d 1353 (J.P.M.L. 2017), the Panel rejected the argument that "33 cases . . . pending in seventeen different districts, with at least eight groups of what appears to be competing plaintiffs' counsel involved" was not numerous enough. *Id.* at 1355.

Nonetheless, the Panel has noted that "[w]here only a minimal number of actions are involved, the proponent of centralization bears a heavier burden to demonstrate that centralization is appropriate." *In re American Bd. of Med. Specialties Maintenance of Certification Antitrust Litig.*, 382 F. Supp. 3d 1353, 1353 (J.P.M.L. 2019).

In *In re Gemcap Lending I, LLC*, 382 F. Supp. 3d 1352 (J.P.M.L. 2019), a plaintiff sought centralization of two actions pending in different districts, both stemming from a loan issued by one of the defendants. While noting that "[n]o party disputes that the actions share common factual and legal issues," the Panel denied centralization, because there were "just two actions involving a single plaintiff, with no indication of more to come." *Id.* at 1352. *Accord, e.g., In re Dry Bean Revenue Protection Crop Ins. Litig.*, 350 F. Supp. 3d 1381, 1382 (J.P.M.L. 2018) (denying MDL treatment of two cases pending in two districts); *In re Time Warner Cable, Inc., Tel. Consumer Prot. Act (TCPA) Litigation.*, 247 F. Supp. 3d 1388, 1388–89 (J.P.M.L. 2016) (denying centralization of seven actions because there were "relatively few actions at issue. . . pending in only two districts, and the factual issues presented [were] neither particularly complex nor numerous").

Another factor is whether the cases include putative class actions. In the class action context, the Panel may be more receptive to transfer, even when there are relatively few cases. *See, e.g., In re Gen. Motors Corp. Air Conditioning Mktg. & Sales*

Practices Litig., 289 F. Supp. 3d 1340, 1341 (J.P.M.L. 2018) (granting centralization of four putative class actions concerning allegedly defective air conditioning systems in defendant's vehicles).

In summarizing the Panel's approach, the Manual for Complex Litigation has noted that "[a]s few as two cases may warrant multidistrict treatment, although those advocating transfer bear a heavy burden of persuasion when there are only a few actions, particularly those involving the same parties and counsel." Manual § 20.131.

H. RELEVANCE OF THE MERITS

A number of cases have addressed whether transfer should be denied based on arguments that the underlying claims are meritless. In general, because the Panel is not empowered to decide the merits, it will not deny transfer on merits-based grounds.

In *In re Wright Medical Technology, Inc., Conserve Hip Implant Products Liability Litigation*, 844 F. Supp. 2d 1371 (J.P.M.L. 2012), the plaintiff moved to centralize five actions pending in five districts involving alleged defects in hip implant products. In opposing transfer, the manufacturer defendants argued that "certain of plaintiffs' contentions regarding [the implant product] are wholly without merit." *Id.* at 1372. In rejecting that argument as a basis for denying transfer, the Panel noted that "[t]he framers of Section 1407 did not contemplate that the Panel would decide the merits of the actions before it and neither the statute nor the implementing Rules of the Panel are drafted to allow for such determinations." *Id.* The Panel explained that the defendants "can seek dismissal or other relief from the transferee judge, who will be intimately familiar with the nuances of this litigation." *Id.*

Similarly, in *In re Kauffman Mutual Fund Actions*, 337 F. Supp. 1337 (J.P.M.L. 1972), the Panel rejected the defendants' argument that centralization should be denied because the litigation was "of questionable merit." *Id.* at 1339. The Panel noted that "[i]f defendants are correct in their contention that the complaints are unmeritorious, the most fair and efficient way for them to obtain dismissal is to place the question before a single judge, rather than allowing ten groups of defendants to proceed separately over the same common factual background before ten different judges." *Id.* at 1340.

In other cases as well, the Panel has granted centralization despite merits-based arguments. *See, e.g.*, *In re Anheuser-Busch Beer Labeling Mktg. & Sales Practices Litig.*, 949 F. Supp. 2d 1371, 1371 n.2 (J.P.M.L. 2013) (granting centralization despite the defendant's argument that "little or no discovery [would] be required in light of the defenses raised in its pending motions to dismiss"); *In re Fluoroquinolone Prods. Liab. Litig.*, 122 F. Supp. 3d 1378, 1380 (J.P.M.L. 2015) (centralizing actions despite the defendants' assertions that the majority of the actions were unmeritorious due to statutes of limitations and other defenses; the Panel explained that it was "not authorized to engage in an assessment of the merits of [those] actions"); *In re*

Viagra (Sildenafil Citrate) Prods. Liab. Litig., 224 F. Supp. 3d 1330, 1332 (J.P.M.L. 2016) (granting centralization despite the argument that MDL would lead to the filing of frivolous cases).

I. SUCCESSIVE REQUESTS

The Panel views successive requests for transfer with skepticism, and is likely to deny MDL treatment when a party has already sought transfer and failed. The Panel has noted that, while a prior denial "does not preclude [it] from" later changing its mind, it will "rarely" grant centralization after previously denying it. *In re Plavix Mktg., Sales Practices & Prods. Liab. Litig. (No. II)*, 923 F. Supp. 2d 1376, 1378 (J.P.M.L. 2013). However, the Panel might reach a different result if "a significant change in circumstances has occurred." *Id.*

In *Plavix*, which involved allegations that defendants falsely promoted the cardiovascular benefits of the drug at issue while failing to disclose its serious risks, the Panel initially denied centralization. 829 F. Supp. 2d 1378 (J.P.M.L. 2011). A year later, after a new centralization motion was filed, the Panel found significant differences from the first motion based on the filing of numerous additional actions in both state and federal courts, as well as a substantial increase in the number of law firms involved on the plaintiffs' side. *Plavix II,* 923 F. Supp. 2d at 1378–79. The Panel granted centralization the second time around. *Id.* at 1379.

Similarly, in *In re Proton-Pump Inhibitor Products Liability Litigation (No. II)*, 261 F. Supp. 3d 1351

(J.P.M.L. 2017), the Panel stated that "several of the grounds on which [it] denied centralization in *Proton-Pump I* remain largely valid[.]" *Id.* at 1354. Nonetheless, on a new transfer motion, the Panel found that "the significantly larger number of involved actions, districts, and counsel, the concomitant increase in burden on party and judicial resources, and the opportunity for federal-state coordination, coupled with most defendants' change in position to now support centralization, tip the balance in favor of creating an MDL." *Id.* The Panel noted that "[c]entralization will facilitate a uniform and efficient pretrial approach to this litigation, eliminate duplicative discovery, prevent inconsistent rulings on *Daubert* and other pretrial issues, and conserve the resources of the parties, their counsel, and the judiciary." *Id.*

A similar sequence occurred in *In re Health Management Associates, Inc. Qui Tam Litigation (No. II)*, 11 F. Supp. 3d 1346 (J.P.M.L. 2014). The lawsuits alleged that the defendants' improper actions led to medically unnecessary tests on emergency room patients and hospital admissions of patients who should have received outpatient care. The Panel granted centralization less than a year after denying it, because the United States Government had subsequently intervened in eight of the nine actions. The Panel noted that "with the Government now having made its intervention decisions, we conclude that centralization will eliminate the possibilities of duplicative discovery and conflicting pretrial rulings[.]" *Id.* at 1348. *See also* Marcus (Tulane) at 2271 (noting that there were five unsuccessful attempts to transfer asbestos cases before a motion to transfer was granted).

J. MASS ACTION LIMITATION

The Class Action Fairness Act (CAFA), allows removal in actions seeking money damages that, while not brought as class actions, involve at least 100 individual plaintiffs who assert common questions of law or fact. 28 U.S.C. § 1332(d)(11)(B)(i). Cases removed to federal court under this so-called mass action provision "shall not thereafter be transferred to any other court pursuant to section 1407, or the rules promulgated thereunder, unless a majority of plaintiffs in the action request transfer pursuant to section 1407." 28 U.S.C. § 1332(d)(11)(B)(i).

In *In re Plavix Mktg., Sales Practices & Products Liability Litigation (No. II)*, 923 F. Supp. 2d 1376, 1380 (J.P.M.L. 2013), the Panel denied without prejudice the transfer of 12 actions that had been removed to federal court on multiple grounds, including that they were mass actions under CAFA. "In these unusual circumstances," the Panel opted to "deny, without prejudice, transfer of these actions at this time, and to await rulings by the two putative transferor courts . . . on the remand motions pending therein." *Id.* at 1380.

A few months after flagging the issue in *Plavix II*, the Panel held that CAFA's mass action limitation does not apply when a case is removed to federal court on multiple grounds, and not just under the mass action provision. As the Panel explained,

"Congress did not intend that actions removed on multiple grounds, grounds which include the mass action provision, would be restricted from Section 1407 transfer." *In re Darvocet, Darvon & Propoxyphene Prods. Liab. Litig.*, 939 F. Supp. 2d 1376, 1381 (J.P.M.L. 2013). The Panel acknowledged that "the provision's language arguably might be read otherwise," but it concluded that "such an interpretation would not square with Congress's intent and would bar transfer (absent a request by a majority of the plaintiffs therein) of cases that presumptively have been transferable, simply because the removing defendant cited CAFA mass action as but one ground supporting federal jurisdiction." *Id.* The Panel reasoned that "reading the provision to restrict transfer of actions properly removed on diversity or federal-question grounds, in addition to the mass action ground, would result in a major change in the Panel's authority and function that is unsupported by the statute's legislative history." *Id.* at 1380.

K. RELEVANCE OF THE LAW THAT WOULD APPLY

In addressing transfer, the Panel has refused to take into account the possibility that the transferee court might apply different substantive law than the transferor court. This can arise, for example, when the district courts are in different circuits and the circuits are divided on an important issue of federal law in the case. *See* § 12.2 (most transferee courts apply the law of the transferee court's circuit on questions of federal law).

For instance, in *In re Equifax, Inc., Customer Data Security Breach Litigation*, 289 F. Supp. 3d 1322 (J.P.M.L. 2017), the Panel considered whether to centralize numerous actions arising from an alleged data breach that compromised the personal information of more than 145 million consumers. The plaintiffs in one potential tag-along action opposed centralization, arguing that there was "a deep circuit split on the issue of Article III standing, making centralization before rulings on motions to dismiss inefficient." *Id.* at 1325. The Panel found that the circuit split was irrelevant. It explained that "[t]ransferee courts consider a wide variety of legal issues that are subject to differing precedent in their transferor courts," and that in any event, "the Panel does not consider the possible implications with respect to standing or other potential rulings when it selects a transferee district." *Id.*

Similarly, the Panel does not consider the possibility (based on prior proceedings) that the transferee court might rule against certain parties. In *In re Beef Industry Antitrust Litigation*, 419 F. Supp. 720 (J.P.M.L. 1976), certain parties opposed transfer to a particular district "because of their displeasure with prior proceedings in that forum." *Id.* at 722. The Panel found that contention "wholly without merit," explaining that "[t]he prospect of an unfavorable ruling by the transferee court or the possibility that another district judge may be more favorably disposed to a litigant's contentions are simply not factors considered by the Panel in determining whether and to where transfer under Section 1407 is appropriate." *Id.*

L. PENDENCY OF DISPOSITIVE MOTIONS

"[T]he Panel has [frequently] held that the pendency of potentially dispositive motions is not an impediment to transfer of actions, because such motions can be addressed to the transferee judge for resolution after transfer." Manual § 20.131. For example, in *In re Bank of New York Mellon Corp. Foreign Exchange Transactions Litigation*, 857 F. Supp. 2d 1371 (J.P.M.L. 2012), one plaintiff asked the Panel to defer transfer until the transferor court ruled on a pending motion to dismiss. *Id.* at 1372. The Panel "decline[d] . . . plaintiff's request for an open-ended delay in the transfer of its action until the issuance of a ruling on a motion to dismiss," reasoning that the "transferee court is fully capable of addressing that motion." *Id.* at 1374.

Similarly, the Panel will not decide the merits of a jurisdictional argument, such as a motion to remand to state court, that will determine whether the cases remain in federal court. For instance, in *In re Eliquis (Apixaban) Products Liability Litigation*, MDL No. 2754, 2017 WL 6569794 (J.P.M.L. May 30, 2017), plaintiffs in 12 cases moved to vacate the Panel's orders conditionally transferring their cases to an existing MDL. The plaintiffs argued that their "actions were improperly removed," and that "remand [was] a near certainty," given that "judges in the Northern District of California [had] ordered remand of similar Eliquis cases[.]" *Id.* at *1. The Panel nonetheless transferred the actions, invoking the "well-established principle that Section 1407 does not empower the MDL Panel to decide questions going to the jurisdiction of the merits of a case, including issues relating to a motion to remand." *Id.*

In some instances, however, the Panel may deny transfer when a motion is pending that would eliminate the eligibility of the actions for transfer. For instance, in *In re Power Balance, LLC, Marketing & Sales Practices Litigation,* 777 F. Supp. 2d 1345, 1346 (J.P.M.L. 2011), the Panel denied centralization, despite common questions of fact, when one plaintiff had a motion pending in the transferor court to approve a proposed nationwide class settlement. And in *In re Deering Milliken Patent*, 328 F. Supp. 504, 505 (J.P.M.L. 1970), the Panel denied centralization when pending motions in transferor courts for change of venue under 28 U.S.C. § 1404(a), if granted, would have resulted in the transfer of all actions to a single district, eliminating the multidistrict character of the actions.

M. ARBITRATION CLAUSES

Consistent with the case law discussed in subsection L above, the Panel has held that the issue of whether lawsuits are subject to dismissal based on arbitration clauses can be decided by the transferee judge and is not a basis for denying transfer. For example, in *In re Uber Technologies, Inc., Data Security Breach Litigation*, 304 F. Supp. 3d 1351 (J.P.M.L. 2018), the defendants opposed transfer "based on the asserted likelihood that their pending and anticipated motions to compel individual arbitration [would] be granted in all actions, prior to the commencement of any discovery, bringing an early end to this litigation." *Id.* at 1353. The Panel rejected that argument, explaining that "such an assessment of the merits is beyond [our] authority." *Id.* at 1354. "[W]here the litigation involves common factual questions," the Panel explained, "centralization may be appropriate even though defendants predict that they will prevail on dispositive motions prior to commencement of discovery." *Id.*

Similarly, in *In re Allura Fiber Cement Siding Products Liability Litigation*, 366 F. Supp. 3d 1365 (J.P.M.L. 2019), the Panel granted centralization despite the defendants' assertion that "their pending and anticipated motions to compel individual arbitration [would] be granted, obviating the need for further pretrial proceedings in any of these actions." *Id.* at 1366. The Panel reasoned that "such an assessment of the merits of the actions is beyond the Panel's authority." *Id.*

On the other hand, in *In re H & R Block Employee Antitrust Litigation*, 355 F. Supp. 3d 1380 (J.P.M.L. 2019), the Panel denied centralization based in part on the fact that the defendant intended to move to compel arbitration or for section 1404(a) transfer, either of which would eliminate the multidistrict character of the litigation. *Id.* at 1381.

And in *In re Uber Technologies, Inc., TCPA Litigation*, 247 F. Supp. 3d 1386 (J.P.M.L. 2016), the Panel denied centralization in a case involving allegations of unsolicited text messages. Despite finding that "the actions appear[ed] to share some factual questions relating to allegations that Uber violated the [Telephone Consumer Protection Act] by sending unsolicited text messages to plaintiffs," the Panel found that "several actions present[ed] significant individualized factual issues concerning . . . the applicability of allegedly mandatory arbitration agreements to certain plaintiffs." *Id.* at 1387.

N. POSSIBILITY THAT NEW CASES WILL BE FILED

In ruling on transfer, the Panel occasionally states that it does not consider the possibility that new cases may be filed.

For instance, in *In re Qualitest Birth Control Products Liability Litigation*, 38 F. Supp. 3d 1388 (J.P.M.L. 2014), plaintiffs moved to centralize litigation arising out of the recall of several birth control products. Plaintiffs alleged that, because of a packaging error, the daily regimen for the contraceptives left them at risk for unwanted pregnancy. The Panel found that centralization was not necessary. Although plaintiffs asserted that there were 113 additional claimants who had not yet filed suit, the Panel found that that "assertion [did] not weigh in favor of centralization" because of the Panel's disinclination to take into account "the mere possibility of future filings in our centralization calculus." *Id.* at 1389.

In *In re Route 91 Harvest Festival Shootings in Las Vegas, Nevada, on October 1, 2017*, 347 F. Supp. 3d 1355 (J.P.M.L. 2018), the defendants sought MDL treatment of cases relating to a highly publicized mass shooting. The gunman shot the victims from his hotel room at the Mandalay Bay Hotel. Various defendants, including MGM Resorts International and Mandalay Bay, LLC, sought transfer of 13 actions pending in eight districts. A number of those actions were declaratory actions brought *by* MGM against approximately 1,977 individuals who had previously sued or threatened to sue. MGM sought a ruling that the claims (based on state law) were barred by the federal SAFETY Act of 2002, 6 U.S.C. §§ 441–444. Despite the small number of suits, MGM argued that MDL transfer was warranted because—based on communications from the plaintiffs' attorneys—MGM expected that as many as 22,000 new lawsuits would be filed against it. In denying transfer, the Panel noted that it "generally does not take into account the mere possibility of future filings when considering centralization." *Id.* at 1358.

Similarly, in *In re Lipitor (Atorvastatin Calcium) Marketing, Sales Practices & Products Liability Litigation*, 959 F. Supp. 2d 1375 (J.P.M.L. 2013), the plaintiffs in various actions alleged that taking the cholesterol drug at issue could result in the development of type 2 diabetes, and that the drug manufacturer had failed to warn consumers. *Id.* at 1376. In arguing for centralization, plaintiffs suggested "that the number of . . . cases" was "likely to expand considerably." *Id.* at 1376. The Panel refused "to take into account the mere possibility of future filings in [its] centralization calculus," especially given the "relative handful of actions" actually brought alleging the link between the drug and diabetes. *Id.* Importantly, the Panel later granted centralization in the litigation after finding that "the number of involved actions, districts, and judges ha[d] grown considerably," "the number of involved plaintiffs' firms ha[d] grown," and related litigation was now pending in at least three state courts. *In re Lipitor (Atorvastatin Calcium) Mktg., Sales Practices & Prods. Liab. Litig. (No. II),* 997 F. Supp. 2d 1354, 1356 (J.P.M.L. 2014).

O. LIKELIHOOD OF DISCOVERY AND MOTION PRACTICE

The Panel has denied transfer when the cases present little likelihood of substantial discovery or motions practice. For instance, in *In re Dry Bean Revenue Protection Crop Insurance Litigation*, 350 F. Supp. 3d 1381 (J.P.M.L. 2018), the plaintiffs sought centralization of two actions pending in two different districts. In denying centralization, the Panel noted that "[d]iscovery, if any, will be limited, as these cases will be decided on the administrative record, and motion practice will consist of motions regarding that record and dispositive motions." *Id.* at 1382.

Similarly, in *In re Clean Water Rule: Definition of "Waters of the United States,"* 140 F. Supp. 3d 1340 (J.P.M.L. 2015), the Panel denied centralization of nine actions involving challenges to a rule promulgated by the Environmental Protection Agency and the U.S. Army Corps of Engineers interpreting the jurisdictional phrase "waters of the United States." The Panel explained that the "resolution of [the] actions [would] involve only very limited pretrial proceedings," and "[d]iscovery, if any, [would] be minimal, as [the] cases [would] be decided on the administrative record." *Id.* at 1341.

And in *In re H & R Block Employee Antitrust Litigation*, 355 F. Supp. 3d 1380 (J.P.M.L. 2019), the Panel denied centralization in a case alleging that the defendants had violated antitrust laws by agreeing not to solicit or recruit each other's employees through a "No Poach Clause" in franchise agreements. The Panel found that the common issues of fact—in particular, the existence of the "No Poach Clause"—"appear[ed] to be largely undisputed, and unlikely to require significant discovery." *Id.* at 1381.

P. SEPARATE MDL FOR CASES RELATED TO AN EXISTING MDL

The Panel has viewed with skepticism requests for separate MDL treatment of claims that are related in some fashion to claims in an existing pending MDL.

For instance, in 2017, the Panel ordered transfer of dozens of cases alleging "improper marketing of and inappropriate distribution of various prescription opiate medications into cities, states and towns across the country." *In re National Prescription Opiate Litig.*, 290 F. Supp. 3d 1375, 1377 (J.P.M.L. 2017). Seven plaintiffs later sought a separate MDL for seven cases involving opiate-addicted infants diagnosed with neonatal abstinence syndrome (NAS). *In re Infants Born Opioid-Dependent Prods. Liab. Litig.*, 350 F. Supp. 3d 1377 (J.P.M.L. 2018). In denying the request, the Panel noted that all of the cases involved allegations of "allegedly improper marking and sale of prescription opiates, as well as their allegedly improper diversion to illicit channels." *Id.* at 1378. As a result, "[t]here [was] substantial overlap between" those seven cases and the cases in the existing *Opiate* MDL. *Id.* The Panel explained that "[f]ew efficiencies [would] be gained by creating a new MDL for NAS plaintiffs," given that "[d]iscovery [in the two cases] . . . will substantially overlap," and "[t]he progress of both MDLs likely would be hindered by the need for two judges to attend to overlapping discovery matters, rule on redundant motion practice and administer both MDLs separately." *Id.* at 1379. In addition, "[n]ew case management protocols and counsel leadership would have to be established in the NAS MDL." *Id.* As a result, "[t]he substantial duplication of activity would be costly, and it likely would slow the pace of [the first MDL], in which discovery and bellwether motion practice [were] underway." *Id.*

Similarly, in *In re Sorin 3T Heater-Cooler System Products Liability Litigation (No. II)*, 289 F. Supp. 3d 1335 (J.P.M.L. 2018), the Panel rejected certain plaintiffs' request to create a separate MDL for their cases. The cases involved allegations that the defendants' medical devices exposed plaintiffs to two types of bacteria. Two plaintiffs argued that the Panel should create a separate MDL for the specific type of bacterial exposure that they alleged. The Panel, however, found that "[d]iscovery and pretrial proceedings will overlap regarding the design, manufacture, operation, and regulation of the . . . device; the sufficiency of the defendants' warnings; and the plaintiffs' theory of general causation regarding the manner of transmission." *Id.* at 1337.

Although the "actions undoubtedly will involve some plaintiff- and hospital-specific factual issues," the Panel noted that "this is not unusual in products liability MDLs, particularly with medical device cases." *Id. See also, e.g., In re Porsche "Clean Diesel" Mktg., Sales Practices, & Prods. Liab. Litig.*, 158 F. Supp. 3d 1369, 1371 (J.P.M.L. 2016) (declining to create a separate MDL from the *Volkswagen "Clean Diesel"* MDL for Porsche vehicles and instead transferring those actions into the *VW* MDL; the Panel explained that a separate MDL was "unnecessary because of the actions' strong factual ties to the Volkswagen MDL and the inefficiencies of establishing a separate MDL"). *But see, e.g., In re Cook Medical, Inc., Pelvic Repair Sys. Prods. Liab. Litig.*, 365 F. Supp. 3d 685, 690–92 (S.D.W.Va. 2019) (describing the Panel's creation of 7 separate, related MDLs involving "similar pelvic mesh products manufactured by different defendants that allegedly caused a variety of injuries").

Q. DIFFERENT DISCOVERY TRACKS

In some instances, the fact that cases are on different discovery tracks will weigh against centralization as an MDL. This could be because the discovery needs in the different cases will be separate and non-overlapping, or because, even though the discovery will be similar, some cases are new and others are nearing completion.

An example of the first situation is *In re CVS Caremark Corp. Wage & Hour Employment Practices Litigation*, 684 F. Supp. 2d 1377 (J.P.M.L. 2010). In that case, which involved wage and hour litigation, the Panel found that discovery in each of the constituent actions was "likely to involve individualized, location-specific examination of things such as a particular assistant manager's job duties and the specific tasks assigned to them in a given store or locality." *Id.* at 1379. The Panel concluded that "the potential for significant individual discovery tilts the balance against centralization." *Id.* at 1379.

An example of the second situation is *In re Ambulatory Pain Pump-Chondrolysis Products Liability Litigation*, 709 F. Supp. 2d 1375 (J.P.M.L. 2010). There, the Panel rejected centralization in mass tort litigation in part because "the constituent actions are at widely varying procedural stages," with fact discovery "either over or nearly over" in some, and with expert discovery "underway . . . or . . . completed in a number of actions." *Id.* at 1378. In *In re Cymbalta (Duloxetine) Prods. Liab. Litig.*, 65 F. Supp. 3d 1393, 1393–94 (J.P.M.L. 2013), the Panel denied centralization, despite the fact that the actions for which MDL treatment was sought were "highly similar," because "the procedural posture of the actions varie[d] significantly." *Id.* at 1393. While the recently filed actions before the Panel were "still in their infancy," the earlier filed actions were much further along and "most, if not all of the common discovery" had already taken place in those cases. *Id.* at 1394.

In other cases, however, discovery complications have not resulted in the denial of transfer. For example, in *In re Toyota Motor Corp. Unintended Acceleration Marketing Sales Practices & Products Liability Litigation*, 704 F. Supp. 2d 1379 (J.P.M.L. 2010), the Panel transferred cases that required both common and individualized discovery. Although "the personal injury and wrongful death claims will require considerable individual discovery in addition to the common discovery in each case," the Panel was "confident that the transferee judge [could] design the kind of distinct discovery tracks often employed to address these concerns." *Id.* at 1382. *See also, e.g., In re Valsartan N-Nitrosodimethylamine (NDMA) Contamination Prods. Liab. Litig.*, 363 F. Supp. 3d 1378, 1382 (J.P.M.L. 2019) (in centralizing economic loss class actions with personal injury actions, the Panel noted that "discovery undoubtedly will overlap among these actions," and that "the individual discovery required in personal injury actions is regularly . . . coordinated within MDLs involving both kinds of actions").

R. RELEVANCE OF OPPOSITION TO TRANSFER

As noted (*see* § 3.4), the Panel has frequently cited wide party support as a basis for centralization. The impact of vigorous opposition by some parties is less clear. In many cases, the Panel has centralized cases despite some opposition. *See, e.g., In re Nat'l Century Financial Enters., Inc.*, 293 F. Supp. 2d 1375, 1376 (J.P.M.L. 2003) (centralizing actions despite the fact that most of the plaintiffs objected); *In re Asbestos Prods. Liab. Litig. (No. VI)*, 771 F. Supp. 415, 416–17 (J.P.M.L. 1991) (centralizing actions when transfer was supported by plaintiffs in approximately 17,000 actions and 30 defendants, and opposed by plaintiffs in at least 5,200 actions and 454 defendants). The Panel has stated that "[i]n an appropriate situation, [it] has the power to order transfer in multidistrict litigation even if all parties are opposed to transfer." *In re Asbestos & Asbestos Insulation Material Prods. Liab. Litig.*, 431 F. Supp. 906, 910 (J.P.M.L. 1977).

There are, however, cases in which the Panel has denied centralization in part because of the extent of the opposition. For example, in *In re CVS Caremark Corp. Wage & Hour Employment Practices Litigation*, 684 F. Supp. 2d 1377 (J.P.M.L. 2010), the Panel denied centralization, among other reasons, because it was opposed by "a clear majority of plaintiffs, as well as all defendants[.]" *Id.* at 1379. For other examples in which the Panel denied centralization in part because of the strong opposition by some parties, *see, e.g.*, *In re "Lite Beer" Trademark Litig.*, 437 F. Supp. 754, 755–56 (J.P.M.L. 1977); *In re Student-Athlete Name & Likeness Litig.*, 763 F. Supp. 2d 1379, 1380 (J.P.M.L. 2011).

S. RELEVANCE OF THE TYPES OF CLAIMS

As the statistics show (*see* § 1.4), transfer is most likely to be granted in certain kinds of cases, with the highest percentages of grants in air crash, antitrust, securities, product liability, and intellectual property cases (all with well over a 50 percent grant rate). Cases with less than a 50 percent grant rate include employment and contract cases.

Certain types of cases tend to be especially strong candidates for centralization. For instance, with respect to air crash cases, the Panel has stated that "[t]here is no doubt that this type of litigation arising out of a single disaster involves common questions of fact or that the convenience of parties and witnesses is generally furthered by consolidation under Section 1407." *In re Air Crash Disaster at Falls City, Neb. on Aug. 6, 1966*, 298 F. Supp. 1323, 1324 (J.P.M.L. 1969).

Nonetheless, the Panel has no formal presumptions in favor of, or against, transferring certain kinds of cases. For example, the Panel has frequently granted centralization in antitrust cases, *see* M.S. Williams at 1268, but has not hesitated to deny centralization when the circumstances do not justify it. *See, e.g., In re Dental Supplies & Equipment Antitrust Litig.*, 289 F. Supp. 3d 1330, 1330–31 (J.P.M.L. 2018) (denying transfer of 36 antitrust actions pending in two districts because the actions were proceeding expeditiously, and there were "few pretrial proceedings remaining that would benefit from centralized treatment").

Similarly, although air crash cases have historically been the most likely to be centralized, *see* M.S. Williams at 1268, just because cases relate to air crashes does not make transfer a foregone conclusion. In fact, a number of air crash cases have been found ill-suited for transfer. *See, e.g., In re Air Crash Near Lake Wales, Fla. on June 7, 2012*, 118 F. Supp. 3d 1374, 1375 (J.P.M.L. 2015) (denying centralization of two actions arising from the crash of a private plane in which the pilot and all five passengers were killed, despite the existence of common issues of fact, because there were "only two actions, with no indication of more to come"); *In re Air Crash Near Islamabad, Pak., on July 28, 2010*, 777 F. Supp. 2d 1352 (J.P.M.L. 2011) (denying centralization of two actions arising from an airplane crash when the two actions had a common plaintiff and alternatives to MDL transfer, such as transfer under 28 U.S.C. § 1404(a), were available).

Ultimately, the Panel decides each transfer motion on the merits. For instance, in *In re CVS Caremark Corp. Wage & Hour Employment Practices Litigation*, discussed in subsection R above, the Panel denied transfer of several actions alleging wage and hour violations under federal and state law. The Panel acknowledged that it had "routinely centralized" such cases. *Id.* at 1378. Yet, it recognized that in some cases alleging wage and hour violations, it had denied centralization. Finding the cases at issue to be ill-suited for centralization, the Panel made clear that "we do not 'rubber stamp' in any docket[.]" *Id.* at 1379.

CHAPTER 4

THE MDL PANEL'S TRANSFER DECISION: SELECTION OF THE DISTRICT COURT AND DISTRICT JUDGE

§ 4.1 OVERVIEW OF THE PANEL'S SELECTION PROCESS

If the Panel determines that transfer is appropriate, it must select both the district where the cases will be sent and the judge who will oversee them. Although the statute provides criteria for transfer (*see* §§ 3.3, 3.4), it provides no guidance on the selection of the transferee district and judge; it simply authorizes transfer "to *any* district." 28 U.S.C. § 1407(a) (emphasis added). Nor do the Federal Rules of Civil Procedure or the JPML Rules address the issue.

This Chapter examines the considerations used by the Panel in selecting the district court and the district judge. It considers those decisions separately, even though the two decisions invariably overlap.

It is often difficult, even for the most experienced MDL advocate, to predict the Panel's selection of district court and judge. In many cases, the Panel simply announces its conclusions on the district and judge with little analysis. And prior cases are generally of little precedential value when the Panel makes its decisions. Ultimately, the Panel exercises its discretion in each case based on all of the facts. Heyburn at 2241.

Nonetheless, it is instructive to review the considerations that the Panel has articulated in selecting the transferee court and judge. Understanding those considerations can help the advocate focus on the strongest arguments favoring or opposing particular districts or judges. Before addressing those considerations, however, several aspects of the Panel's selection process warrant discussion.

First, the Panel has authority to pick the transferee court and transferee judge in either order or simultaneously. That is, the Panel may pick a particular judge and settle on the district as a consequence, or it may select an appropriate district and thereafter select an appropriate judge within that district.

For instance, the Panel's main consideration may be the suitability of a particular judge. If that judge is selected, then the district is necessarily selected as well (unless, as discussed below, the judge is temporarily assigned to a different district). By contrast, the Panel's main focus may be on the suitability of a particular district (*e.g.*, because it is where the parties and witnesses are located). In that event, the Panel first identifies a suitable district, and it then focuses on selecting a judge from within that district (or, as noted below, possibly a judge from another district who can be temporarily reassigned to that district). Because the Panel uses similar factors for both decisions, and because the transferee court and judge are both named in the Panel's order, it is often difficult to determine whether the choice of district dictated the choice of judge or vice-versa. Williams & George at 436, 449; Herr (MDL) § 7:5.

Second, section 1407(b) provides two ways for the Panel to select a transferee judge. Typically, the Panel selects the district court and a district judge within that district. The second (much less common) method allows the Panel to petition either the Chief Justice of the United States or the Chief Judge of the U.S. Court of Appeals for the circuit in which the transferee court resides to appoint a judge from outside the transferee district to conduct the MDL proceedings. For example, in *In re San Juan, Puerto Rico Air Crash Disaster*, 316 F. Supp. 981 (J.P.M.L. 1970), the Panel—after securing the proper approval—designated a judge from the Southern District of New York to preside over litigation in the District of Puerto Rico. The Panel noted the District of Puerto Rico's "heavy docket" and the fact that both judges in that district had declared their "preference . . . not to participate in this litigation to avoid any possible conflict of interest[.]" *Id.* at 982; *see* Herr (MDL) § 7:2.

Third, the Panel has discretion with respect to the number of judges to appoint. Typically, the Panel assigns a single judge, but it has sometimes assigned more than one judge. *See, e.g., In re Janus Mut. Funds Inv. Litig.*, 310 F. Supp. 2d 1359, 1361–62 (J.P.M.L. 2004) (appointing three transferee judges to MDL that "encompasse[d] complex claims against multiple mutual funds by a vast number of plaintiffs/

putative class members which could potentially (i) present various disqualification issues and/or (ii) consume much attention from one transferee judge"); *In re Antibiotic Drugs*, 320 F. Supp. 586, 589 (J.P.M.L. 1970) (the Panel appointed a second judge in an MDL involving numerous antitrust actions, finding that "this litigation has simply become too massive and burdensome for any one judge to process efficiently and expeditiously"); *see also In re Asbestos Prods. Liab. Litig. (No. VI)*, 771 F. Supp. 415, 423 (J.P.M.L. 1991) (noting the Panel's "willingness to appoint additional transferee judges in litigations whose size and complexity make it difficult for the original transferee judge to handle § 1407 proceedings alone"); Herr (MDL) § 7:14.

Finally, before selecting a transferee judge, a Panel member will first contact the prospective transferee judge to ensure that the judge is ready, willing, and able to serve. Heyburn at 2242. The Panel must also obtain the consent of the chief judge of the transferee district that is selected. *Id.* at 2243 (citing 28 U.S.C. § 1407(b) (requiring "consent of the transferee district court")).

§ 4.2 SELECTION OF THE DISTRICT COURT

As noted, after the Panel decides to centralize cases, it must select the district court to manage the pretrial proceedings. The Panel has discretion to select any federal district court from among the 94 districts. Selection of a transferee district is not restricted by section 1407 or by traditional limitations of personal jurisdiction and venue. *See* §§ 13.1–13.4. Thus, it is not surprising that parties are sometimes unable to predict the Panel's selection of the federal district where the MDL proceeding will take place.

Selection of a transferee district can be contentious, with the various parties at odds over the proper assignment of the district court (and district judge). Because the transferee court, as a practical matter, will resolve all or most of the cases (*see* § 1.1), the Panel's decision on where to send the cases has profound consequences. Yet the parties have limited opportunities to persuade the Panel to select their preferred districts, and no Panel selection has been successfully challenged on appeal. Burch (NYU) at 73; Williams & George at 426–27.

Although the process for selecting a transferee court is not fully transparent, the Panel usually explains its decisions, albeit briefly. It is critical for advocates to understand both the general trends as well as the specific factors cited by the Panel in explaining its selections.

A. GENERAL TRENDS

Few empirical studies have been conducted regarding the Panel's transfer selection process. Nonetheless, two significant trends should be noted.

First, although all 94 federal district courts are available as transferee courts, most centralizations take place within a relatively limited number of major urban areas. Courts within the Second, Third, and Ninth Circuits receive the most transfers, with most going to New York City, San Francisco, Chicago, Los Angeles, and Philadelphia. Districts within or near these cities account for roughly half of all transferee courts. Williams & George at 444; M.S. Williams at 1277.

Second, the composition of the Panel—which changes over time—can impact the likelihood that a district is selected. Each district that is represented on the Panel by one of the seven judges has a 14 percent greater chance of being selected than other districts, with all other variables controlled. Williams & George at 449, 457; *see also* M.S. Williams at 1249.

B. FACTORS USED BY THE PANEL

The Panel invokes a variety of factors when selecting a transferee court. Understanding these factors will enable advocates to sharpen their presentations when arguing for a specific district or judge. But even though the Panel frequently invokes particular factors, such as the location of the witnesses or evidence, it has no set formula or standard for selecting the district or judge. Depending on the case, the Panel may be persuaded by a single factor or a confluence of factors. Given the Panel's broad discretion, advocates must consider how the specific facts surrounding their litigation may impact the Panel's analysis. Herr (MDL) §§ 6:2, 6:23; Richards at 320–29.

(1) Party Preferences

While the Panel may select any federal district court, it is far more likely to select a court for which the parties have expressed a preference. One study covering 2005 to 2009 found that more than 90 percent of transferee courts selected by the Panel were recommended by at least one party. In general, the likelihood of transfer to a particular court or judge increases with party support. Williams & George at 446, 449.

For example, in *In re Equifax, Inc., Customer Data Sec. Breach Litigation,* 289 F. Supp. 3d 1322 (J.P.M.L. 2017), the Panel selected the Northern District of Georgia as the transferee court in part because that district was "supported by defendants and the vast majority of responding plaintiffs." *Id.* at 1326. In *In re Xarelto (Rivaroxaban) Products Liability Litigation*, 65 F. Supp. 3d 1402 (J.P.M.L. 2014), the Panel chose the Eastern District of Louisiana as the transferee court, noting that the district had "the support of a number of plaintiffs and also [was] supported by the opposing defendants as an appropriate alternative." *Id.* at 1405. And in *In re Daily Fantasy Sports Marketing & Sales Practices Litigation*, 158 F. Supp. 3d 1375 (J.P.M.L. 2016), the Panel concluded that the District of Massachusetts was the appropriate transferee district, where that district was "supported by both defendants and plaintiffs in at least seven actions." *Id.* at 1380.

Although party preferences often play a role in the Panel's selection, the relative weight of this factor varies depending on the circumstances. Nearly one in five transfer orders acknowledge joint party recommendations as supporting a particular court. The Panel gives especially significant weight to the preference of the defendants. The defendants' support for a particular court almost doubles the odds that the Panel will select that court. Williams & George at 448 (finding that a defendant's support for a particular district increased the probability of selection from 22 percent to 42 percent). Unsurprisingly, unanimous party agreement is more significant than non-unanimous support. On the other hand, heated disagreement between the parties has sometimes led the Panel to select a court other than one recommended by one or more parties. *Id.* at 445, 449; Herr (MDL) § 6:18.

An empirical analysis of the Panel's transfer orders shows even greater complexity. Party preference is cited frequently in transfer orders involving antitrust, product liability, and securities cases. Yet, for whatever reason, in intellectual property MDLs, the Panel rarely cites party preferences. Richards at 332–35.

The motives underlying party support are often critical to the Panel. On the one hand, the Panel gives weight to party preferences when the parties appear to be genuinely concerned about finding a district that can handle the cases efficiently and fairly. On the other hand, the Panel has routinely declined to adopt a party's preference when that preference appears to be an attempt to gain an advantage in the litigation, such as recommending a district because the advocate has been successful there in earlier phases of the litigation (or in related litigation). *See* Heyburn at 2241 ("The Panel is particularly alert . . . to parties who may venture to use the MDL process for some substantive or procedural advantage, and will act to avert or deflect attempts by a party or parties to 'game' the system.").

A party's preference need not be emphatic to have an impact. A party's lack of opposition to (or acquiescence in) a suggested district can carry significant weight. Furthermore, the Panel's consideration of party preferences often merges with other factors. For example, parties often advocate for a court in or near districts where parties, witnesses, or evidence are located. Similarly, the filing of a large number of actions in a particular district implicitly reveals party preferences. These types of factors—discussed below—can bolster the likelihood of the Panel following a party's recommendation. Herr (MDL) §§ 6:18, 6:23; Williams & George at 440.

(2) Location of Parties, Witnesses, and Evidence

A significant factor is whether a particular district is close to the location of parties, witnesses, and evidence. The Panel frequently cites this factor in selecting a transferee court. Rhodes at 722; Richards at 343. Empirical studies reveal that the Panel has identified the location of parties and witnesses as an important factor in 41.5 percent of transfer orders, and has referred to the location of evidence in 35 percent of transfer orders. Williams & George at 445.

(a) Location of Parties

The Panel often tries to select a transferee court that is convenient for the litigants. Convenience is generally considered in terms of geography and accessibility. One analysis revealed that 11.4 percent of transfer orders identified the central location of a transferee district as supporting the panel's choice. Williams & George at 445. When parties are dispersed nationwide, making no district an obvious choice for consolidation, a compromise choice in the middle of the country may make sense. For example, in one case in which constituent actions spanned the country, with many actions in California and on the East Coast, the Panel transferred all actions to the Northern District of Illinois, noting that "there is . . . something to be said for the convenience of a geographically central forum in coast-to-coast litigation." *In re Library Editions of Children's Books*, 297 F. Supp. 385, 387 (J.P.M.L. 1968). In addition, if party preferences are strong, the Panel may interpret those preferences as indicating the convenience of the preferred forum. Williams & George at 440; Herr (MDL) § 6:7.

The Panel's concern with providing a convenient transferee court for litigants includes concerns about accessibility. In many circumstances, it is not sufficient that a district be physically central; what may be even more important is whether that district has easy transportation access for litigants from across the country. Large international airports, such as those in New York, Los Angeles, or Chicago, support the selection of nearby districts. One authoritative source recommends that advocates provide evidence of the accessibility of the recommended court. *See* Herr (MDL) § 6:7. For example, attorneys can submit relevant portions of the Official Airline Guide with their briefing to the Panel to show the extent of airline service to particular districts. Such evidence can support one district, or identify a significant accessibility issue with another potential district. The significance of accessibility increases with the geographic dispersion of litigants, and is of particular concern for litigation involving foreign litigants. *Id.* Also, the Panel's concern for accessibility tends to push it in favor of urban over rural locations, because the former are presumably more convenient to various modes of transportation. Herr (MDL) § 6:7.

The Panel has noted that the convenience of the attorneys generally "coincides" with considerations of party convenience. *In re Air Crash Disaster Near Chicago, Ill., on May 25, 1979*, 476 F. Supp. 445, 449 n.4 (J.P.M.L. 1979). According to the Panel, "[t]he convenience of counsel . . . is not by itself a factor to be considered under Section 1407[.]" *In re Anthracite Coal Antitrust Litig.*, 436 F. Supp. 402, 403 (J.P.M.L. 1977). The Panel may select a transferee district that is suitable for the parties even if it is inconvenient to counsel (or experts). *Id.*

The location of the defendant's headquarters has been an important consideration in selecting the transferee district. For example, in *In re Toyota Motor Corp. Unintended Acceleration Marketing Sales Practices & Products Liability Litigation*, 704

F. Supp. 2d 1379, 1382 (J.P.M.L. 2010), the Panel selected the Central District of California as the transferee district in part because defendant Toyota maintained its U.S. headquarters in that district, and "relevant documents and witnesses [were] likely located there." *Id.* at 1382. In *In re Valsartan N-Nitrosodimethylamine (NDMA) Contamination Products Liability Litigation*, 363 F. Supp. 3d 1378 (J.P.M.L. 2019), the Panel selected the District of New Jersey as the transferee court, in part because "[m]any of the defendants have their U.S. headquarters in New Jersey[.]" *Id.* at 1382. And, in *In re Equifax, Inc., Customer Data Security Breach Litigation*, 289 F. Supp. 3d 1322 (J.P.M.L. 2017), the Panel selected the Northern District of Georgia as the transferee district in part because "Equifax is headquartered in that district[.]" *Id.* at 1326. *Accord, e.g., In re Stryker Orthopaedics LFIT V40 Femoral Head Products Liability Litigation*, 249 F. Supp. 3d 1353, 1356 (J.P.M.L. 2017) (relying on a defendant's headquarters); *In re Nat'l Football League's "Sunday Ticket" Antitrust Litig.*, 148 F. Supp. 3d 1358, 1359–60 (J.P.M.L. 2015) (same).

(b) Location of Witnesses and Evidence

A former chair of the Panel has recognized that a court's proximity to potential witnesses and evidence can be a significant factor in selecting the transferee district. Heyburn at 2239. These factors are likely considered in the vast majority of transfer decisions. *Id.*; Herr (MDL) §§ 6:5, 6:23.

The location of parties often overlaps with the location of witnesses and evidence, because the Panel assumes that, in most cases, relevant witnesses and evidence will be located near the places where the parties reside. When the issue is ascertaining where relevant evidence is likely to be found, the Panel generally construes "location" broadly. Operational offices may qualify as a likely location for potential evidence, as would executive offices or headquarters. Richards at 329, 344. Nonetheless, this factor has arguably lost significance—especially in cases centering mainly on documentary evidence—due to the prevalence of electronic evidence and the ability to instantly transmit and access voluminous amounts of information anywhere. Herr (MDL) § 6:5.

In mass tort litigation involving a singular incident and numerous claims, such as an airline crash, the location of evidence and witnesses frequently causes the Panel to select the district where the accident occurred. Herr (MDL) § 6:6. For example, in *In re Oil Spill by the Oil Rig "Deepwater Horizon" in the Gulf of Mexico*, 731 F. Supp. 2d 1352 (J.P.M.L. 2010), the Panel centralized economic and personal injury litigation involving the BP Deepwater Horizon oil spill in the Eastern District of Louisiana. The Panel noted that "if there is a geographic 'center of gravity' in this docket, the Eastern District of Louisiana is closest to it." *Id.* at 1355.

In certain circumstances, the proximity of a potential transferee court to evidence may support its selection even if the district is not where the evidence is located. For example, assume that the Panel is seriously considering only two potential districts, and neither one is where the evidence is located. If those districts are in other respects relatively equal, the relative proximity of one court to a likely source of evidence may tilt the scales in favor of that court. Herr (MDL) § 6:5.

The Panel has frequently cited the location of relevant documents and witnesses as an important consideration in selecting the transferee district. *See, e.g., In re Uber Techs., Inc., Data Sec. Breach Litig.*, 304 F. Supp. 3d 1351, 1355 (J.P.M.L. 2018); *In re BP p.l.c. Sec. Litig.*, 734 F. Supp. 2d 1376, 1379 (J.P.M.L. 2010); *In re Avandia Mktg., Sales Practices & Prods. Liab. Litig.*, 528 F. Supp. 2d 1339, 1341 (J.P.M.L. 2007); *In re Long Distance Tel. Serv. Fed. Excise Tax Refund Litig.*, 469 F. Supp. 2d 1348, 1350 (J.P.M.L. 2006). Of course, if the witnesses and evidence are dispersed across the country, this factor necessarily takes on much less significance. *See, e.g., In re Volkswagen "Clean Diesel" Mktg., Sales Practices, & Prods. Liab. Litig.*, 148 F. Supp. 3d 1367 (J.P.M.L. 2015) (noting that "any number of transferee districts could ably handle this litigation," given that the controversy "touches multiple districts across the United States and that the various VW entities hold ties to many districts").

(3) Location of Pending Actions

The Panel has often found the location of the various actions to be relevant to the choice of transferee court. By one analysis, there is a 93 percent chance that a transferee court will be one that has either a pending action or a pending potential tag-along action. Richards at 339.

For example, in *In re National Arbitration Forum Antitrust Litigation*, 682 F. Supp. 2d 1343 (J.P.M.L. 2010), the Panel selected the District of Minnesota, in part because seven of the ten actions were already pending in that district. *Id.* at 1345–46. Similarly, in *In re Total Body Formula Products Liability Litigation*, 582 F. Supp. 2d 1381 (J.P.M.L. 2008), the Panel found that the Northern District of Alabama was an appropriate transfer district, given that 14 of the 20 actions were pending there. *Id.* at 1382.

If cases are concentrated in a particular region, the Panel is likely to select a district within that region. For example, in *In re Pamidronate Products Liability Litigation*, 657 F. Supp. 2d 1368 (J.P.M.L. 2009), in which the litigation was "concentrated on the east coast," the Panel selected the Eastern District of New York as the transferee district. *Id.* at 1369.

The location of filed actions is less important, however, when potential plaintiffs and putative class members reside throughout the country. For example, in *In re BP p.l.c. Securities Litigation*, 734 F. Supp. 2d 1376 (J.P.M.L. 2010), the Panel noted that "[b]ecause potential plaintiffs and putative class members will reside in every corner of the country, the location of the currently filed cases is not a particularly important factor in our decision." *Id.* at 1379. Similarly, in *In re Porsche Cars North America, Inc., Plastic Coolant Tubes Products Liability Litigation*, 787 F. Supp. 2d 1349 (J.P.M.L. 2011), in which the cases were spread across the country, the Panel chose the Southern District of Ohio as the transferee district, because that district was "geographically centrally located[.]" *Id.* at 1349.

The location of pending actions is often related to other factors used by the Panel. For example, a party's choice of forum implicitly reflects that party's preference and perception of convenience. A wide geographic distribution of pending cases, however, undercuts the significance of a particular district as indicative of preferences or convenience. *See, e.g.*, *In re Nat'l Prescription Opiate Litig.*, 290 F. Supp. 3d 1375, 1379 (J.P.M.L. 2017) ("Most parties acknowledge that any number of the proposed transferee districts would be suitable for this litigation that is nationwide in scope.").

It should also be underscored that the Panel evaluates the current locations of pending actions at the time of transfer. If a change of venue has already occurred under 28 U.S.C. § 1404(a), the Panel will consider the new venue as the location of the action, not the district where the case was originally filed. Moreover, the Panel will consider the section 1404(a) ruling as a reflection of the trial judge's determination that the district selected is a convenient one. Herr (MDL) § 6:8.

Other considerations related to pending actions may influence the Panel's selection of a transferee court. For example, if pending actions are concentrated in a particular district, the Panel will have fewer actions to transfer by selecting that district, and, ultimately, fewer cases to transfer back if the cases are not resolved by the transferee court prior to trial. Herr (MDL) § 6:8. In addition, when there are multiple districts with pending cases, the Panel will often favor a district in which a broad, comprehensive action (as opposed to a more limited action) is pending. Herr (MDL) § 6:10.

The relative progress of the pending actions at the time of transfer can also be an important factor. Almost 15 percent of transfer orders discuss the progress of constituent actions as supporting a particular transferee district. Williams & George at 445. The Panel considers the specific progress made in discovery as well as the general progress made toward trial. When evaluating the progress of pending actions, the Panel takes note of various steps indicating that the cases are heading to trial—for example, the resolution of class certification, the adjudication of significant legal issues, or the completion of expert discovery. If multiple districts are equally possible, one district's progress in a pending action may break the tie. *Id.*; Herr (MDL) § 6:16.

The Panel may also consider the pendency of important motions in potential transferee courts. For example, in one case the Panel acknowledged that a pending motion for a preliminary injunction in the Eastern District of Texas supported transferring the MDL proceedings to that district under principles of comity. *In re L. E. Lay & Co. Antitrust Litig.*, 391 F. Supp. 1054, 1056 (J.P.M.L. 1975).

Despite the relevance of where pending cases are located, that factor is not necessarily controlling. The

Panel has the authority to transfer all of the cases to a district where no case is pending. Herr (MDL) § 6:2; Richards at 343–44; M.S. Williams at 1257.

(4) Docket Conditions of Potential Transferee Courts

According to one study, the Panel has cited the workload of a transferee district in 11.4 percent of transfer orders. Williams & George at 445. When considering workload, the Panel focuses on the backlogs of the dockets of possible transferee courts, emphasizing the median time to disposition rather than overall caseload. Advocates are well advised to present evidence to the Panel of the docket conditions of potential district courts. For example, in *In re Maxim Integrated Products, Inc., Patent Litigation,* 867 F. Supp. 2d 1333 (J.P.M.L. 2012), the Panel selected the Western District of Pennsylvania as the transferee district in part because that district "enjoy[ed] favorable caseload conditions." *Id.* at 1336. The Annual Report of the Director of the Administrative Office of the United States Courts is a useful source, and the Panel has cited it when considering docket conditions. Herr (MDL) § 6:17.

The Panel may also consider the MDL dockets of possible transferee courts. If a district has few or no pending MDL cases, the Panel may find it an attractive candidate for that reason. *See, e.g., In re Chantix (Varenicline) Prods. Liab. Litig.*, 655 F. Supp. 2d 1346, 1346 (J.P.M.L. 2009) (noting that the transferee district "currently is home to only one multidistrict litigation proceeding"); *In re Total Body*

Formula Prods. Liab. Litig., 582 F. Supp. 2d 1381, 1382 (J.P.M.L. 2008) (selection of transferee district was supported by the fact that "no multidistrict litigation dockets [were] currently pending" there).

To be sure, while case volume is important, a high volume of cases in a district is not disqualifying. What matters is whether the district court and transferee judge have the capacity and ability to perform the work that the MDL will require. For example, in *In re Toyota Motor Corp. Unintended Acceleration Marketing, Sales Practices & Products Liability Litigation*, 704 F. Supp. 2d 1379 (J.P.M.L. 2010), the Panel rejected the argument that "docket conditions" in the Central District of California made the district undesirable for an MDL. It noted that it had consulted with the transferee judge and the chief judge of the district in making its selection, and concluded that the transferee judge "is positioned to devote all the time necessary to manage and decide the important issues that these cases raise." *Id.* at 1382.

(5) Location of First-Filed Action

Related to the general consideration of the location of pending actions is the location of the first-filed action. Over 20 percent of transfer orders refer to the location of the first-filed action as supporting a particular transferee court. Williams & George at 445; *see also, e.g.*, *In re Smith & Nephew BHR & R3 Hip Implant Prods. Liab. Litig.*, 249 F. Supp. 3d 1348, 1352 (J.P.M.L. 2017) (selecting transferee district in part because the first-filed action was pending there); *In re GMAC Ins. Mgmt. Corp. Overtime Pay Litig.*, 342 F. Supp. 2d 1357, 1358 (J.P.M.L. 2004) (same). This preference relates to the relative progress of pending actions, because the first-filed action is often the most advanced case. Williams & George at 445; Herr (MDL) § 6:16.

(6) Coordination with Other Federal Proceedings or with Related State Court Proceedings

When evaluating potential transferee districts, the Panel will frequently consider the possibility of coordinating MDL proceedings with other judicial proceedings. If a potential district is located where criminal or civil proceedings related to the MDL are taking place, the Panel may be inclined to transfer the MDL to that district. *See, e.g.*, *In re Orthopaedic Implant Device Antitrust Litig.*, 483 F. Supp. 2d 1355, 1355 (J.P.M.L. 2007) (transferee district was "where related grand jury proceedings [were] located"); *In re Neurontin Mktg. & Sales Practices Litig.*, 342 F. Supp. 2d 1350, 1351–52 (J.P.M.L. 2004) (transferee district was "where a False Claims Act qui tam action predicated on the same facts as those at issue in the [MDL] actions had been pending for eight years" prior to settlement).

This preference applies, even in the absence of formal proceedings, if the Panel is aware of pending government investigations that will necessitate discovery similar to that involved in the MDL. Also, if multiple state actions are pending in a particular state, a district within that state is more likely to be chosen, thereby facilitating coordination between the federal MDL judge and state judges who have related cases on their dockets. Herr (MDL) §§ 6:12–6:13.

(7) Location Designated in a Forum-Selection Clause

In some instances, the parties have previously agreed that, in the event of litigation, any dispute will be resolved in a particular jurisdiction. Such clauses (known as forum-selection clauses) are generally enforceable, even in the context of a consumer signing a form contract with a sophisticated corporation. *See Carnival Cruise Lines, Inc. v. Shute,* 499 U.S. 585 (1991) (enforcing forum selection clause printed on cruise ticket sold to consumers; the clause required that disputes arising under the contract be resolved in Florida). Yet, all bets are off in the MDL context. Because the cases are ostensibly transferred only for pretrial proceedings (even though, as noted in § 1.1, few cases return to the transferor courts), forum-selection clauses do not constrain the Panel's selection. Bock at 1673.

For example, in *In re Park West Galleries, Inc., Marketing & Sales Practices Litigation*, 655 F. Supp. 2d 1378 (J.P.M.L. 2009), the defendant moved to vacate a Panel order transferring two actions to an MDL in the Western District of Washington, pointing to a forum-selection clause designating Miami, Florida, as the mandatory location for any litigation between the parties. The Panel rejected that argument, explaining that "contractual forum selection clauses . . . do not limit the Panel's authority with respect to the selection of a transferee district, or, by the same token, our authority to transfer tag-along actions to an existing MDL." *Id.* at 1379. The Panel added that "because Section 1407 transfer is for pretrial purposes only," MDL transfer "in no way precludes [the defendant] from seeking enforcement of the forum selection clauses for purposes of trial." *Id. Accord, e.g., In re Disposable Contact Lens Antitrust Litig.*, 109 F. Supp. 3d 1369, 1371 (J.P.M.L. 2015) (a "forum selection clause does not affect [the Panel's] authority to transfer" the case to a different district).

These authorities make some sense if one views the MDL transfer as truly for pretrial purposes, with the likelihood that the cases will be returned to the transferor court for trial. On the other hand, given the low likelihood that cases centralized in an MDL will be returned to the transferor courts, it arguably becomes harder to defend the Panel's failure to abide by a forum-selection clause.

C. EXAMPLES OF TRANSFEREE COURT SELECTIONS

The above discussion has isolated specific factors that may bear on the Panel's selection of a transferee court. In reality, however, the Panel often balances a variety of factors in making its decision on the proper district court. One factor is rarely dispositive. Several Panel transfer orders illustrate the interplay of the foregoing factors in the Panel's selection decisions.

In *In re Uber Technologies, Inc., Data Security Breach Litigation,* 304 F. Supp. 3d 1351 (J.P.M.L. 2018), the Panel selected the Central District of California as the appropriate transferee district for ten data breach actions pending in five districts involving 57 million alleged victims and two defendants. The Panel's transferee selection was influenced by several of the factors discussed above. Three actions were already pending in the Central District of California. Plaintiffs were split between preferring the Northern District of California and the Northern District of Illinois, while defendant Uber preferred the Central District of California. Because California was the location of Uber's headquarters, and thus was where much of the common evidence and witnesses were located, and because the Illinois plaintiffs identified the Central District of California (Uber's choice) as their second choice, the Panel selected the Central District of California for transfer. *Id.* at 1355.

In *In re Ford Motor Co. DPS6 PowerShift Transmission Products Liability Litigation*, 289 F. Supp. 3d 1350 (J.P.M.L. 2018), the Panel emphasized that the "vast majority" of actions were pending in the Central District of California, and that choosing that district would facilitate coordination between state and federal litigation. *Id.* at 1353.

In *In re Dicamba Herbicides Litigation,* 289 F. Supp. 3d 1345 (J.P.M.L. 2018), a product liability MDL involving ten pending actions and two tag-along actions, the Panel selected the Eastern District of Missouri. This selection was based on several factors: four of the pending actions were located in that district; numerous plaintiffs preferred that district; and the defendant was amenable to the district as an alternative preference. Moreover, the defendant was headquartered in the district and had informed the Panel that much of its activity relevant to the litigation had occurred there. *Id.* at 1347.

And in *In re NeuroGrafix ('360) Patent Litigation*, 936 F. Supp. 2d 1376 (J.P.M.L. 2013), which involved ten actions alleging patent infringement, the Panel transferred the cases to the District of Massachusetts because half of the ten actions were pending there, one defendant was headquartered in the district, and the district was "relatively convenient" for all of the defendants. *Id.* at 1378.

§ 4.3 SELECTION OF DISTRICT JUDGE

The foregoing section discussed the Panel's considerations in selecting a particular district. This section discusses the Panel's considerations in selecting a particular district judge. Like the prior section, the discussion focuses first on general trends and then on specific factors.

A. GENERAL TRENDS

Some academics and MDL judges believe that the Panel tries to pick the best and brightest judges to serve as MDL judges. *See* Gluck at 1673, 1693 (discussing interviews with 15 federal and 5 state MDL judges (all with federal MDL or analogous state law experience)). Obviously, it is a plus if the judge is familiar to the Panel, and is known for having excellent management skills. Williams & George at 449–56; Gluck at 1693.

Other trends should also be noted. Senior district judges "are less than half as likely" as active judges to be selected as transferee judges. Williams & George at 455–56. Chief judges (both present and former) and Panel members (both present and former) are more likely to be selected than judges without those credentials. *Id.* at 456.

Judicial experience in complex cases has, historically, been important to the Panel. Thus, in selecting the first MDL Panel, Chief Justice Warren picked judges who had been involved in the electrical equipment antitrust cases. Williams & George at 433–34. Some of them had worked on the original Manual for Complex Litigation. As discussed below, a judge's prior complex litigation experience continues to be an important consideration under the statute.

At the same time, the Panel has begun assigning MDL cases to a wider group of judges, and not simply to a small group of judges who already have had MDL experience. For instance, in 2012, "about 27 percent of all active judges and about 20 percent of senior judges [had] an MDL assignment." Heyburn & McGovern at 30. As of July 16, 2019, 158 district judges had MDL cases (out of 199 MDL dockets), revealing the breadth of the federal bench currently overseeing MDLs. MDL Statistics Report, July 16, 2019. *See* § 1.4. Also, the pool of MDL judges has become increasingly diverse in terms of gender and race. *See* M.S. Williams at 1285–86 (noting "the increasing diversity of transferee judges" in recent years); § 17.6 (discussing diversity trends).

B. FACTORS USED BY THE PANEL

This section discusses the factors that have been important in the Panel's selection of transferee judges. In some cases, the Panel clearly identifies its reasons for selecting a particular judge; in other cases, the selection receives minimal analysis and explanation. Nonetheless, it is possible to identify factors that frequently influence the Panel's decisions.

(1) Transferee Judge Presides over Some Pending Cases

A commonly cited factor in the selection of a transferee judge is that the judge is already presiding over one or more of the pending cases. For example, in *In re Natrol, Inc. Glucosamine/Chondroitin Marketing & Sales Practices Litigation*, 26 F. Supp. 3d 1392 (J.P.M.L. 2014), the Panel noted that the transferee judge selected was "presid[ing] over two MDLs that raise[d] similar factual and legal claims concerning the effectiveness of dietary supplements containing glucosamine and chondroitin in promoting joint health." *Id.* at 1394. *Accord, e.g.*, *In re Ford Motor Co. DPS6 PowerShift Transmission Prods. Liab. Litig.*, 289 F. Supp. 3d 1350, 1353 (J.P.M.L. 2018) (noting that the transferee judge was already presiding over several actions); *In re Lipitor (Atorvastatin Calcium) Mktg., Sales Practices & Prods. Liab. Litig. (No. II)*, 997 F. Supp. 2d 1354,

1357 (J.P.M.L. 2014) (same); *In re Chantix (Varenicline) Prods. Liab. Litig.*, 655 F. Supp. 2d 1346, 1347 (J.P.M.L. 2009) (same).

(2) Party Preferences

In contrast to the selection of the transferee district, in which party preferences can make a difference, the Panel normally gives little weight to the litigants' preferences with respect to the specific transferee judge. The Panel may take note of the parties' suggestions, but these suggestions appear to have little impact in most cases. The Panel has even refused to select judges to whom all parties have stipulated. Herr (MDL) § 7:7.

Advocates seeking to influence the Panel's selection of a transferee judge must proceed with caution. Most likely, the Panel will not respond favorably to arguments that a particular judge lacks the skills, experience, or objectivity to preside over an MDL or suffers a disabling conflict of interest. The Panel understands that attacks on a particular judge (and praise for another) may be motivated not by a desire to obtain a neutral judge but by the hope of securing a judge who will favor the particular party's position in the litigation. If the Panel thinks that a party is trying to secure a favorably disposed judge, it will likely make sure that that judge is *not* selected. Herr (MDL) § 7:7.

(3) Experience of the Judge

The experience of potential transferee judges is often a significant factor in the Panel's selection determination. One analysis showed that in nearly 14 percent of transfers, the Panel selected the transferee district because of that judge's experience. Williams & George at 445. And in over one-third of transfer orders, the Panel referred to prior experience as one ground for appointing a specific transferee judge. *Id.* at 450. *See also* M.S. Williams at 1283 (from 1968 to 2017, "nearly half of the assignments made by the Panel were to judges receiving a subsequent assignment").

Indeed, prior judicial experience is so significant that the Panel has selected transferee judges on that basis despite a lack of constituent or tag-along actions in their district. *See, e.g., In re Silica Prods. Liab. Litig.*, 280 F. Supp. 2d 1381, 1383 (J.P.M.L. 2003) (assigning centralized actions to a particular judge even though none of the actions were pending in the judge's district; the Panel noted that the judge was "an experienced transferee judge for multidistrict litigation" and "a seasoned jurist with a relatively low civil caseload").

Of course, consideration of "experience" begs the question of what kind of experience is relevant. In fact, the type of experience cited by the Panel varies from case to case.

(a) Experience in Complex Litigation

The Panel occasionally cites a judge's general "experience," without greater detail. *See, e.g., In re Dollar Gen. Corp. Motor Oil Mktg. & Sales Practices Litig.*, 190 F. Supp. 3d 1361, 1363 (J.P.M.L. 2016); *In re Ashley Madison Customer Data Sec. Breach Litig.*,

148 F. Supp. 3d 1378, 1380 (J.P.M.L. 2015); *In re Nat'l Football League's "Sunday Ticket" Antitrust Litig.*, 148 F. Supp. 3d 1358, 1360 (J.P.M.L. 2015). At other times, however, the Panel refers to the judge's specific experience in handling other MDLs or complex litigation. *See, e.g., In re Silica Prods. Liab. Litig.*, 280 F. Supp. 2d 1381, 1383 (J.P.M.L. 2003) (judge selected was "an experienced transferee judge for multidistrict litigation"); *In re Chrysler-Dodge-Jeep EcoDiesel Mktg., Sales Practices & Prods. Liab. Litig.*, 273 F. Supp. 3d 1377, 1379 (J.P.M.L. 2017) (judge selected was "well-versed in the nuances of complex and multidistrict litigation").

The Panel does not focus entirely on prior judicial experience. At times, the Panel will note a judge's experience as a lawyer before taking the bench. For example, in *In re Toyota Motor Corp. Unintended Acceleration Marketing Sales Practices & Products Liability Litigation*, 704 F. Supp. 2d 1379 (J.P.M.L. 2010), the Panel noted that the transferee judge's "28 years of private law practice at the highest levels and in some of the most complex cases leaves him well prepared for a case of this magnitude." *Id.* at 1382.

The significance of prior experience helps to explain the Panel's tendency to appoint past or present members of the Panel to serve as MDL judges. Herr (MDL) §§ 7:6, 7:10, 7:14–7:15; Richards at 342–45; Williams & George at 450, 452.

(b) Experience with Related Litigation

Experience in litigation related to the pending MDL is also a significant factor supporting the appointment of a transferee judge. The Panel generally prefers to select judges who are already familiar with the issues in the litigation at the time of transfer. This familiarity often arises from a judge having presided over either a constituent case or a related action. If a judge is already handling a related action and is making good progress on it, the Panel may be inclined to appoint that judge to oversee the entire MDL. This inclination applies even if the related or underlying action has been dismissed or settled. Such experience is so significant that it may guide the Panel's selection of a transferee judge despite strong arguments for a different selection. Herr (MDL) §§ 7:9–7:10.

The Panel construes "related" actions broadly. A related action may be a tag-along case or potential tag-along case, but it may also be a relevant criminal case or a civil case that is not one of the cases in which transfer was sought. The cases may involve different facts or parties, yet present similar issues. Familiarity with the issues in the pending MDL is the general standard, and no formula binds the Panel's consideration of a judge's relevant experience. As a general matter, however, the Panel views experience handling similar MDL litigation, or other actions related to the proposed MDL, as the strongest kind of "relevant" experience. Herr (MDL) §§ 7:6, 7:10–7:15.

Finally, litigants should understand that prior rulings by judges in related or underlying actions are generally irrelevant to the selection of a transferee judge. If a potential transferee judge has ruled against one party in a related matter, that party cannot disqualify the judge from presiding over the MDL as a consequence. Herr (MDL) § 7:11. *See, e.g., In re Beef Indus. Antitrust Litig.*, 419 F. Supp. 720, 722 (J.P.M.L. 1976) (finding "wholly without merit" defendants' opposition to transferee judge based on "their displeasure with prior proceedings in the actions in that forum"); *In re Air Crash Disaster at Paris, France, on Mar. 3, 1974*, 386 F. Supp. 1404, 1405 (J.P.M.L. 1975) ("The prospect of an unfavorable ruling by the transferee court . . . is not a factor considered by the Panel in determining whether transfer under Section 1407 is appropriate.").

(4) The Judge's Workload

Nearly 18 percent of transfer orders refer to the docket conditions of a transferee judge as a factor supporting that judge's appointment. Williams & George at 450. When evaluating the caseload of a potential transferee judge, the Panel generally considers whether, given the judge's available time and experience, the judge is able to handle the burdens of the MDL. Presumably driven in part by workload considerations, the Panel has tried in recent years to distribute the burdens of MDL cases among a wider group of judges, including judges without prior MDL experience. Herr (MDL) §§ 7:8, 7:15; M.S. Williams at 1283–84; *see* § 1.4.

Docket conditions are one avenue for advocacy by litigants. Because arguments attacking particular judges must be nuanced and tactful, information about the current caseload of a potential transferee judge—especially a judge's pending MDL caseload—may be the safest and most effective route for a lawyer to support or oppose a particular judge. Herr (MDL) §§ 7:7–7:9.

(5) Alleged Bias

Challenging a potential MDL judge on grounds of bias is a difficult task. For example, in *In re Oil Spill by the Oil Rig "Deepwater Horizon" in the Gulf of Mexico*, 731 F. Supp. 2d 1352 (J.P.M.L. 2010), the Panel rejected the argument of some parties that a particular judge in the Eastern District of Louisiana would be biased. The Panel noted its "experience . . . that transferee judges impartially carry out their duties and make tough decisions time and time again[.]" *Id.* at 1356. Turning to the specific case, the Panel rejected the arguments of certain defendants that the judge in question was biased. It pointed out that "the Fifth Circuit [had] recently denied the petition of certain defendants for a writ of mandamus directing [that judge] to recuse himself." *Id.* at 1355.

C. EXAMPLES OF TRANSFEREE JUDGE SELECTIONS

A brief overview of several transfer orders illustrates the interplay of the foregoing factors in the Panel's selection of transferee judges.

In one mass tort litigation, involving 26,639 asbestos actions with 14,000 plaintiffs and nearly 500 defendants pending in 87 federal districts, the Panel selected a judge from the Eastern District of

Pennsylvania. *In re Asbestos Prods. Liab. Litig. (No. VI)*, 771 F. Supp. 415 (J.P.M.L. 1991). In its ruling, the Panel noted that no district presented a "clear nexus" for pretrial proceedings, and that three factors supported the particular judge's appointment: (1) his "thorough familiar[ity] with the issues in asbestos litigation"; (2) his "track record of accomplishment and successful innovation" in managing MDLs; and (3) the support he garnered from a majority of the plaintiffs and defendants. *Id.* at 422–23. Although unmentioned in the transfer order, the judge appointed was also a prior member of the Panel.

In *In re Verizon Wireless Data Charges Litigation,* 701 F. Supp. 2d 1380 (J.P.M.L. 2010), a case alleging overcharging by Verizon, the Panel emphasized the selection of the judge as guiding the selection of the district. The Panel transferred three pending actions in two districts to a judge in the District of New Jersey. It noted various rationales for selecting the District of New Jersey but ultimately made clear that choosing that district allowed the Panel to assign the cases to the particular judge, "an experienced transferee judge who is already presiding over the three actions pending in the District of New Jersey." *Id.* at 1382.

In *In re New Motor Vehicles Canadian Export Antitrust Litigation,* 269 F. Supp. 2d 1372 (J.P.M.L. 2003), a conspiracy case against General Motors, the Panel noted that no "geographic focal point" stood out as an appropriate transferee district (there were 10 constituent actions and 16 potential tag-along actions in various districts). As a consequence, the Panel "searched for a transferee judge with the time and experience to steer th[e] litigation on a prudent course." *Id.* at 1373. Without further explanation, the Panel selected a judge from the District of Maine, whom it called "an exceedingly able jurist[.]" *Id.*

An especially instructive case is the Panel's decision in *In re Silicone Gel Breast Implants Products Liability Litigation*, 793 F. Supp. 1098 (J.P.M.L. 1992). That decision demonstrates how overzealous advocacy can impact the Panel's selection process in unintended ways. The parties in the 78 actions at issue were split three ways between requesting: (1) a judge from the Northern District of California; (2) a judge from the District of Kansas; or (3) a judge from the Southern District of Ohio. The Panel ultimately selected a judge from the Northern District of Alabama (a prior member of the Panel), even though no party had advocated for him. *Id.* at 1099. The Panel initially determined that "either the Northern District of California or the Southern District of Ohio could be an appropriate forum . . . ." *Id.* at 1100. The Panel further acknowledged that the requested judges associated with those districts were "well-qualified to handle th[e] litigation." *Id.* However, the "volume and tone" of the advocates' arguments had "threatened" to cloud and taint the proceedings. *Id.* at 1100–01. Consequently, the Panel looked beyond the preferences of the parties. Because no other district stood out as especially appropriate, the Panel focused on finding a transferee judge with the "ability and temperament" to manage the contentious proceedings; this search "embraced the universe of federal district judges." *Id.* at 1101. Ultimately, the Panel selected a judge who had not been involved in the litigation, because of his extensive experience as an MDL judge. The Panel also mentioned the judge's previous membership on the Panel, his chairmanship of the Board of Editors of the Manual for Complex Litigation, and his role as Chairman of the Judicial Conference's Advisory Committee on Civil Rules. *Id.*

CHAPTER 5

APPELLATE REVIEW OF PANEL TRANSFER DECISIONS AND OTHER ORDERS

This Chapter addresses the availability of appellate review of Panel rulings. The primary focus is on whether an appellate remedy exists for the Panel's decision granting or denying transfer. With respect to the granting of transfer, the Chapter addresses the further issue of whether an appellate remedy exists for the Panel's selection of the transferee district court and judge. Finally, the Chapter considers possible appellate remedies for other Panel decisions.

Because the Panel is neither a trial court nor an appellate court, appealing orders of the Panel raises threshold questions. As one commentator has stated, analyzing appellate options "creates a puzzle[.]" Marcus (Tulane) at 2281. The Panel consists of seven judges, all from different circuits. At times, one or more of the judges on the Panel have been federal court of appeals judges. Nonetheless, despite the Panel's odd configuration, there are some limited options to challenge certain Panel orders by way of extraordinary writ. Some Panel decisions, however, are entirely unreviewable. And even though an extraordinary writ is theoretically available to challenge some Panel orders, that route is virtually never successful.

The statutory section governing appeals and extraordinary writs relating to Panel rulings is 28 U.S.C. § 1407(e). That subsection provides:

> No proceedings for review of any order of the panel may be permitted except by extraordinary writ pursuant to the provisions of title 28, section 1651, United States Code. Petitions for an extraordinary writ to review an order of the panel to set a transfer hearing and other orders of the panel issued prior to the order either directing or denying transfer shall be filed only in the court of appeals having jurisdiction over the district in which a hearing is to be or has been held. Petitions for an extraordinary writ to review an order to transfer or orders subsequent to transfer shall be filed only in the court of appeals having jurisdiction over the transferee district. There shall be no appeal or review of an order of the panel denying a motion to transfer for consolidated or coordinated proceedings.

Id.

This Chapter discusses the implications of section 1407(e) for various types of Panel orders. As explained below, the statute differentiates between: (1) orders denying transfer, from which no review is available; (2) orders granting transfer, from which mandamus review is available; and (3) other Panel orders, from which mandamus review is available. These categories are discussed below. This Chapter then discusses specific cases in which federal appellate courts have been asked to grant mandamus in connection with various Panel orders.

§ 5.1 APPEAL OR MANDAMUS FROM PANEL DECISIONS DENYING CENTRALIZATION

The MDL statute makes clear that no appeal or review is available for an MDL Panel decision denying a motion to transfer. 28 U.S.C. § 1407(e). It provides that "[t]here shall be *no appeal or review*" of an order denying a motion to transfer. *Id.* (emphasis added). This means that a Panel order denying transfer cannot be reviewed even if the Panel egregiously errs—for instance, by saying there are no common questions of fact when scores of common factual issues exist, or denying transfer because none of the parties want that result when in fact all of the parties want transfer. Of course, it is almost inconceivable that the Panel—composed of highly respected judges, handpicked by the Chief Justice—would make such egregious and obvious errors. Yet, the Panel could conceivably err by failing to understand the enormous efficiencies of centralization, thereby denying the parties the benefits of the statute that Congress intended to make available.

Congress, however, has chosen to rely entirely on the sound judgment of the Panel when the Panel chooses not to order centralization. And it is difficult to argue that the parties have suffered genuine prejudice in such circumstances. The statute provides no *right* to transfer, and a denial of transfer simply maintains the status quo. *See* Sen. Rep. No. 90-454 (1967), at 2, 6 (explaining that subsection (e) makes clear that there is no appeal or review of an order of the panel denying transfer, "[s]ince such an order would not affect the ordinary course of legal proceedings[.]"). When the Panel declines to transfer cases, the parties simply proceed as they would have had transfer never been sought.

Attorneys and litigants have taken the unambiguous language of section 1407(e) seriously. Research has failed to identify a single instance in which a party has attempted to seek appeal or mandamus from the Panel's denial of centralization.

§ 5.2 APPEAL OR MANDAMUS FROM PANEL DECISIONS GRANTING CENTRALIZATION

Although the MDL statute makes clear that no appeal or mandamus lies from a Panel order denying transfer, it takes a different approach to a decision granting transfer. Under section 1407(e), a decision granting transfer can be challenged, but only "by extraordinary writ" pursuant to 28 U.S.C. § 1651.

§ 5.3 APPEAL OR MANDAMUS FROM OTHER PANEL ORDERS

The only order specifically excluded even from mandamus review under section 1407(e) is an order denying transfer. The statute appears to permit writs challenging all other orders prior to transfer and all "orders subsequent to transfer[.]" The statute specifically mentions "an order of the panel to set a transfer hearing" as one that is subject to mandamus attack. *Id.* Other orders that would be subject to mandamus challenges include orders setting transfer hearings, orders remanding cases to the transferor judge and orders refusing to remand cases to the transferor judge.

§ 5.4 PROPER APPELLATE COURT FOR MANDAMUS FROM PANEL ORDERS

For orders that can be challenged by mandamus, the statute prescribes the court where the petition must be filed. For orders issued prior to an order granting or denying transfer, appellate review is "only in the court of appeals having jurisdiction over the district in which a hearing is to be or has been held." 28 U.S.C. § 1407(e). For instance, if the hearing on transfer is scheduled to occur in Philadelphia, then a petition challenging a Panel order issued prior to transfer would be filed in the Third Circuit. For orders transferring the cases, or orders issued after transfer, the mandamus petition "shall be filed only in the court of appeals having jurisdiction over the transferee district." *Id.* For instance, if the Panel orders that all cases be transferred to the Southern District of New York, the mandamus petition challenging that order would be filed in the Second Circuit.

§ 5.5 STANDARDS FOR MANDAMUS

Mandamus is the only route for challenging a Panel order. As this section discusses, mandamus is an extraordinary remedy, and the standards for obtaining it are stringent. To secure a writ of mandamus, a petitioner must satisfy three elements.

First, the petitioner must establish that there are no other adequate means to attain the relief it seeks. *Cheney v. U.S. Dist. Court for the Dist. of Columbia*, 542 U.S. 367, 380 (2004). This factor is typically met, since 28 U.S.C. § 1407(e) prescribes mandamus as the sole means of obtaining review of Panel orders. No other avenues for relief are available. *See, e.g.*, *FedEx Ground Package Sys., Inc. v. U.S. Judicial Panel on Multidistrict Litig.*, 662 F.3d 887, 890 (7th Cir. 2011) (finding this element met when a party sought appellate review of a Panel remand order).

Nonetheless, to satisfy this element when challenging the denial of a motion to remand cases to the transferor court, the party must first seek a suggestion of remand from the transferee court to fully exhaust all practical means of obtaining relief. *In re Patenaude*, 210 F.3d 135, 141 (3d Cir. 1999) (so holding, and noting that the petitioner "ha[d] a practical but untried avenue for relief").

Second, the petitioner must show that it has a clear and indisputable right to the issuance of a writ. *Cheney v. U.S. Dist. Court for the Dist. of Columbia*, 542 U.S. at 381. Unlike the first element, this element is exceedingly difficult to demonstrate, because the statute leaves virtually unfettered discretion to the Panel. For instance, it is hard to imagine that the Panel's finding of a common question of fact supporting transfer would be so egregiously incorrect as to warrant mandamus relief. Similarly, it is virtually inconceivable that a party could demonstrate that centralization would be so inefficient that mandamus is warranted.

Third, the court must find that the writ is appropriate under the circumstances. *Id.* at 381. Again, given the Panel's broad discretion under the MDL statute, it is virtually inconceivable that a party could show the appropriateness of extraordinary relief.

§ 5.6 CASES IN WHICH MANDAMUS WAS SOUGHT

Not surprisingly, there are few cases in which mandamus has been sought attacking a Panel order, and almost no cases in which mandamus has been successful. As discussed below, only one case has been found in which mandamus has been granted challenging any Panel order. In all other instances, mandamus petitions challenging Panel orders have been denied.

A. DECISIONS DENYING MANDAMUS

In *In re Regents of the University of California*, 964 F.2d 1128 (Fed. Cir. 1992), the Regents of the University of California challenged an order centralizing five patent-related cases to which it was a party in the Southern District of Indiana. (The Federal Circuit has exclusive appellate jurisdiction in patent cases, *see* 28 U.S.C. § 1295.) The Regents argued that the Northern District of California would be a more efficient district to hear the cases than the district selected by the Panel. *Id.* at 1136. The Federal Circuit held that it had jurisdiction to hear the petition, but it refused to second-guess the Panel's order. *Id.* at 1130, 1136. Although the Federal

Circuit found the Regents' argument to be reasonable, the argument was insufficient to meet the burden of showing "a clear and indisputable right to selection of the Northern District of California as transferee forum." *Id.* at 1136. The Panel had a sufficient basis to consolidate the cases in the Southern District of Indiana as the best way to serve the objectives of efficiency and convenience.

In *In re Ivy,* 901 F.2d 7 (2d Cir. 1990), state court plaintiffs sued defendant chemical companies in Texas state court, alleging harm from exposure to Agent Orange and other herbicides. Defendants removed the case to the Eastern District of Texas, and then asked the Panel to transfer the case to the ongoing *Agent Orange* MDL in the Eastern District of New York. The Panel granted a conditional transfer order, which the plaintiffs then moved to vacate. The Panel heard oral argument and then issued an order transferring the case into the MDL. Plaintiffs petitioned the Second Circuit for a writ of mandamus directing the Panel to vacate the transfer order on the ground that the removal of the case to federal court had been improper. The Second Circuit denied the writ of mandamus, holding that "the MDL Panel has jurisdiction to transfer a case in which a jurisdictional objection is pending, [with] that objection to be resolved by the transferee court." *Id.* at 9.

In *In re Wilson*, 451 F.3d 161 (3d Cir. 2006), a group of plaintiffs whose cases had been transferred into a product liability MDL sought a writ of mandamus from the Third Circuit directing the

Panel to remand their cases to the transferor courts. The plaintiffs argued, first before the Panel and then before the Third Circuit, that the common discovery phase of the MDL had concluded, and that their cases should be remanded for case-specific discovery and trial. *Id.* at 163–64. The Third Circuit found that the plaintiffs had met the first element of mandamus, "in that they have no other adequate means to attain relief from the JPML's order refusing to remand their cases." *Id.* at 168. However, because the plaintiffs did not show a clear and indisputable right to mandamus relief, the Third Circuit denied their petition. *Id.* at 173. Plaintiffs pointed to the language of section 1407(a), which refers to "coordinated or consolidated pretrial proceedings," arguing that, because common discovery was completed, the consolidated pretrial phase of their cases was over, and the Panel abused its discretion in refusing to remand the cases. The Third Circuit disagreed, finding that the test for whether "coordinated or consolidated" proceedings are ongoing "is not whether proceedings on issues common to all cases have concluded; it is whether the issues overlap, either with MDL cases that have already concluded or those currently pending." *Id.* at 170. "Moreover, the overlapping issues do not necessarily need to touch the petitioners' particular cases." *Id.* Applying that standard, the Third Circuit found adequate evidence that the proceedings in the MDL qualified as "coordinated or consolidated." *Id.* The appellate court saw "no evidence that petitioners' cases have languished impermissibly on the MDL court's docket." *Id.* at 173. Although the court "recognize[d] the petitioners' frustration" that the transferee court had not suggested remand, it concluded that "the standards of mandamus ... limit[ed] [its] ability and inclination" to find that the Panel committed a clear error of law. *Id.*

B. DECISION GRANTING MANDAMUS

Research has revealed only one case in which a writ of mandamus was granted after review of a Panel order. In *In re Food Lion, Inc., Fair Labor Standards Act "Effective Scheduling" Litigation*, 73 F.3d 528 (4th Cir. 1996), the Panel transferred claims for unpaid overtime under the Fair Labor Standards Act for coordinated pretrial proceedings in the Eastern District of North Carolina. The transferee court granted partial summary judgment against the plaintiffs in approximately half of the cases and suggested remand. The Panel followed the suggestion and ordered remand of eight cases. In all of the remanded cases, there were some claims that had not been dismissed. Two cases remained in the transferee court; one was pending and another was completed. In the transferor courts, some parties attempted to appeal the dismissed claims under Federal Rule of Civil Procedure 54(b), urging the transferor courts to declare final judgments on the claims that had been resolved. *See* § 14.1 (discussing Rule 54(b)). Some district courts rejected that request, thereby prohibiting immediate appeals. Other district courts, however, allowed the plaintiffs to obtain a final order satisfying Rule 54(b), and those plaintiffs could then appeal the dismissed claims to the circuit courts in which the transferor courts were located. Various plaintiffs whose cases were remanded sought a writ of mandamus in the Fourth Circuit, seeking to have the cases re-transferred to the transferee court. The argument was that all appeals should go to the Fourth Circuit to avoid piecemeal rulings by different appellate courts. The Fourth Circuit granted mandamus relief. It reasoned that allowing several federal appellate courts to review the summary judgment orders of the transferee court would frustrate the aims of 28 U.S.C. § 1407. Providing for review by one appellate court was much more efficient. The Fourth Circuit ordered that the remanded cases be returned to the transferee court so that the appeals from the summary judgment rulings could all be heard by the Fourth Circuit. 73 F.3d at 533.

Food Lion itself, however, was distinguished in an unsuccessful attempt to seek mandamus. In *FedEx Ground Package System, Inc. v. U.S. Judicial Panel on Multidistrict Litigation*, 662 F.3d 887 (7th Cir. 2011), drivers of FedEx trucks brought a class action lawsuit seeking a determination that they were employees, not independent contractors, and that they were entitled to reimbursement for business expenses, backpay, overtime, and other wages. The Panel consolidated the cases in the Northern District of Indiana. The transferee court granted summary judgment for FedEx on all claims in 22 of the cases, but granted summary judgment to plaintiffs on some claims in 12 cases, leaving other claims for trial. FedEx moved for partial final judgments under Rule 54(b) in the 12 cases so that plaintiffs would have to appeal immediately. The appeals would all go to the Seventh Circuit, along with the cases that had been fully resolved on summary judgment. The transferee court denied the Rule 54(b) motion, and instead recommended that the Panel remand the 12 cases to the transferor courts, since the cases were ready for trial. FedEx sought a writ of mandamus from the Seventh Circuit, citing *Food Lion*, but the court denied relief. According to the court, *Food Lion* did not hold that all appeals of claims in an MDL must go to the circuit with jurisdiction over the MDL court. In *Food Lion*, all of the appeals were governed by a single uniform federal law, the Fair Labor Standards Act, while the appeals in *FedEx* involved state laws from multiple states. Because of that difference, FedEx failed to show that it had "a clear and indisputable right to the writ[.]" *FedEx*, 662 F.3d at 891.

CHAPTER 6

TAG-ALONG ACTIONS

§ 6.1 OVERVIEW OF TAG-ALONG ACTIONS

The Panel's procedural rules define a "tag-along action" as a "civil action pending in a district court which involves common questions of fact with either (1) actions on a pending motion to transfer to create an MDL or (2) actions previously transferred to an existing MDL, and which the Panel would consider transferring under Section 1407." JPML Rule 1.1(h). In other words, tag-alongs include actions "filed after the initial hearing on transfer and actions that were then pending but were not brought to the attention of the Panel." Herr (MDL) § 8:1.

Tag-along actions form a significant part of many MDLs. On average, the Panel considers 5,000 tag-along actions per year, and it transfers the vast majority of them without objection. Heyburn & McGovern at 31. Despite this efficiency, tag-along actions present significant issues, which are the focus of this Chapter.

§ 6.2 TAG-ALONG TRANSFER MECHANISMS

There are two primary mechanisms for centralizing tag-along actions: (1) traditional transfer orders under section 1407; and (2) direct filings.

A. TRADITIONAL TRANSFER ORDERS

The traditional transfer mechanism is section 1407, which treats tag-along actions as a routine part of the MDL process. Transferring tag-alongs—and including them with the cases that were initially part of the MDL—promotes the purposes of section 1407 by ensuring coordinated discovery and consistent rulings on motions.

(1) Notice of Tag-Along Actions

JPML Rule 7.1 requires parties and counsel in consolidated cases to "promptly notify" the Clerk of the Panel of "any potential tag-along actions" in which they are involved. JPML Rule 7.1(a). Notice of these tag-alongs may also come from the clerks of courts in which the tag-alongs were originally filed. Once the Panel is notified of a potential tag-along action, or learns of the action on its own, Rule 7.1(b) authorizes the Panel to take one of three actions.

First, the Clerk of the Panel may serve a conditional transfer order on the parties in the tag-along action. This order transfers the action to the transferee court unless a party opposes transfer within seven days. Opposition to transfer results in briefing and oral argument before the Panel. A lack of response to, or acceptance of, the order serves to transfer the action into the existing MDL proceeding. Approximately 90 percent of conditional transfer orders receive no opposition and are transferred automatically. Heyburn at 2233. It should be noted that if the Clerk of the Panel fails to serve a conditional transfer order on "all plaintiffs or defendants or their counsel," the Panel can either: (1) have the Clerk of the Panel reinstate the conditional transfer order; or (2) permit a party to seek remand to the transferor court under 28 U.S.C. § 1407(c). *See* JPML Rule 7.2(b).

Second, the Clerk of the Panel may serve the parties with a show cause order, which asks the parties to show cause why their actions should not be transferred. Parties have 21 days to respond to the order, and failure to respond is considered acquiescence to transfer. *See* JPML Rule 8.1(a)–(c).

Third, the Panel may decide to do nothing after being notified of potential tag-along actions. Rule 7.1(a) provides no criteria for this determination, but the Panel may conclude that the proposed tag-along actions are too unrelated to an existing MDL to warrant transfer under the section 1407 criteria. Practical considerations may also lead the Panel to take no action, such as the advanced progress of the MDL cases versus the lack of progress of the potential tag-along cases. If the Panel declines to act after being notified of a potential tag-along, or if the Panel has not yet been notified, the parties can themselves move for transfer.

Occasionally, the Panel declines to transfer a tag-along action but leaves open the possibility for a party to file a subsequent motion for transfer. *See, e.g., In re Nexium (Esomeprazole) Prods. Liab. Litig.*, 908 F. Supp. 2d 1362, 1364 (J.P.M.L. 2012) ("[W]e will not conditionally transfer th[is] action to the MDL. If any involved party believes that [it] should be centralized, it may file a separate motion to that effect." (citing JPML Rule 7.1(b)(i))).

(2) The Standards for Transfer

To warrant transfer, a potential tag-along action must share a common question of fact with actions in which a transfer motion has either been granted or is pending. In addition, the Panel frequently examines whether the status of the tag-along action is similar to the status of the transferred cases. Finally, additional factors (discussed below) may make transfer of a tag-along action inappropriate. Herr (MDL) § 8:4.

(a) Common Factual Question

A potential tag-along action must be related to the MDL by virtue of common questions of fact. Relatedness is assessed on a case-by-case basis, and is a fundamental requirement for transfer. For example, the Panel has rejected transfer because of an absence of significant common questions of fact. Herr (MDL) § 8:4 (citing cases). By contrast, the Panel has found that the common presence of the defendant in each action, combined with common questions of fact, was enough for transfer. *Id.* (citing cases).

The case-by-case nature of the Panel's relatedness inquiry is illustrated by contrasting the Panel's consideration of tag-along actions in *In re Nexium (Esomeprazole) Products Liability Litigation*, 908 F. Supp. 2d 1362 (J.P.M.L. 2012), and in *In re Swine Flu Immunization Products Liability Litigation*, 453 F.

Supp. 648 (J.P.M.L. 1978). In *Nexium*, the Panel held that the injury claimed in one potential tag-along (hypomagnesemia) was outside the scope of the MDL, which dealt with claims of bone injuries allegedly caused by the same prescription drug. *Nexium*, 908 F. Supp. 2d at 1364. In *Swine Flu*, by contrast, the Panel found the uniqueness of an alleged injury did not preclude transfer because of the "substantial" commonality of factual questions—such as issues "concerning the development, production, testing and administration of the swine flu vaccine," and "[s]cientific knowledge concerning the efficacy of the swine flu vaccine and the potential risks involved in administration of the vaccine[.]" *Swine Flu*, 453 F. Supp. at 649. The Panel in *Swine Flu* also noted that the tag-along action would result in duplicative discovery absent transfer. *Id.*

As another example of the Panel's fact-specific inquiry, in *In re Deepwater Horizon*, the Panel denied a plaintiff's motion to vacate its conditional transfer order. MDL No. 2179 (Doc. 2005) (J.P.M.L. July 31, 2019). In his lawsuit, the plaintiff alleged that leadership attorneys and BP had colluded to maximize plaintiffs' counsel's attorneys' fees and limit BP's liability, and asserted "multiple challenges to the conduct of the litigation generally." *Id.* at 1. Although the plaintiff argued that his action was separate from the *BP Deepwater Horizon* MDL, the Panel disagreed, finding that "[p]laintiff's wide-ranging allegations concerning defendant's wrongdoing go to the core of the MDL itself, including the prosecution and settlement of tens of thousands of claims in the litigation." *Id.* Noting that "a transferee judge has an undeniable interest in policing the conduct of attorneys involved in an MDL," *id.*, the Panel found that transfer was appropriate.

(b) Similarity of Status

In addition to the statutory requirement of a common question of fact, the Panel often considers the progress made by the MDL transferee judge and the progress of the tag-along action. Although a major objective of section 1407 is the efficient conduct of discovery, the Panel is sensitive to the potential for disruption of the MDL by the transfer of tag-along actions. If the MDL has proceeded significantly—particularly if disposition or remand is near—the Panel may be reluctant to transfer new tag-along actions. In those circumstances, the interest in efficiency may be dwarfed by the disadvantages of unnecessarily extending and complicating the MDL process.

However, the fact that a tag-along party will need to "catch up" to the MDL does not necessarily preclude transfer. Herr (MDL) § 8:4. There must be a "great disparity" in the status of the cases to warrant a prudential denial of transfer on this basis. *Id.* Of course, if the MDL is finished—that is, if the transferred cases have been fully disposed of or remanded to their transferor courts for trial—then there would no longer be an active MDL to adjudicate the tag-along actions. *Id.*

The Panel may similarly deny transfer if the tag-along action has progressed substantially—for instance, if it is ready for trial. The Panel must assess, on a case-by-case basis, whether the benefits of transfer are outweighed by the disadvantages to the parties in the MDL and the tag-along action. Ultimately, the Panel must decide each case on its facts. Herr (MDL) § 8:4.

(c) Other Factors

Even if commonality of facts and similarity in status are established, the Panel may deny transfer of tag-along actions if it finds that the goals of the MDL statute would be undermined. Such denials have resulted when a tag-along action would inject novel or burdensome issues into an MDL or, conversely, when a simple action would not fit within an MDL composed of complicated issues. Nonetheless, the inclusion of some different claims does not necessarily preclude transfer. Herr (MDL) § 8:4.

In addition, the Panel may deny transfer of a tag-along action if the party requesting transfer has not been timely and diligent in seeking this relief. Herr (MDL) § 8:4. Likewise, the Panel may deny transfer of a tag-along action based on input by the transferee court. Because transferee courts have first-hand knowledge of the issues and procedural challenges involved in their MDLs, they can provide valuable information to the Panel. Heyburn & McGovern at 31; Heyburn at 2244.

The Panel is also likely to deny transfer if a tag-along action is actually an attempt to circumvent a prior ruling by the transferee court. For example, in one case a transferee judge denied a party's motion to include a cross-claim in pretrial proceedings, and that party subsequently filed an individual suit based on that claim. The Panel denied the party's motion to transfer that suit into the MDL. *In re Cessna Aircraft Distributorship Antitrust Litig.*, 460 F. Supp. 159 (J.P.M.L. 1978). The Panel disapproved of the party's effort to circumvent the transferee judge's ruling, noting that the MDL system requires "trust, confidence, comity and good will" to function. *Id.* at 162. The transferee judge's original refusal to include the cross-claim received "great weight" in the Panel's decision to deny transfer. *Id.*

The Panel's transfer decision on a tag-along action may also depend in part on other case-specific characteristics. For instance, if a class action is filed after centralization, the Panel may be more likely to transfer it into a preexisting MDL than it would be for a single-plaintiff case. Herr (MDL) § 8:4.

B. DIRECT FILING

The second mechanism for centralizing tag-along actions (in addition to transfer orders under section 1407) is through "direct filing" in the MDL. Rule 7.2(a) states that "[p]otential tag-along actions filed in the transferee district do not require Panel action." Rather than proceeding through the section 1407 transfer mechanism outlined above, a party may choose to file a tag-along action directly in the transferee district and file a motion to have the action assigned to the transferee judge under the district court's local rules. Bradt (Notre Dame) at 795–96; Gluck at 1699–1700.

A direct filing does not guarantee that the case will become part of the MDL. A party "requests" transfer to the transferee judge following the direct filing in the transferee district court. However, the assignment of the action is an administrative matter left to that district court. If a directly filed case is assigned to a judge unassociated with the MDL, the Panel is unlikely to order the case transferred, since doing so would show lack of respect for the transferee court's internal administration. Wright & Miller et al. § 3865.

Direct filings have the advantage of sidestepping the burdens traditionally associated with transfer under section 1407. But that approach is not automatically available for parties in tag-along actions. Unless the transferee court has personal jurisdiction and venue over the defendant(s), the defendant(s) must waive personal jurisdiction and venue defenses. Absent these waivers, the tag-along can be filed only in a court with personal jurisdiction and venue and then transferred by the Panel, as detailed above. Bradt (Notre Dame) at 795–98.

To avoid inefficiencies and complications, defendants sometimes stipulate to allowing tag-along actions to be filed directly in the transferee court. Such stipulations (and plaintiffs' own filings) sometimes make clear that defendants do not waive their right to argue for transfer to a court with personal jurisdiction and venue at the time when other cases in the MDL are remanded to the transferor courts.

Some courts issue general orders regarding direct filing at the outset of the MDL. *See, e.g.*, CMO No. 7, *In re Tylenol (Acetaminophen) Mktg., Sales Practices & Prods. Liab. Litig.*, MDL No. 2436 (E.D. Pa. July 17, 2013); Fourth Amended CMO No. 9, *In re Yasmin & Yaz (Drospirenone) Mktg., Sales Practices & Prods. Liab. Litig.*, MDL No. 2100 (S.D. Ill. Mar. 19, 2012). In *In re Vioxx*, the MDL judge encouraged the use of stipulations allowing direct filing to "promote judicial efficiency" and "eliminate . . . delays . . . ." *In re Vioxx Prods. Liab. Litig.*, 478 F. Supp. 2d 897, 903 (E.D. La. 2007). With more than 2,000 directly-filed cases in that litigation, the MDL judge's use of stipulations likely saved substantial judicial resources. Bradt (Notre Dame) at 798.

C. POST-TRANSFER CONSEQUENCES

Once the Panel has transferred a tag-along action under section 1407, the Panel relinquishes control over that action unless and until the Panel must decide whether to remand the action to the transferor court. After transfer of a tag-along action to the transferee court, the details of integrating that action into the existing MDL are left to the transferee judge. Wright & Miller et al. § 3865. And for cases that were directly filed in the MDL district, the Panel has no role to play, JPML Rule 7.2(a), although the Panel no doubt continues to monitor the various MDLs. Heyburn & McGovern at 31–32.

Upon transfer of a tag-along action, the transferor court loses jurisdiction over the tag-along (unless and until the case is remanded). Nonetheless, rulings made by the transferor court prior to transfer remain in effect unless modified by the transferee court. Of course, the transferee court may revisit the transferor court's orders, just as a court may reconsider its own prior orders. *Cf.* Herr (MDL) § 9:3. *See* § 8.1 (discussing law of the case).

At the conclusion of MDL proceedings, the distinction between direct-filed actions and transferred cases becomes highly relevant. Unless transferred cases have been resolved, they are remanded by the Panel to the transferor court. By contrast, tag-along actions that are directly filed remain with the transferee court for final adjudication—assuming that the transferee court has personal jurisdiction and venue over the case (or the defendant has waived personal jurisdiction and venue). Bradt (Notre Dame) at 796. As noted, a defendant's stipulation (or the plaintiffs' own filings) will sometimes contemplate that the case will be transferred when other cases are remanded. It is not uncommon for fact sheets, short form complaints, and other filings to state where venue would be proper for purposes of post-MDL proceedings. *See, e.g.*, Amended Case Mgmt. Order No. 2, *In re Stryker LFIT V40 Femoral Head Prods. Liab. Litig.*, No. 1:17-md-02768-IT (Doc. 307) (D. Mass. Oct. 23, 2010), at 5 (short form complaint must specify "[t]he federal district court in which the action otherwise would have been filed absent the direct filing procedures adopted by this Court").

D. COMPLICATIONS

Tag-along actions are subject to complications that may occur in all cases transferred into MDL proceedings. However, three potential complications of tag-along cases should be noted: (1) issues relating to cases removed to federal court; (2) issues stemming from lack of service of process; and (3) issues involving choice-of-law.

(1) Removal Complications

The transfer process for tag-along actions can frustrate parties who are in the midst of challenging the removal of a case to federal court. Once the Panel has notice of a potential tag-along action, it can start to transfer the case via a conditional transfer order or show cause order. The presence of unresolved motions (including a remand motion to state court) before the transferor court poses no barrier to transfer. *See* § 3.5. A plaintiff who filed a lawsuit in state court may find that, after the defendant initially removed the case to federal district court, the plaintiff must then address the possibility of the case being transferred to another federal district for pretrial proceedings, including ruling on a motion to remand. Heyburn & McGovern at 31. Of course, the transferor court has authority to rule on remand motions before transfer is effectuated. Also, "[t]he Panel has sometimes delayed ruling on transfer to permit the court in which the case is pending to decide critical, fully briefed and argued motions." Manual § 20.132.

(2) Complications from Lack of Service of Process

Transfer of tag-along actions can occur even if one or more defendants have not been served in accordance with Rule 4 of the Federal Rules of Civil Procedure. JPML Rule 7.2(b) provides that an action may be transferred despite lack of service, unless a party can establish prejudice, in which case the Panel may deny the transfer. The criteria used by the Panel in assessing prejudice are discussed in § 3.5.

(3) Choice-of-Law Complications

A third complication in the tag-along context deals with choice-of-law determinations for tag-along actions filed directly with the transferee court. Ordinarily, in MDL actions that are in federal court based on diversity, the transferee court is required to apply the substantive law of the transferor court's state, including that state's choice-of-law rules. *See* § 12.1. This approach is consistent with the derivative basis of the transferee court's jurisdiction. For MDLs based solely on federal question jurisdiction, however, most courts hold that the transferee court should apply its own circuit's interpretation of federal law (although some transferee courts apply the federal law of a different circuit in certain narrow circumstances, *see* § 12.2).

When a plaintiff files a tag-along action directly in the transferee court, the application of choice-of-law principles becomes more difficult. If the transferee court has no contacts with the parties, meaning that personal jurisdiction and venue would ordinarily constitute strong defenses (had the defendant not agreed to the direct filing), it is not obvious which choice-of-law rules should apply. As one transferee court has acknowledged, "there technically is no prior proper forum whose choice-of-law rules should apply." *Sanchez v. Boston Sci. Corp.*, No. 2:12-CV-05762, 2014 WL 202787, at *4 (S.D.W. Va. Jan. 17, 2014). Most courts "treat foreign direct filed cases as if they were transferred from a judicial district sitting in the state where the case originated[.]" *In re Yasmin & Yaz (Drospirenone) Mktg., Sales Practices & Prods. Liab. Litig.*, MDL No. 2100, 2011 WL 1375011, at *6 (S.D. Ill. Apr. 12, 2011). *Accord, e.g., Wahl v. Gen. Elec. Co.*, No. 3:13-CV-0329, 2013 WL 604818, at *4 (M.D. Tenn. Nov. 14, 2013).

Of course, this problem arises only when personal jurisdiction and venue do not exist and have not been waived. When the MDL transferee court has personal jurisdiction and venue over the defendant, then it is legitimate to treat the MDL court as the court of original jurisdiction (thus avoiding the issue of where the case would have been filed absent an MDL). In that circumstance, the MDL context poses no unique issues, and the MDL court can then follow *Erie Railroad Co. v. Tompkins*, 304 U.S. 64 (1938), and other choice-of-law principles.

§ 6.3 TRANSFEREE COURT'S INITIAL CASE MANAGEMENT ORDERS INVOLVING TAG-ALONG ACTIONS

As noted by the Manual for Complex Litigation, "[t]he "transferee judge's management plan for the

[MDL] should include provisions for handling tag-along actions transferred by the Panel after the initial transfer." Manual § 20.132. According to the Manual:

> Ordinarily, it is advisable [for the transferee court] to order that (1) tag-along actions shall be automatically made part of the centralized proceedings upon transfer to, or filing in, the transferee court; (2) rulings on common issues—for example, on the statute of limitations—shall be deemed to have been made in the tag-along action without the need for separate motions and orders; and (3) discovery already taken shall be available and usable in the tag-along cases.

Manual § 20.132. The MDL court's process of establishing a case management plan for the MDL is discussed in §§ 8.1–8.11.

CHAPTER 7

ROLE OF TRANSFEREE JUDGE: DESIGNATION OF LEAD ATTORNEYS AND COMMITTEES

Chapters 2 to 6 focused on the role of the Panel in determining whether cases are suitable for centralization. This Chapter, and Chapters 8 to 12, assume that the Panel has created an MDL and selected the transferee court and judge. Now the chosen judge must oversee potentially massive litigation, previously spread out among multiple federal districts, and figure out how to make order out of the chaos.

With potentially thousands of cases, and many plaintiffs' attorneys, an MDL cannot operate efficiently by giving each attorney in each case an equal role. In most MDLs, it is necessary for MDL judges to appoint lead attorneys and one or more committees to take the lead on various aspects of the litigation. Such leadership will commonly focus on, *inter alia*, conducting common discovery, briefing and arguing key motions, taking the lead in bellwether trials, appearing at major conferences and hearings, conducting settlement discussions, and making decisions and recommendations on the overall management of the litigation. Fallon at 373.

The MDL court's leadership appointments are of major importance. This small group of attorneys plays a crucial role. Although some of the remaining attorneys will be designated by the leadership to work on the cases as a whole, most end up having little or no ongoing role other than interacting with their individual clients. Those not selected for leadership thus usually "become bystanders in their own lawsuits." Mueller at 537.

In addition to the prestige of leading a major MDL, plaintiffs' attorneys selected for leadership roles are far more likely to receive the largest attorneys' fee awards, because their task is to perform common-benefit work for the MDL as a whole. By contrast, attorneys who primarily represent individual clients and do not secure leadership positions or otherwise participate in common-benefit work must rely for compensation on the contingency fee agreements with their clients. The issue of attorneys' fees is addressed in § 11.2, but it is important to understand, in studying this Chapter, that attorneys' fees drive much of the competition for leadership appointments.

Taking on a leadership role in an MDL can involve significant risk. MDLs can be lengthy and can present enormous financial burdens. Dismissal of an MDL can eviscerate the investments of leadership attorneys, both in time and in money (including payment of consulting and testifying experts, salaried attorneys, and essential support staff). *See* § 11.3. It is generally accepted that attorneys accept this financial risk when they decide to seek leadership positions. MDL Standards at 45–46; Dodge at 361.

This Chapter addresses the MDL process for appointing leadership committees and attorneys. The primary focus is on the appointment of leadership for the plaintiffs. Section 7.1 discusses the models for selecting MDL leadership; section 7.2 discusses responsibilities of leadership attorneys; and section 7.3 discusses the various categories and designations of lead attorneys. MDL judges frequently appoint leadership positions for the defense as well, and that topic is addressed in section 7.4. Section 7.5 then provides examples of the leadership structure and appointments in a number of MDLs.

Most MDL judges and practitioners recognize that appointing attorneys to leadership positions is an inevitable part of the process. And most MDL judges are comfortable that their selections are merit-based, and that the attorneys who are appointed generally do an excellent job. In the past several years, however, some academics have raised concerns about the leadership appointment process, arguing (sometimes with empirical support) that there is an elite group of attorneys who are repeatedly selected for MDL leadership positions and who are willing to compromise the plaintiffs' interests to maximize their own attorneys' fees. This growing debate regarding leadership appointments is discussed in Chapter 17, which addresses MDL reform proposals. *See* § 17.6.

§ 7.1 MODELS FOR SELECTION

The power to appoint lead lawyers and committees "exists as a matter of federal common law," and arguably traces back to a Second Circuit shareholder derivative case, in which the court stated that the trial court could appoint a "general counsel" to "supervise and coordinate" the litigation. Mueller at 536 (citing *MacAlister v. Guterma*, 263 F.2d 65, 66 (2d Cir. 1958)).

Despite the significance of committees and other leadership appointments, there are no statutory or rule-based guidelines for an MDL judge's selection of lead counsel and committees. The MDL judge retains broad discretion on this issue (and many others). Dodge at 355.

Because each MDL has unique needs and issues, there are wide variations in leadership structures. For instance, small MDLs may have few committees and lead attorneys, while large MDLs may have numerous committees and leadership positions. As an example of one highly complex situation, a federal judge in West Virginia was assigned to oversee seven related MDLs involving pelvic mesh litigation. The court appointed a "large 61-attorney" plaintiff steering committee (commonly called the "PSC") "that was responsible for leading all of the litigation under a coordinated leadership structure." *In re C.R. Bard, Inc., Pelvic Repair System Prods. Liab. Litig.*, MDL No. 2187 (S.D.W.Va. Jan. 30, 2019) (Pretrial Order No. 298), at 5. The PSC was tasked "to address common issues that affected all seven of the MDLs[.]" *Id.*

The responsibilities that attach to MDL leadership may be stated generally or with great particularity, depending on the governance and committee structure of the particular MDL. "[T]here is no one-size-fits-all solution." MDL Standards at 27.

Although it is impossible to generalize about leadership structure, given the wide variety of cases, there are basically three methods for selecting lead counsel and committees. *See generally* MDL Standards at 34. First, under the "consensus method," the MDL judge "relies on informal attorney networks to identify necessary leadership positions and select their own leaders; the judge then confirms the proposed slate." Burch & Williams at 1460. Second, under a competitive selection method, the judge "invites submissions and chooses among them." *Id.* at 1460–61. Third, under the "hybrid" method, the MDL judge may designate temporary or interim lead counsel, who designate others to serve in interim committee roles as well, but at the same time the judge conducts "an open application process." *Id.* at 1460. For methods two and three, some judges allow attorneys to object to nominees who have been named. *Id.* at 1461. When MDL judges assess applicants, they frequently look at "experience, cooperative tendencies, and ability to finance the litigation." *Id.*

This selection process inevitably leads to some of the same plaintiffs' attorneys appearing in leadership positions in numerous MDL cases. As noted, concerns have been raised (mainly by some academics) about so-called repeat players. *See* § 17.6 (discussing those criticisms). Such concerns include the absence of adequate checks and balances governing the decisions of these repeat players. One response to such concerns is that MDL judges simply " 'want[ ] to have [attorneys] with expertise.' " Gluck at 1702 (quoting interview with an MDL judge). *See also* Bradt & Rave II at 23–26 (explaining the advantages of plaintiffs having repeat players as leaders).

One source urges MDL judges to "[p]ut[ ] a leadership structure in place promptly[,]" and then to add attorneys to committees, as needed, during the course of the MDL proceedings. MDL Standards at 28, 33. In addition, that source notes that in some cases, it may be necessary to "reconstitute the leadership team," a step MDL judges "should not hesitate" to take if the need arises. MDL Standards at 49.

That source also argues that, in general, the MDL judge should appoint specific lawyers to leadership posts, as opposed to designating law firms. That way, the judge knows that "individual lawyers . . . can be held accountable" and that "the case receives consistent attention of a senior partner." MDL Standards at 29.

Management and litigation skills are important. MDL Standards at 39. MDL judges should appoint lead counsel who have "excellent management skills," and it may be useful to choose attorneys "who have worked together previously[.]" *Id.* at 40–41. On the other hand, the same source notes that "ensuring diversity in the leadership of the cases will enhance public trust in the courts." *Id.* at 44. Because achieving greater diversity may mean appointing lawyers with less MDL experience, that goal is arguably in tension with focusing on lawyers who have previous MDL leadership experience.

In addition, the leadership selection process should be "as transparent as possible," and when the judge requires applications, such applications should be made public. MDL Standards at 37–38.

Needless to say, the appointment of lead counsel is not an easy task. A federal district judge (and former Director of the Federal Judicial Center) advises courts to consider several factors in selecting lead counsel, including: the attorneys' relevant knowledge, experience and resources; agreements among the attorneys; whether the interests of the parties are fairly represented; and the ability of the attorneys to "work cooperatively with opposing counsel and the court." Rothstein Pocket Guide at 12–13. That judge also notes that, "[w]hile prior MDL experience is valuable," an MDL judge should "[c]onsider including attorneys who may bring new perspectives." *Id.* at 13. *See also* Manual for Complex Litigation § 22.62 ("Including plaintiffs' attorneys with different perspectives and experience in lead or liaison counsel or as committee members can be helpful.")

§ 7.2 RESPONSIBILITIES OF LEADERSHIP GENERALLY

Although the responsibilities of lead counsel and committees are not the same in every case, some characteristics are common across many MDLs. *See* Manual § 40.22.

A. FUNDING

While funding burdens of MDLs vary from case to case, in virtually all instances, MDL leadership is responsible for financing the litigation. MDL Standards at 31. This responsibility is so important, and the commitment is so substantial, that MDL transferee judges are encouraged to consider the financial capabilities of potential appointees when selecting lead counsel. *See, e.g.*, MDL Standards at 31.

MDLs frequently use "common-benefit funds." These funds, which are created and overseen by MDL judges, compensate counsel based on their proportional contributions to the litigation. The legal basis for these funds is unclear, although some courts and scholars analogize them to the "common-benefit funds" in class actions. Fallon at 375–76; *but see* Silver & Miller at 121 (arguing that common-benefit funds in non-class MDLs are not analogous to common-benefit funds in class actions). MDL judges also rely on their inherent authority in managing MDLs to justify establishing such funds. Fallon at 377.

The idea behind the common-benefit fund is that attorneys who represent individual clients on a contingent-fee basis—known as Individually Retained Private Attorneys (IRPAs)—receive a benefit from work performed by attorneys who are undertaking tasks for the litigation as a whole. For instance, attorneys who depose corporate executives are often performing work that benefits many or all of the cases. For that reason, such a fund taxes the attorneys who benefit from such work. Fallon at 376.

A common-benefit fund is typically set up by the MDL court early in the case, although "it will usually remain unfunded until much later in the litigation process, when cases are resolved through trial or settlement." MDL Standards at 52–53. The federal MDL judge may wish to coordinate with state judges who have related cases, perhaps to require IRPAs in state cases to contribute to the common-benefit fund. *Id.* at 58. The topic of common-benefit funds is related to the broader issue of attorneys' fees in MDL cases. The latter topic is discussed in § 11.2.

In addition to compensating the attorneys for their common-benefit work, in most MDLs the common-benefit fund also compensates for common-benefit litigation expenses, such as experts and travel costs that benefit the litigation as a whole. *See* MDL Standards at 50 ("[A] common benefit fund is meant to compensate attorneys for the costs borne and work performed for the common benefit of all plaintiffs and their counsel.").

As a separate matter, MDL plaintiffs' leadership attorneys usually create a "housekeeping fund," which is used to pay for "communal litigation expenses," such as special master fees. Unlike common-benefit funds, these housekeeping funds are typically managed by the leadership attorneys, not by the court. MDL Standards at 52. MDL lead counsel and the committee members pay into this fund, and also pay for their own expenses going forward, such as travel expenses. *Id.* The plaintiffs and defendants may also have a joint fund to pay for "common expenses like special master fees[.]" *Id.*

In a large, hard-fought MDL, leadership attorneys can incur potentially millions of dollars in funding expenses, such as deposition costs and hiring of expert witnesses. For example, in *In re Syngenta AG MIR 162 Corn Litigation*, No. 2:14-md-02591-JWL-JPO, 2018 WL 6839380 (D. Kan. Dec. 31, 2018), the plaintiffs' attorneys incurred expenses of more than $48 million. *See id.* at *15. In *In re Deepwater Horizon*, MDL No. 2179, 2016 WL 6215974 (E.D. La. Oct. 25, 2016), the plaintiffs' attorneys incurred more than $44 million in expenses. *Id.* at *1 & n.4. And in *In re Vioxx Products Liability Litigation*, 760 F. Supp. 2d 640 (E.D. La. 2010), expenses were more than $40 million. *See id.* at 642 n.1.

There is little authority governing the formation and use of common-benefit funds, except for orders entered in individual MDL cases. Those orders, of course, are not binding on other MDL judges, and they may not even be persuasive in some respects, given the differences from one MDL to another. MDL Standards at 53; Dodge at 356; Silver (Fordham) at 1991.

Funding for MDLs may also come from third-party funders, *i.e.*, investors who provide funds to plaintiffs' law firms to prosecute civil cases in exchange for a portion of the recovery. *Cf.* Hensler at 501 (discussing various types of third-party funding). Third-party funding in complex litigation is controversial. One commentator argues that such funding "helps to manage principal-agent problems" by "(1) unbundling the attorney's competing roles as investor and advisor, (2) shifting financial risk to a third party . . ., and (3) putting in place a sizeable stakeholder with the sophistication and incentive to monitor the agents." Burch (NYU II) at 1277. On the other hand, some have argued that third-party funding "undercut[s] the plaintiff's control over his or her own claim because investors inherently desire to protect their investment and will therefore seek to exert control over strategic decisions in the lawsuit." Beisner, Miller & Rubin at 7. *See* § 17.5 (discussing reform proposal requiring disclosure of third-party funders).

B. COMMITMENT

MDL lead counsel on the plaintiffs' side are responsible for efficiently managing their cases and fairly representing the claimants involved. *But see* subsection D, *infra* (explaining that there is a dispute whether such attorneys have strict fiduciary duties to non-clients). Multidistrict litigation carries immense oversight and management burdens. Those appointed to leadership roles in MDL cases must manage their cases efficiently and, in many instances, must delegate work to non-leadership attorneys. Leadership attorneys in an MDL are responsible for making the MDL a professional priority for the duration of the litigation. MDL Standards at 34–35, 42, 49.

C. PERFORMANCE AND SUPERVISION OF KEY LITIGATION TASKS

A major role of lead counsel is collaborating with all attorneys involved in the litigation, including those who are not on leadership committees but are representing individual clients. In a large MDL, there might be a dozen or so attorneys on leadership committees, but perhaps hundreds of other attorneys who are representing individual plaintiffs.

Among other things, lead counsel is charged with keeping other attorneys informed of major litigation developments. This requires active and timely communication of litigation updates, deadlines, and other important information. It is also critical that lead counsel properly manage the common benefit work done by attorneys who are not in leadership roles.

Most importantly, appointed lead counsel is responsible for the overall management of the MDL litigation. Scholars and practitioners emphasize this critical responsibility in encouraging judges to consider management capabilities when appointing lead counsel. Lead counsel must be able to manage the litigation efficiently and respond to the various actors in the litigation, including other leadership components, non-lead attorneys, opposing counsel, and the court. MDL Standards at 25–26. One source also recommends that transferee judges, in making appointments, consider the potential "harmony" among lead attorneys, opposing counsel, and the court. *Id.* at 40–41, 47. *But see* § 17.6 (discussing concerns raised by some scholars about repeat players).

A significant function of attorneys in leadership roles is to delegate work to other attorneys. Tasks should be delegated to non-lead attorneys whenever possible, but attorneys in leadership roles bear ultimate responsibility for ensuring high-quality work as well as overall efficiency. Because, as noted in the introduction to this Chapter, attorneys in leadership roles incur the greatest financial risks, it is in their interest to ensure efficient delegation of the work throughout the litigation. MDL Standards at 41, 47.

D. LEGAL RELATIONSHIP OF MDL LEADERSHIP TO NON-CLIENT PLAINTIFFS

The nature of the relationship between leadership attorneys and plaintiffs not represented by those attorneys has been the subject of significant debate. Some argue that it would be incorrect to characterize leadership attorneys' obligations to other plaintiffs as "fiduciary" obligations in the traditional sense. Under that view, the role of leadership attorney differs from "common law fiduciary relationships of agency and trust." Herman at 8. Moreover, imposing fiduciary duties would be "extremely burdensome for the attorneys and the court." *Id.* Thus, it is argued, leadership attorneys should not be deemed "subject to instruction or control" of non-client plaintiffs. *Id.* at 10. Holding leadership attorneys to fiduciary standards would lead to "an endless series of . . . dispute[s]" among the various players in MDLs. *Id.*

at 11. Consequently, leadership attorneys should be under no obligation to share "confidential and sensitive information" that they gain in leadership roles, absent a "compelling reason[.]" *Id.* at 19. At the same time, that view acknowledges that leadership attorneys attempting to negotiate a global settlement lack authority to bind non-clients, and when they engage in settlement negotiations, they must not skew the proposals to favor their clients over other plaintiffs. *Id.* at 22.

Others, however, believe that the relationship between leadership attorneys and non-client plaintiffs is indeed a fiduciary relationship. As one scholar argues, non-clients "are at risk of being exploited and require the protection the fiduciary duty provides." Silver (Fordham) at 1990.

The extent to which leadership attorneys serve as fiduciaries can have important ramifications. Under a fiduciary approach akin to a traditional attorney-client relationship, leadership attorneys are required to keep all plaintiffs' counsel involved in all strategic decisions and perhaps day-to-day activities. Yet while leadership attorneys should keep other attorneys apprised of major developments, *see* MDL Standards at 47, the Manual for Complex Litigation cautions that "too much communication [between leadership attorneys and the other attorneys and their clients] may defeat the objectives of efficiency and economy." Manual § 10.222. Given these competing concerns, the MDL judge is well advised to set forth clearly, in appointing leadership attorneys, the extent to which leadership attorneys can—and cannot—bind non-clients. *See* Herman at 10 & n.29 (discussing pretrial order in *BP Deepwater Horizon MDL* limiting the ability of leadership attorneys to bind non-client plaintiffs). *See also* Burch (Mass Tort Deals) at 96 (discussing importance of setting forth duties owed by leadership to nonclients).

§ 7.3 TYPES OF DESIGNATIONS

A. LEAD COUNSEL

The most significant appointment for MDL leadership is the lead counsel. In most cases, an MDL judge will appoint one lead attorney (or a very small number of lead attorneys) to oversee the overall MDL proceedings. Many of the preceding obligations and risks apply with particular force to lead counsel. As the top of the organizational pyramid, lead counsel steers the litigation throughout the MDL proceedings. Not surprisingly, appointment as lead counsel is extremely competitive.

B. STEERING OR EXECUTIVE COMMITTEES AND OTHER COMMITTEES

If the MDL is particularly complex, or if the plaintiffs require separate representation due to differences in their legal interests, the MDL judge may consider establishing a steering or executive committee in addition to appointing lead counsel. The judge may establish as many committees as are necessary, and may establish the committee(s) in any form that the judge finds beneficial to the overall litigation.

Executive committees "typically consist of three to five attorneys who work closely with lead counsel on managing the litigation." MDL Standards at 30. By contrast, steering committees "are often composed of a broader set of attorneys who each focus on specific aspects of the day-to-day ligation," including briefing, discovery, technology issues, and interfacing with attorneys in related state cases. *Id.* at 31. One source contends that, apart from "exceptional cases," steering committees should not have more than 20 members. *Id.* at 31–32. Smaller committees may be appropriate to avoid unwieldiness.

Although the court may appoint an executive committee and other committees, the lead attorneys are free—absent court instruction—to augment the formal committee structure as needed in the particular litigation. MDL Standards at 32.

C. LIAISON COUNSEL

The transferee judge may also appoint a liaison counsel for the plaintiffs. Liaison counsel is usually responsible for communicating between the court and other counsel as well as for recording filings and developments. MDL Standards at 29–30. Liaison counsel also coordinates with the clerk of the court. If an MDL involves related state court actions as well, the MDL transferee judge may assign liaison counsel the task of updating the MDL judge on the progress of the state court actions. *Id.* at 79.

For liaison counsel, one source recommends appointing someone "who has practiced before the transferee judge," because that attorney "will already be familiar with the local rules, the judge's practices and preferences, and other court-specific procedures." MDL Standards at 5. Only "rarely" should the court appoint more than one attorney as liaison counsel for the plaintiffs. *Id.*

§ 7.4 LEADERSHIP APPOINTMENTS ON THE DEFENSE SIDE

Although MDL judges routinely make leadership appointments on the plaintiffs' side, such appointments are less common on the defense side. They do occur, however, particularly in cases involving numerous defendants. MDL Standards at 28. Even when an MDL judge appoints a defense leadership team, the functions of the designated attorneys are often more limited than those on the plaintiffs' side. *See* Manual § 10.221 ("The role of a defense leadership team in multi-defendant cases is often one of coordination, in contrast to the more substantive and strategic role of plaintiffs' leadership.")

In many cases, the MDL court will simply designate lead defense counsel, who is primarily responsible for coordinating information among defense counsel and serving as a "point of contact" for interacting with plaintiffs' lead counsel. MDL Standards at 28–29. In addition, when the MDL judge appoints liaison counsel for plaintiffs, the judge may appoint liaison counsel for defendants as well.

In complicated cases, however, the MDL judge may create a committee structure on the defense side as well. *Id.*

§ 7.5 EXAMPLES OF LEADERSHIP ARRANGEMENTS

Several examples of leadership structures in actual MDL cases illustrate the broad discretion given to MDL judges in organizing the litigation.

A. *IN RE VOLKSWAGEN "CLEAN DIESEL"*

In a marketing, sales practices, and product liability MDL involving fraudulent emissions systems in hundreds of thousands of VW and Audi diesel vehicles, the MDL judge appointed a plaintiffs' lead counsel and steering committee. *In re Volkswagen "Clean Diesel" Mktg., Sales Practices, & Prods. Liab. Litig.*, No. 3:15-md-02672-CRB (Doc. 1084) (N.D. Cal. Jan. 21, 2016). After receiving 150 applications, the court selected 22 lawyers for these leadership positions. The MDL judge appointed a prominent plaintiffs' attorney as the sole lead counsel, based on her "extensive experience" with MDLs. *Id.* at 1. The court noted that she had "held leadership positions in seventeen different MDLs, including several that involved" similar legal issues. *Id.* at 1–2. The court further emphasized that its choice of lead counsel was supported by "a great number" of other plaintiffs' counsel in the MDL, and that the court's previous experience working with her demonstrated "first-hand" her leadership abilities. *Id.* at 2.

In the *Volkswagen "Clean Diesel"* MDL, the authority and duties assigned to lead counsel were broad. In addition to serving as chair of the plaintiffs' steering committee (PSC), she was assigned responsibility for "coordinat[ing] and oversee[ing] the [PSC's] responsibilities . . .; schedul[ing] PSC meetings and keep[ing] minutes or transcripts of these meetings; . . . appear[ing] at periodic Court-noticed status conferences and hearings; . . . sign[ing] and fil[ing] all pleadings relating to all actions; . . . bind[ing] the PSC in scheduling settlement discussions and discovery, setting agendas, entering into stipulations, and in other necessary interactions with the settlement master, defense counsel, and the PSC"; maintaining a depository for pleadings, transcripts, and documents; and designating attorneys to interact with (and set depositions and agendas with) attorneys for plaintiffs, the defendants, and government entities. *Id.* at 2.

The PSC was responsible for creating its own internal structure and conducting pretrial proceedings. The size of the committee (21 attorneys plus lead counsel) was based on the court's perception of "the amount of work th[e] litigation may entail" and "the need for" expediency. *Id.* at 4. In appointing attorneys to the committee, the court considered each attorney's resources, including the resources of that attorney's law firm. *Id.*

In its order appointing lead counsel and the steering committee, the MDL judge instructed Volkswagen to name its own liaison counsel. The court also designated coordinating counsel for the

Department of Justice, which had a case in the MDL. *Id.* at 5.

B. *IN RE QUALCOMM*

In an antitrust MDL, the MDL judge established a smaller governance structure than in the *Volkswagen "Clean Diesel"* case. *In re Qualcomm Antitrust Litig.*, No. 17-MD-02773-LHK, 2017 WL 2222531 (N.D. Cal. May 15, 2017). This structure consisted of a plaintiffs' steering committee and co-lead counsel. From five attorney motions for leadership positions, the court established a committee of three attorneys. Of those three, two attorneys were appointed as co-lead counsel. The court did not spell out the responsibilities of those leadership positions.

The court, however, was very detailed in explaining its particular selections of the two co-lead attorneys. For both attorneys, the court identified several significant elements that supported the selections: (1) both had "performed considerable work in identifying or investigating potential claims" within the litigation; (2) both "demonstrated experience in handling complex class actions" as well as an "adequate knowledge of the applicable law"; and (3) both were "willing[ ] to commit significant resources" to the litigation. *Id.* at *1. One of the attorneys was further found suitable for leadership because she had "considerable experience" with complex litigation, including litigation involving a similar technological focus. Furthermore, she was the only plaintiffs' counsel in the case who had previously appeared before the MDL judge and, according to the court, she "was excellent at trial." *Id.*

C. *BP DEEPWATER HORIZON*

The *BP Deepwater Horizon* MDL involved the largest oil spill in history, in which hundreds of thousands of people suffered personal injuries or economic and business losses. Immense effort was needed to maintain efficiency due to the number and diversity of claims. To this end, the MDL judge established multiple leadership roles and committees for both the plaintiffs and the defendants. *See BP Deepwater Horizon* MDL website (listing orders in the MDL).

For plaintiffs, the MDL judge established a governance structure composed of co-liaison counsel, an executive committee, and a steering committee. The court appointed two attorneys as co-liaison counsel; those attorneys were also members of the executive committee and served on the steering committee as ex officio members. In addition to the traditional tasks of liaison counsel, those attorneys worked with the defendants' liaison counsel to make joint recommendations to the court. *In re Oil Spill by the Oil Rig Deepwater Horizon in the Gulf of Mexico, on Apr. 20, 2010*, No. 2:10-md-02179-CJB-SS (Doc. 110) (E.D. La. Aug. 27, 2010) (pretrial order no. 6); *see id.* (Doc. 600) (E.D. La. Oct. 26, 2010) (pretrial order no. 12) (liaison counsel for both parties stipulated to protocols for service of documents). Those attorneys also had executive leadership authority by virtue of their positions on the executive committee (discussed below). *Id.* (pretrial order no. 6).

The court also appointed a 15-member PSC. The court detailed the responsibilities of the PSC members, which were categorized as "[d]iscovery," "[h]earings and [m]eetings," "[t]rial," and "[m]iscellaneous." Collectively, those responsibilities encompassed the overall management of the pretrial proceedings. *Id.* (Doc. 506) (E.D. La. Oct. 8, 2010) (pretrial order no. 8), at 3–4.

Finally, on the plaintiffs' side, the MDL judge appointed a four-member executive committee as opposed to a traditional lead counsel. This executive committee included plaintiffs' co-liaison counsel, as well as two members of the steering committee. The executive committee was tasked with "coordinat[ing] the responsibilities" of the steering committee. *Id.* at 2. The appointments to the steering committee and executive committee were "personal"; the court's order barred members from substituting others (including other members of their own law firms) to serve. *Id.*

For the defendants, the MDL judge appointed a steering committee composed of 13 attorneys, along with nine attorneys appointed as liaison counsel. Six attorneys were appointed to both groups, while three additional non-committee attorneys served as liaison counsel. *Id.* (Doc. 567) (E.D. La. Oct. 19, 2010) (pretrial order no. 10).

D. *NATIONAL PRESCRIPTION OPIATE LITIGATION*

In *In re National Prescription Opiate Litigation*, No. 1:17-md-02804-DAP (Doc. 37) (N.D. Ohio Jan. 4, 2018), one of the most highly publicized MDLs in history, plaintiffs filed a motion (later amended) to approve co-lead and co-liaison counsel, and an executive committee. The court noted that the process leading to the motion and proposed slate was "open and transparent" and included discussions among "attorneys representing the vast majority of the filed cases across the country, counsel with extensive trial and resolution experience, and counsel with decades of leadership experience in MDL proceedings." *Id.* at 2–3. The court subsequently held an open meeting for all counsel of record for plaintiffs, attended by 150 attorneys from 97 law firms. At the meeting, counsel made nominations for various positions, and a motion was made to adopt a slate that plaintiffs' counsel had developed.

At the court's request (after three objections were filed), the plaintiffs revised their original motion. As revised, the proposed leadership structure included "three co-leads and a diverse executive committee to serve as a superstructure and provide oversight for various committees populated from a steering committee." *Id.* at 4. The proposal contemplated the nomination of a 16-member plaintiffs' executive committee, *id.* at 10–20, and three attorneys as co-lead counsel, *id.* at 20–22. The proposal detailed the qualifications and tasks for all elements of the leadership structure, including prior MDL experience (and in most instances, prior MDL leadership experience). *Id.* at 4–21. The MDL judge approved the revised proposal.

A few days earlier, the court had appointed leadership positions for the defendant manufacturers and distributors. *See* Docket Entries for Case No. 1:17-md-02804-DAP (N.D. Ohio) (order granting the defendants' motions to approve liaison counsel and steering committee and appointing two additional steering committee representatives for individual defendants).

On August 19, 2019, the MDL judge designated two plaintiffs' attorneys to serve as co-lead attorneys for a proposed "negotiation class" to pursue settlements with defendants in the MDL. Order Appointing Interim Class Counsel, *In re Nat'l Prescription Opiate Litig.*, No. 1:17-md-02804-DAP (Doc. 2490) (N.D. Ohio Aug. 19, 2019). The court certified the negotiation class on September 11, 2019. Order Certifying Negotiation Class and Approving Notice, *In re Nat'l Prescription Opiate Litig.*, No. 1:17-md-02804-DAP (Doc. 2591) (N.D. Ohio Sept. 11, 2019).

CHAPTER 8

ROLE OF TRANSFEREE JUDGE: CASE MANAGEMENT

This Chapter focuses on issues that an MDL judge should address from the outset: how to design and implement proper case management for the MDL.

§ 8.1 CASE MANAGEMENT: OVERVIEW

When the MDL Panel enters a transfer order (and the order is filed with the transferee court), the transferor court loses jurisdiction over the case (unless and until the case is remanded by the Panel). Before the transfer order is entered, the transferor court remains free to enter orders that the court deems appropriate, including an order remanding the case to state court for lack of subject matter jurisdiction.

Upon transfer, the transferee court has the power to administer all pretrial aspects of the case, including discovery, class certification, and dispositive motions (such as motions to dismiss and motions for summary judgment). The transferee court also has the power to rule on unresolved jurisdictional issues, such as motions to remand to state court for lack of subject matter jurisdiction. The transferee court may also be involved in trying to secure a global settlement. This power is important, as reflected in the fact that only about three percent of MDL cases get remanded to the transferor courts. *See* § 1.1.

One limitation on the transferee court's authority is that the court is normally bound by the rulings of the transferor court. Herr (MDL) § 9.3. Under law of the case doctrine, a court cannot "revisit the determinations of an earlier court unless (i) the evidence in a subsequent trial was substantially different, (ii) controlling authority has since made a contrary decision of the law applicable to such issues, or (iii) the decision was clearly erroneous and would work . . . [a] manifest injustice." *In re Ford Motor Co.*, 591 F.3d 406, 411–12 (5th Cir. 2009).

In the early stages of an MDL, the court must consider a variety of issues, including a timeline for ruling on pending motions; a discovery plan; a schedule for dispositive motions; and numerous other issues discussed in this Chapter. Because of the volume and complexity of many MDLs, devising a case management order may be more challenging than devising such an order for a single case under Federal Rule of Civil Procedure 16. As one MDL judge aptly put it, "It's like Rule 16 on steroids." Gluck at 1688. It is not a stretch to characterize MDL judges as more like "modern administrator[s]" than traditional judges. *Id.* at 1673. Yet anecdotal evidence suggests that MDL judges do not favor the enactment of special Federal Rules to govern case management issues in MDLs. *Id.* at 1689.

Federal appellate courts recognize the special management tasks facing MDL judges. For that reason, while appellate courts traditionally give deference to trial court case management orders even in non-MDL cases, that deference is at its zenith in the MDL context. *See, e.g., In re Asbestos Prods. Liab. Litig. (No. VI),* 718 F.3d 236, 243 (3d Cir. 2013) (reviewing the district court's case management orders "with deference, particularly in the MDL context"); *In re Fannie Mae Secs. Litig.*, 552 F.3d 814, 822 (D.C. Cir. 2009) (same); *In re Deepwater Horizon*, 907 F.3d 232, 235 (5th Cir. 2018) (same).

Extra deference is appropriate in MDL cases because such cases are often highly complex. The Panel looks for MDL judges who have the skills, temperament, and judgment to manage complicated litigation. It would substantially undermine the MDL process if appellate courts interfered with MDL judges' day-to-day management of cases without compelling reasons.

§ 8.2 INITIAL CASE MANAGEMENT ORDERS

When the Panel centralizes cases before a single MDL judge, that judge must promptly create an orderly process and develop a plan. The attorneys involved in the cases contribute substantially to this effort, but ultimately the MDL judge must decide how the transferred cases should proceed.

It is not possible, especially in a Nutshell, to delineate all of the issues that the MDL judge and counsel should consider in developing initial case management orders. Much depends on the facts and circumstances of the particular cases. Local rules or orders may also affect what should be included in the orders. *See, e.g.*, N.D. Cal. Civil Local Rule 16–2(c) ("When a civil action is transferred to this district, the Court shall issue . . . an Order Setting Initial Case Management Conference[.]"). Although no definitive checklist exists, one authoritative source notes that the MDL court's initial case management order should set dates for the following:

- "filing of a consolidated amended complaint (when appropriate),
- responding to motions to remand to state court,
- filing and briefing on motions to dismiss,
- . . . fact-discovery . . .,
- . . . resolution of any class certification motions,
- expert disclosures and discovery . . ., and
- . . . summary judgment motions[.]"

Rothstein Pocket Guide at 16–17.

That source also notes that, in addition to setting specific dates, the MDL judge should consider a number of tasks, including: developing a service list of counsel; directing counsel to provide preliminary reports on key factual and legal issues and on affiliated companies and counsel (for recusal purposes); directing attorneys who are seeking leadership positions to submit relevant information; and determining whether to designate a magistrate judge (and for what purposes). Rothstein Pocket Guide at 17–18. The court should also focus early in the MDL process on *Daubert* issues; class certification issues (if class actions are involved);

choice-of-law issues; and possible dispositive issues, such as statutes of limitations. *Id.* at 17. *See also* Smith at 227–29 (offering suggestions for initial case-management issues, focusing on mass tort cases).

One source recommends regular status conferences, with status reports prepared by leadership attorneys in advance of each conference. MDL Standards at 4–5.

§ 8.3 CRITICAL CASE MANAGEMENT TECHNIQUES

Commentators have emphasized two areas as especially important for MDL judges to consider at an early stage: (1) focusing on the common issues; and (2) determining the strength of individual cases.

A. FOCUSING EARLY ON COMMON ISSUES

One commentator has explained that, even if resolving common issues does not dispose of the litigation, great efficiencies can be achieved by focusing on them up front, possibly "eliminating whole categories of claims" or "obviate[ing] the need for certain types of discovery[.]" Smith at 253. A careful focus on common issues can also identify the need for, and parameters of, bellwether trials, and can help sharpen discovery and motions practice.

One technique that some MDL judges employ for focusing attention on the common issues is the use of master complaints. As the Supreme Court explained in *Gelboim v. Bank of America*, 135 S. Ct. 897 (2015), "Parties may elect to file a 'master complaint' and a corresponding 'consolidated answer,' which supersede prior individual pleadings. In such a case, the transferee court may treat the master pleadings as merging the discrete actions for the duration of the MDL pretrial proceedings." *Id.* at 904 n.3. Merger does not occur, however, "when the master complaint is not meant to be a pleading with legal effect but only an administrative summary of the claims brought by all the plaintiffs." *Id.*

Typically, a master complaint is filed by the MDL leadership to encompass the claims of all plaintiffs, while "short form" complaints are filed to address plaintiff-specific claims. *See, e.g.*, Master Long Form Complaint, *In re Lipitor (Atorvastatin Calcium) Mktg., Sales Practices & Prods. Liab. Litig.*, No. 2:14-mn-02502-RMG (Doc. 160) (D.S.C. May 30, 2014) (setting forth generalized allegations, factual background, and causes of action). As discussed in the context of MDL reform (§ 17.4), the legal effect of master complaints has generated controversy, including whether defendants can move to dismiss such complaints (*e.g.*, for failure to state a claim upon which relief can be granted). Most MDL judges have allowed defendants to file dispositive motions in response to master complaints. *See* § 17.4 (citing examples); *but see In re Nuvaring Prods. Liab. Litig.*, No. 4:08MD1964, 2009 WL 2425391, at *2 (E.D. Mo. Aug. 6, 2009) (denying defendants' motion to dismiss a master complaint because that complaint was "simply meant to be an administrative tool to place in one document all of the claims at issue in this litigation").

B. ASSESSING THE STRENGTH OF INDIVIDUAL PLAINTIFFS' CLAIMS

Courts in MDLs may wish to adopt approaches for assessing the strength of individual plaintiffs' claims. It is usually impractical to file a motion to dismiss for each individual case pending before an MDL judge. A concern raised by the defense bar, however, is that if there is no way to screen the merits of each case, there will be little or no deterrent to filing baseless cases. *See* § 17.2.

Several screening devices are available. One is to require plaintiffs to submit fact sheets outlining the evidentiary support for the claims. *See, e.g., In re Silica Prods. Liab. Litig.,* 398 F. Supp. 2d 563, 567 (S.D. Tex. 2005) ("[A]ll Plaintiffs in recently-transferred actions must submit sworn Fact Sheets within 60 days from the date of transfer by the Panel[.]").

The Ninth Circuit, in *In re Phenylpropanolamine (PPA) Products Liability Litigation*, 460 F.3d 1217 (9th Cir. 2006), described the plaintiff fact sheet process used in that litigation:

> [The court] adopt[ed] a "Plaintiff's Fact Sheet" (PFS) protocol in lieu of interrogatories to streamline the process. The PFS is a questionnaire to be signed under oath seeking information about the plaintiffs' injuries, medical history, current medical condition, identification of the product claimed to have caused injury, specifics of the injury suffered, and the identity of the plaintiffs' healthcare

> providers. It also includes blank authorizations to be signed by plaintiffs to allow defendants to collect medical and other records. . . . The PFS was the starting point for defendants' assessment of plaintiffs' claims and the precondition for proceeding with further discovery . . . .

Id. at 1224. The Ninth Circuit held that the MDL court did not abuse its discretion by dismissing certain cases with prejudice for failure to comply with this process. *Id.* at 1233–34. *See also In re Guidant Corp. Implantable Defibrillators Prods. Liab. Litig.*, 496 F.3d 863, 868 (8th Cir. 2007) (same).

One variation is the issuance of a so-called *Lone Pine* order. That name is derived from a New Jersey trial court order requiring plaintiffs in a toxic tort suit to produce detailed information to support the claims and then dismissing the suits when sufficient evidence was not produced. *See Lore v. Lone Pine Corp.,* No. L33606-85 (N.J. Super. Ct. Law Div., Monmouth Cnty., Jan. 1, 1986), *reprinted in* 1 Toxic L. Rep. (BNA) 726. *Lone Pine* orders have been entered in a number of MDLs. *See, e.g., In re Zimmer NexGen Knee Implant Prods. Liab. Litig.*, No. 1:11-cv-05468, 2016 WL 3281032, at **1–2 (N.D. Ill. June 10, 2016) (finding a *Lone Pine* order "necessary to ensure that certain cases [in the MDL] have sufficient merit to proceed to trial"); *In re Rezulin Prods. Liab. Litig.,* 441 F. Supp. 2d 567, 570 (S.D.N.Y. 2006) (after the court granted a defendant's motion to exclude the plaintiffs' proposed expert's testimony, the court issued a *Lone Pine* order requiring "each plaintiff to consider whether good grounds existed to continue prosecuting his or her claim[.]"); *In re Vioxx Prods. Liab. Litig.,* 557 F. Supp. 2d 741, 743 (E.D. La. 2008) (noting that "*Lone Pine* orders have been routinely used by courts to manage mass tort cases" and citing examples).

Some argue that *Lone Pine* orders can help MDL judges to "weed out" meritless claims and concentrate on the claims that have potential merit. Smith at 230–31. *See also In re Vioxx Prods. Liab. Litig.,* 557 F. Supp. 2d 741, 743 (E.D. La. 2008) (*Lone Pine* orders are designed to "identify and cull potentially meritless claims"). One source has noted that *Lone Pine* orders are especially important "where multiple alternative potential causes of the alleged injuries exist." MDL Standards at 13.

One commentator explains that, although *Lone Pine* orders and plaintiff fact sheets serve similar purposes, the two devices differ in several ways. First, *Lone Pine* orders, unlike plaintiff fact sheets, require evidence of scientific causation. Second, and related, *Lone Pine* orders require plaintiffs to supply information from qualified experts, as opposed to fact sheets, which require information that is usually within the plaintiff's possession or easily obtainable. Third, because of the requirement to provide information from qualified experts, *Lone Pine* orders impose greater costs on plaintiffs than do fact sheets. In general, *Lone Pine* orders are more controversial among the plaintiffs' bar than plaintiff fact sheets. Engstrom at 20–21; *see also* Burch (Mass Tort Deals) at 118–119 (relying on data to argue that *Lone Pine* orders are used to coerce non-settling plaintiffs to settle).

§ 8.4 DISCOVERY COORDINATION

One of the most important functions of an MDL judge is to coordinate discovery. *See, e.g.*, *In re Activated Carbon-Based Hunting Clothing Mktg. & Sales Practices Litig.*, 840 F. Supp. 2d 1193, 1198 (D. Minn. 2012) ("The primary purpose behind assigning multidistrict litigation to a transferee court is to promote efficiency through the coordination of discovery."); *Faircloth v. Merck & Co., Inc.*, No. 2:06-CV-184-RDP, 2006 WL 8437244, at *1 (N.D. Ala. Mar. 3, 2006) (same); Gluck at 1683 (same). Discovery should be productive, yet efficient for all parties. Duplication should be avoided whenever possible. *See, e.g.*, *In re Vioxx Prods. Liab. Litig.*, 360 F. Supp. 2d 1352, 1354 (J.P.M.L. 2005) (centralization was "necessary . . . to eliminate duplicative discovery"); *Wilk v. Am. Med. Ass'n*, 635 F.2d 1295, 1297 n.3 (7th Cir. 1980) (same). As one example, a CEO or other high-level corporate executive whose testimony is relevant in an MDL could be deposed just once, instead of multiple times, with the testimony applying to all of the transferred cases. Likewise, document productions can be made more efficient by creating document depositories that are available for all of the transferred cases.

In creating a discovery plan, the MDL judge may not be starting from scratch. In many instances, some (or even substantial) discovery will have occurred before MDL transfer. The filing of a motion for transfer will not mean a stay of discovery, unless the transferor judge chooses to order a stay pending resolution of the motion. According to the Manual for Complex Litigation, when a transferor court is notified that a motion to transfer has been filed, it "should not automatically stay discovery[.]" Manual § 20.131.

Regardless of whether discovery in the transferor court was temporarily stayed, the MDL judge will want to assess, early on, what discovery has occurred, what discovery is still necessary, and how best to manage discovery going forward. According to one source, discovery issues the MDL judge may wish to address include: (1) prioritizing (and possibly bifurcating) discovery; (2) determining deposition guidelines (including videotaping certain depositions); (3) establishing privilege and confidentiality protocols; (4) identifying ways of reducing duplicative discovery; and (5) possibly requiring fact sheets from plaintiffs or other early mandatory disclosures. MDL Standards at 3–9. Other topics that the MDL judge may wish to address are the establishment of document depositories; protocols for electronic discovery; and standards for interrogatories and requests for admission. Rothstein Pocket Guide at 25. According to the Manual for Complex Litigation, "[f]or effective discovery control, initial discovery should focus on matters—witnesses, documents, information—that appear pivotal . . . . [T]his initial discovery may render other discovery unnecessary or provide leads for further necessary discovery." Manual § 11.422.

See also MDL Standards at 8 (urging phased discovery).

The MDL judge should also focus at an early stage on expert discovery. One experienced judge has noted that "[t]he use of common experts, along with consolidated expert disclosures and expert discovery, is . . . sometimes worthwhile." Rothstein Pocket Guide at 25. In complex cases, "only a limited number of persons may be available to provide certain kinds of opinions." *Id.* at 26. Moreover, "high expert fees can provide an incentive for parties to join together in selecting their experts on common issues and to establish reasonable parameters on expert discovery." *Id.*

In some instances, related cases will be pending in state courts. In those situations, discovery coordination with the relevant state courts will be important. Key areas on which the MDL judge should focus for such coordination include: creation of joint federal/state document depositories; coordinating the taking of discovery in federal and state courts; coordinating federal and state court document production and scheduling of depositions; and coordinating rulings on discovery issues. Rothstein Pocket Guide at 25. Federal/state coordination is discussed in detail in Chapter 16.

§ 8.5 *DAUBERT* RULINGS

One key task in many MDLs is determining the admissibility of expert testimony. The seminal case in this area is *Daubert v. Merrill Dow Pharmaceuticals, Inc.* 509 U.S. 579 (1993). *Daubert* directs federal courts to perform a gatekeeping function with respect to expert testimony. *Daubert* and its progeny instruct courts to consider whether the expert's theory or methodology: (1) can be tested; (2) has been published or peer-reviewed; (3) has a known rate of error; and (4) is generally accepted within the "relevant scientific community." *Id.* at 589–95. In a subsequent case, the Court held that *Daubert* is not limited to scientific testimony, but applies to all expert testimony. *Kumho Tire Co., Ltd. v. Carmichael*, 526 U.S. 137, 147 (1999).

Daubert rulings can make or break a lawsuit (or an entire MDL). Without admissible expert testimony on crucial points, plaintiffs may be unable to prove crucial elements of their claims. *Daubert* issues will often be the same (and controlling) in all or many of the constituent cases in the MDL. Many MDL judges focus intensively on *Daubert* issues, often early in the MDL. In some instances, MDL judges grant *Daubert* motions, thus either terminating or at least sharply restricting the litigation. In other instances, judges deny the motions, giving the green light to the experts to testify at trial. The importance of *Daubert* rulings is reflected in the fact that the defense bar has urged proposals to make such rulings immediately appealable in at least some MDLs when final judgments do not otherwise result. *See* § 17.1.

In recent years, defendants in MDL cases have frequently sought early expert discovery and early *Daubert* rulings, particularly when causation is at issue. An example of a court granting crucial *Daubert* motions by the defense is *In re Prempro Products*

Liability Litigation, 738 F. Supp. 2d 887 (E.D. Ark. 2010). In that MDL, plaintiffs alleged that the estrogen hormone replacement therapies Prempro and Premarin can cause breast cancer. In support of their theory of general causation, plaintiffs offered two experts. The court concluded that neither expert's testimony satisfied the *Daubert* standard, and thus granted defendants' motions to exclude those experts. The court found that neither expert could sufficiently challenge the results of a decade-long clinical study conducted by the Women's Health Initiative, a subdivision of the U.S. Department of Health and Human Services, which found that estrogen hormone replacement therapies did not increase the risk of breast cancer. *Id.* at 893, 895.

An example of a court allowing much of plaintiffs' expert testimony to go forward is *In re Abilify (Aripiprazole) Products Liability Litigation*, 299 F. Supp. 3d 1291 (N.D. Fla. 2018). In that case, the plaintiffs alleged that the drug Abilify caused "impulsive and irrepressible urges to engage in certain harmful behaviors, including gambling, eating, shopping, and sex." *Id.* at 1300. The plaintiffs offered five experts to support their assertion of general causation between the drug and the behaviors at issue (*i.e.,* that the drug can cause such behavior). The defendants filed *Daubert* motions challenging all five experts. The court issued a lengthy ruling, addressing each expert in detail. Although it excluded certain portions of the expert testimony, it found that core testimony from some of plaintiffs' experts was admissible. The court concluded that plaintiffs had offered "reliable evidence of a broad scientific consensus regarding the existence of an association between Abilify and increased risk of impulse control problems." *Id.* at 1372. The court also addressed *Daubert* motions filed by the plaintiffs with respect to five experts proffered by the defendants, finding some of the testimony admissible and some inadmissible.

Although the *Prempro* and *Abilify* rulings reached opposite *Daubert* conclusions, each ruling greatly advanced the overall progress of the particular MDL. These are only two of many cases in which MDL judges have addressed crucial *Daubert* issues. *See, e.g.*, Smith at 231–43 (summarizing numerous MDLs in which *Daubert* issues were adjudicated).

§ 8.6 RULINGS ON SUMMARY JUDGMENT MOTIONS AND OTHER DISPOSITIVE MOTIONS

Another key task in many MDLs is ruling on summary judgment motions and other dispositive motions. For example, in *In re Mirena IUS Levonorgestrel-Related Products Liability Litigation (No. II)*, 341 F. Supp. 3d 213 (S.D.N.Y. 2018), the court excluded numerous expert witnesses submitted by plaintiffs on general causation. The lawsuits alleged that Mirena, an intrauterine device manufactured by Bayer, caused an increase in cerebrospinal fluid pressure in the skull. After the court excluded those experts, Bayer moved for summary judgment based on the lack of evidence of general causation. In a comprehensive opinion, the court granted the motion and closed all cases that were still in the MDL. *In re Mirena IUS Levonorgestrel-Related Prods. Liab. Litig. (No. II)*, 387 F. Supp. 3d 323 (S.D.N.Y. 2019). The plaintiffs attempted to piece together a theory of general causation despite the exclusion of their experts, but the court rejected all of plaintiffs' arguments. It found that "plaintiffs [had] not come forward with sufficient reliable, non-speculative evidence from which a reasonable factfinder could determine, by a preponderance of the evidence, that Mirena caused plaintiffs' injuries." *Id.* at 356.

In *Fox v. Ethicon, Inc.*, No. 2:12-cv-0878, 2016 WL 3748509 (S.D.W.Va. July 8, 2016), the court addressed summary judgment in the context of an individual lawsuit within one of seven pelvic mesh MDLs. (At one point, those seven MDLs involved more than 100,000 lawsuits.) The MDLs alleged injury from the use of transvaginal surgical mesh to treat pelvic organ prolapse and stress urinary incontinence. The defendants moved for summary judgment, attacking multiple claims filed by the plaintiff. The court granted summary judgment with respect to several claims, but denied summary judgment with respect to various others.

There are numerous other examples of summary judgment rulings within MDLs. *See, e.g.*, Smith at 244–46 (providing examples).

Similarly, it is common for MDL judges to rule on other dispositive motions, such as motions to dismiss for failure to state a claim. *See, e.g.*, *In re Keurig Green Mountain Single-Serve Coffee Antitrust Litig.*, 383 F. Supp. 3d 187 (S.D.N.Y. 2019) (granting in part and denying in part defendant's motions to dismiss antitrust actions under Rule 12(b)(6) in MDL); *In re Biomet M2a Magnum Hip Implant Prods. Liab. Litig.*, MDL No. 2391, 2019 WL 1077291 (N.D. Ind. Mar. 7, 2019) (granting defendants' motions to dismiss 23 cases for lack of personal jurisdiction and failure to state a claim).

MDL judges should devise an orderly approach for the resolution of dispositive motions. This is an area in which creativity at the outset can achieve great efficiencies and pave the way for early settlements. It is difficult to identify specific strategies for MDL judges to adopt in connection with dispositive motions. Much will depend on the complexities and other circumstances of the specific litigation. Nonetheless, some general practices are instructive.

First, it may be useful to require parties to notify the MDL judge before filing motions. That approach was taken in the *Marriott Data Breach* MDL. *In re Marriott Int'l Customer Data Sec. Breach Litig.*, No. 19-md-2879 (Doc. 334) (D. Md. July 16, 2019). The MDL judge instructed the parties in a letter order that any party wishing to file a motion (including a dispositive or discovery motion) had to first file a letter (not exceeding three single-spaced pages) describing the motion and the grounds for it. The court would then decide whether a response to the letter was required and whether the matter could be resolved without formal briefing. If the court determined that a motion was appropriate, it would issue an order directing the filing of the motion.

Second, it may be useful to identify a specific procedure for dispositive motions. In the *Marriott Data Breach* case, which involved numerous tracks, the court issued an order authorizing one motion to dismiss, one opposition brief, and one reply brief for each track. *In re Marriott Int'l Customer Data Sec. Breach Litig.*, No. 19-md-2879 (Doc. 279) (D. Md. June 10, 2019). For the consumer track, securities track, and derivative track, the court set page limits of 35 pages for the motion and opposition, and 20 pages for the reply. For the financial institutions track, the court set page limits of 25 pages for the motion and opposition and 12 pages for the reply. For the consumer track, the court limited the motion to dismiss to 10 claims (5 selected by plaintiffs and 5 selected by defendants), and ruled that any motions for class certification would be limited to those 10 claims. For all of the tracks, the court set deadlines for various tasks, including the filing of amended complaints, selection of bellwether claims (for the consumer cases), and the filing of dispositive motions.

§ 8.7 RULING ON PREEMPTION MOTIONS

One type of dispositive motion that warrants special mention is a motion to dismiss on preemption grounds. Preemption motions are frequently filed in MDL cases, especially in certain mass tort cases, and they can potentially resolve the entire litigation.

In 2019, the U.S. Supreme Court addressed preemption in litigation arising out of an MDL. *Merck Sharp & Dohme Corp. v. Albrecht*, 139 S. Ct.

1668 (2019). The MDL involved Fosamax, a drug that, according to plaintiffs, causes "atypical femoral fractures" (fractures in the femoral shaft, located in the thigh). Merck argued that the plaintiffs' state law failure to warn claims were preempted by federal law. Specifically, Merck claimed that the federal Food and Drug Administration (FDA) would have rejected Merck's attempt to amend the Fosamax label to warn of the risk of atypical femoral fractures, given the FDA's prior rejection of a warning on Fosamax's label of a risk of stress fractures. Because the FDA would not have allowed the warning about atypical femoral fractures, plaintiffs' state law failure to warn claims were preempted. The district court agreed with Merck's argument and dismissed hundreds of claims. 951 F. Supp. 2d 695 (D.N.J. 2013) .

The Third Circuit reversed the MDL judge based on prior circuit precedent, holding that "whether the FDA would have rejected a proposed label change is a question of fact that must be answered by a jury." 852 F.3d 268, 286 (3d Cir. 2017). The court indicated, however, that Supreme Court review would be useful in clarifying the law. *Id.* at 284.

The Supreme Court granted review and vacated the Third Circuit's opinion. Although there were two concurring opinions, the Court was unanimous that the preemption defense was a legal issue for the court. *Id.* at 1679.

As another example, in the *Monsanto Roundup* MDL, the judge rejected Monsanto's argument that the Federal Insecticide, Fungicide and Rodenticide Act preempted plaintiffs' claim that the company did not adequately warn them about the risk of non-Hodgkin's lymphoma caused by its herbicide. *In re Roundup Prods. Liab. Litig.*, 364 F. Supp. 3d 1085 (N.D. Cal. 2019). Although the ruling arose in the context of three bellwether trials, it impacted the entire MDL, which included more than a thousand cases. The ruling may also have an impact on the Roundup litigation pending in the state courts, which involves more than 11,000 plaintiffs.

For other examples of preemption rulings in MDLs, *see* Smith at 246–47.

§ 8.8 RULING ON FORUM NON CONVENIENS MOTIONS

Another type of motion that may dispose of multiple MDL cases is a motion to dismiss based on the doctrine of forum non conveniens. This occurred in *In re Air Crash Over Southern Indian Ocean*, 352 F. Supp. 3d 19 (D.D.C. 2018).

The case arose from "one of the greatest aviation mysteries of modern times: the disappearance of Malaysia Airlines Flight MH370 somewhere in the southern Indian Ocean in the early morning hours of March 4, 2014." 352 F. Supp. 3d at 23. Following the flight's disappearance, numerous plaintiffs filed suit, both in Malaysia and in the United States. The U.S. cases were centralized in the District of Columbia district court. The defendants then moved to have the U.S. cases dismissed under the doctrine of forum non conveniens, and the transferee court granted the motion, dismissing all of the cases without prejudice. In a detailed opinion, the court found that "on balance, the claims asserted in the consolidated complaints have a substantial and overriding nexus to Malaysia that outweighs the less substantial connection to the United States." *Id.* at 24. As a result, the court concluded that "litigation of these claims in the United States is comparatively inconvenient[.]" *Id.*

§ 8.9 USE OF FEDERAL MAGISTRATE JUDGES

In many MDLs, the volume of work will convince the MDL judge to rely on a federal magistrate judge to assist with discovery, conduct status hearings, issue reports and recommendations on motions, and help on numerous other tasks. Some MDL judges also rely on special masters, a topic discussed in § 8.10.

An empirical study focusing on MDLs that were terminated in 2011 and 2012 found that MDL judges used federal magistrate judges in 54 percent of the MDL cases surveyed. Hanks at 50. A more recent anecdotal study sheds a different light on the use of federal magistrate judges. Based on interviews with a number of federal and state judges, one scholar found that many MDL judges are reluctant to involve magistrate judges in MDLs. The MDL judges enjoy the cases and "see themselves as essential players[.]" Gluck at 1693–94. The interviews suggested, however, that MDL judges may not be similarly reluctant to use special masters. *Id.*

Despite the recent anecdotal study, many examples can be found of federal magistrate judges playing a major role in MDL litigation. For instance, in the *BP Deepwater Horizon* litigation, a federal magistrate judge oversaw weekly discovery conferences and was involved in negotiations between the parties that led to a class settlement. 910 F. Supp. 2d 891, 901 (E.D. La. 2012). *See also, e.g.*, *In re Activated Carbon-Based Hunting Clothing Mktg. & Sales Practices Litig.*, 840 F. Supp. 2d 1193, 1199 (D. Minn. 2012) (noting "yeoman efforts by the Magistrate Judge" to encourage settlement); *In re Asbestos Prods. Liab. Litig. (No. VI)*, 830 F. Supp. 2d 1377, 1380 (J.P.M.L. 2011) (describing large groups of MDL cases in which "the parties [were] proceeding to pursue settlement under the supervision of a Magistrate Judge").

§ 8.10 REFERENCE TO A SPECIAL MASTER

Another option for MDL judges seeking assistance in case management is the appointment of a special master. MDL judges interviewed for a scholarly study indicated that their reluctance to use magistrate judges did not extend to special masters. Gluck at 1693–94. However, one empirical study suggests otherwise. It found that special masters were used in only 20 percent of the MDLs terminated in 2011 and 2012 (as opposed to use of federal magistrate judges in 54 percent of the cases). Although 9 percent of the cases involved the use of both magistrates and special masters, magistrate judges alone were used in 45 percent of the MDLs, while special masters alone were used in only 11 percent of the MDLs. Hanks at 50, 59.

Nonetheless, even if federal magistrate judges are used more frequently than special masters, there can be no doubt that special masters have played crucial roles in many MDL cases. For example, in *In re Volkswagen "Clean Diesel" Marketing, Sales Practices, & Products Liability Litigation*, the special master helped guide the massive litigation to settlement within only seven months. *See* 895 F.3d 597, 604 (9th Cir. 2018) (noting role of special master).

In some cases, MDL judges have appointed multiple special masters to perform various functions. For example, in *In re National Football League Players' Concussion Injury Litigation*, the MDL judge appointed an experienced financial expert to assess the settlement, a retired federal judge to mediate the settlement, and another retired federal judge to investigate allegations of fraud. *See* 961 F. Supp. 2d 708, 710–11 (E.D. Pa. 2014) (describing two of the appointments); Order Appointing Special Investigator, No. 2:12-md-02323-AB (Doc. 10355) (E.D. Pa. Dec. 10, 2018), at 2 (naming fraud special investigator). In *In re National Prescription Opiate Litigation*, No. 1:17-md-02804-DAP (Doc. 69) (N.D. Ohio Jan. 11, 2018), the MDL judge appointed three special masters to assist in the "extremely complex litigation." *Id.* at 1. And courts have appointed special masters to review the time and expense records submitted by attorneys performing common-benefit work. *See, e.g.*, Pretrial Order No. 20, *In re Taxotere (Docetaxel) Prods. Liab. Litig.*, No. 2:16-md-02740-KDE-MBN (Doc. 265) (E.D. La. Feb. 24, 2017) (appointing a special master to oversee and make recommendations to the court regarding common-benefit expenses); MDL Standards at 5–6 (citing examples of special master appointments).

An MDL judge appointing a special master should address several subjects, including: the scope of the assignment and delegated powers; compensation; and "the circumstances under which ex parte communications with the court or a party will be appropriate[.]" Rothstein Pocket Guide at 39.

In addition to appointing special masters, some MDL judges have "appoint[ed] a [certified public accountant] early in the litigation to assist . . . with tracking fees and costs." MDL Standards at 46.

§ 8.11 MDL COURT WEBSITE

Many MDL judges establish special websites for their MDLs. For example, the court in the *Volkswagen "Clean Diesel"* MDL established a website with links to numerous case documents of special interest. *See Volkswagen "Clean Diesel"* MDL website; *see also* Appendix C. Similarly, in *In re Ashley Madison Customer Data Security Breach Litigation*, the MDL court established a website with case documents, contact information, and a schedule of hearings and conferences. *See Ashley Madison* MDL website. Some districts have websites that include links to MDLs pending in that district. *See, e.g.*, N.D. Ill. MDL links (Northern District of Illinois). One commentator found that out of 245 MDLs pending in December 2016, 111 had MDL-specific websites. Gluck at 1690. Large MDLs were more likely to have MDL-specific websites than smaller MDLs. *Id.*

One authoritative source advises that the contents of MDL websites should include information about the claims, relevant court orders, reports of leadership attorneys, contact information for the court and counsel, transcripts, and settlement information. Also, this source suggests including links to local rules, PACER, state courts handling related cases, the Panel's website, and the Manual for Complex Litigation. Rothstein Pocket Guide at 8.

CHAPTER 9

ROLE OF TRANSFEREE JUDGE: BELLWETHER TRIALS

Most MDL judges view their job as attempting, whenever possible, to dispose of the cases so that they are not remanded to the transferor courts. Some judges have been clear about this objective, noting early on their goal of achieving a global settlement. For instance, in the widely publicized *National Prescription Opiate* MDL, the transferee judge strongly suggested at his initial hearing as MDL judge that his goal was to oversee a comprehensive settlement. He noted that "[p]eople aren't interested in figuring out the answer to interesting legal questions like preemption and learned intermediary, or unraveling complicated conspiracy theories. . . . [M]y objective is to do something meaningful to abate this crisis and to do it [quickly]." Transcript of Proceedings at 4, *In re Nat'l Prescription Opiate Litig.,* No. 17-CV-2804 (E.D. Ohio Jan. 9, 2018).

Of course, merely creating an MDL will not bring the parties to the settlement table. In some instances, focused discovery and a few dispositive motions will provide a basis to begin discussions. In other instances, however, the parties will need to understand how the cases may be assessed by a trier of fact. If the latter situation exists, there is often no substitute for a trial of one or more cases before the MDL court.

This Chapter discusses the common MDL practice of having "bellwether" trials. It focuses initially on the general concept of a bellwether trial. It then discusses how cases are selected for bellwether trials, including issues stemming from the fact that the MDL statute limits the MDL judge's authority to overseeing pretrial proceedings. Next, it discusses the legal effect of bellwether verdicts on other cases in the MDL. Finally, this Chapter provides examples of how bellwether trials have been useful to the resolution of MDL dockets.

§ 9.1 OVERVIEW OF THE CONCEPT OF A "BELLWETHER" TRIAL

A "bellwether" trial is a trial of a limited number of plaintiffs' cases in an MDL. The results provide useful information, but generally are not binding on the remaining cases. Fallon, Grabill & Wynne at 2325; Lahav at 186. Even without binding effect, the hope is that the results of the trial will allow both sides to "evaluate the strengths and weaknesses of their arguments and evidence," and to assess "the risks and costs associated with the litigation." Fallon, Grabill & Wynne at 2325; *see also* Bellwether Guide at 3–7.

By gathering information about the strengths and weaknesses of the claims, the parties may be able to reach an acceptable settlement structure, thereby reducing attorneys' fees and litigation costs. Of course, bellwether trials can themselves be expensive. And because the cases are being tried in the transferee court's district, the outcomes and jury pools may not be representative of jury pools in other parts of the country, where cases would be tried upon remand to the transferor courts.

The term "bellwether" trial derives from an ancient shepherding practice. A male sheep, a wether, would wear a bell around his neck to lead the other sheep to safe locations. Fallon, Grabill & Wynne at 2324. In the same way, the cases that go forward as bellwether trials are designed to lead the parties to evaluate their cases and understand the risks of litigation.

The prevalence of bellwether trials is a relatively recent development. They are common today, but were less frequent even a decade ago. Gluck at 1689. Many recent bellwether trials have involved mass tort MDLs, including product liability cases involving medications or medical devices. Brown, Holian & Ghosh at 668.

For a bellwether trial to be useful, both parties must find the results to be reasonably representative of the MDL cases as a whole. If the cases are representative, the parties can use the information to formulate a global settlement. Brown, Holian & Ghosh at 670. Of course, the nuances of a particular case may make it hard for a bellwether trial of that case to serve as a proxy for all of the other cases in the MDL. *Id.*

Although the focus of this Chapter is on individual jury trials (to verdict) against defendants on all issues and claims in a case, other variations for deciding issues can yield useful information. Two such variations are: (1) a trial on common issues with subsequent procedures for resolving individual cases, *see, e.g.*, *In re Gypsum Cases*, 386 F. Supp. 959, 963–64 (N.D. Cal. 1974) (describing trial on liability issue in antitrust MDL, followed by a second phase of trial to determine damages); and (2) a "stipulated resolution of all elements of individual claims" based on "a formula or by a hearing before an arbitrator, special master, or magistrate judge." Rothstein Pocket Guide at 47. More commonly, however, courts use the bellwether trial approach described in this Chapter.

§ 9.2 SELECTION OF THE CASES

Selecting the cases that will proceed to a bellwether trial involves three preliminary steps. First, all of the existing cases in the MDL are identified and their important variables recognized. Second, a pool of possible cases that are representative of the whole are selected for case-specific pretrial discovery and for consideration as trial cases. Third, a predetermined number of cases from the pool are selected to proceed to trial.

A. IDENTIFYING THE EXISTING CASES

All of the cases in the MDL should be identified, and the critical variables should be categorized. Fallon, Grabill & Wynne at 2345; Bellwether Guide at 19–20. "A bellwether trial is most effective when it can accurately inform future trends and effectuate an ultimate culmination to the litigation; therefore, it is imperative to know what types of cases comprise the MDL." Fallon, Grabill & Wynne at 2344. If the transferee court and the attorneys do not accurately ascertain the universe of relevant cases, they "risk trying an anomalous case, thereby wasting substantial amounts of both time and money." *Id.*

This process is not as clear as it might appear. Simply looking at cases within the MDL may not be adequate. There may be many relevant cases in state court as well. The number of those cases, and the issues they entail, must be factored into the overall identification of the existing cases. Otherwise, the results of a bellwether trial might be insufficient to facilitate a broad settlement.

B. CREATE THE POOL OF POTENTIAL CASES

(1) General Considerations

After identifying the existing cases, the parties and the court must decide on the number of cases necessary for the bellwether trial selection pool. While there is no set number of cases, it might be appropriate, for example, to choose approximately 20 cases for the selection pool if the court intends to have six bellwether trials. Fallon, Grabill & Wynne at 2347; *see also* Bellwether Guide at 22–24.

Choosing the selection pool can be challenging. There must be enough different variables included to make the bellwether trials representative of the whole, but not so many as to become inefficient. One of three methods is usually used to select the pool: random selection; the court's choice; or the parties' choice. Fallon, Grabill & Wynne at 2348–51; Lahav at 188–96; Bellwether Guide at 24–28; Hellerstein, Henderson & Twerski at 148–52.

Random choice avoids bias in the selection of the cases for the bellwether pool. However, a totally random selection may make it difficult to get cases with all of the representative variables. Since the bellwether trials are designed to be representative, if the randomly chosen cases are missing important variables, the parties may consider the results inadequate for generalizing about other cases. Burch (Mass Tort Deals) at 108 (raising concerns about usefulness of bellwether trials with small sample size). Nonetheless, the Manual for Complex Litigation favors random selection of cases "[t]o obtain the most representative cases from the available pool[.]" Manual § 22.315. *See also* MDL Standards at 19–20 (discussing examples of random selection of bellwether cases).

Alternatively, the transferee judge can choose the cases for the bellwether pool. While this approach also avoids party selection bias, it burdens the court, which must spend time and resources scrutinizing the cases and deciding on a suitable pool. In addition, the parties may be concerned that they had no say in the decision and may conclude that the chosen cases are not representative.

Finally, the attorneys can make the selection of the cases for the bellwether pool. This approach can lead to selection bias. Each side may pick the cases most favorable to its position, rather than identifying truly representative cases.

Attorney selection of cases can be handled in various ways. Under one approach, the plaintiffs can designate half of the cases while the defendants designate the other half. Alternatively, one side, either plaintiffs or defendants, can pick all of the cases. Or the court can require both sides to agree on all the cases in the pool. The last option is perhaps the fairest, but it may be difficult to get the opposing sides to agree. *See* Rubenstein (Newberg) § 11:15 2.

Allowing each side to select some of the cases is a common method for identifying bellwether plaintiffs. Lahav at 191. For instance, in *In re General Motors LLC Ignition Switch Litigation*, No. 14-MC-2543 (JMF), 2016 WL 1441804 (S.D.N.Y. Apr. 12, 2016), each side selected nine cases for discovery and trial, with the parties allowed to strike each other's selections until each side was left with three of its selections. Lahav at 191.

Some methods for selecting the pool of cases for bellwether trials may be more complex than the three approaches described above. For instance, in *In re Fosamax Products Liability Litigation*, No. 1:06-md-1789 (S.D.N.Y. Jan. 30, 2007), 25 cases were to be chosen. Each side proposed 12 cases, and another was chosen at random. If any of the plaintiffs withdrew or dismissed their claims, the defendants chose a replacement; if any defendants settled, plaintiffs chose a replacement. Brown, Holian & Ghosh at 675. *See also* Bellwether Guide at 28–30 (describing various selection strategies employed by MDL judges in specific cases).

(2) *Lexecon* Complications

The fact that MDL transfers are only for *pretrial* proceedings poses complications in selecting the pool of potential trial cases. In *Lexecon, Inc. v. Milberg Weiss Bershad Hynes & Lerach*, 523 U.S. 26 (1998), the Supreme Court held that MDL courts do not have authority to transfer cases to themselves for trial under 28 U.S.C. § 1404(a). *See* § 15.2 (discussing *Lexecon* decision in detail). In light of *Lexecon*, five options are potentially available to MDL judges. MDL Standards at 17–18; Sherman (Louisiana) at 458–59; Bellwether Guide at 11–15; Herr (Annotated Manual) § 20.14 (citing case law on ways MDL courts have conducted trials notwithstanding *Lexecon*).

First, the parties can waive their right to object to a trial on the ground that it violates *Lexecon*. MDL Standards at 17. But *Lexecon* waivers can raise complications. A *Lexecon* waiver must be "clear and unambiguous." *In re Depuy Orthopaedics, Inc.*, 870 F.3d 345, 351 (5th Cir. 2017). In a given case, issues may arise regarding the validity and clarity of a waiver. In addition, issues may arise if a party attempts to revoke a *Lexecon* waiver. For example, in *In re Fosamax Products Liability Litigation*, 815 F. Supp. 2d 649 (S.D.N.Y. 2011), 25 cases were selected for bellwether trials. *Lexecon* waivers were obtained for all 25 cases. One of the cases the defendants chose for trial was *Raber v. Merck & Co., Inc.*, 06 Civ. 6295(JFK). Before the *Raber* bellwether trial, however, the plaintiff moved to revoke her *Lexecon* waiver. The transferee court denied the motion, saying that a party must show good cause for withdrawal once a *Lexecon* waiver is given. 815 F. Supp. 2d at 651. Despite the court's ruling, a bellwether trial that is not supported by all parties may be of limited value.

The second option is to allow new plaintiffs to file their claims directly in the MDL transferee court. Under this direct-filing option, the court can "select any [directly filed] case for a potential bellwether trial and then at that point ask the parties in that case to waive any objections to conducting a trial in the MDL proceeding venue." MDL Standards at 18. This saves judicial resources, as the MDL judge is not required to obtain *Lexecon* waivers from the entire pool. *Id.* Alternatively, the bellwether trial can involve a case that was filed in the MDL district before the creation of the MDL. This approach will not work, however, if there is no personal jurisdiction or venue over the defendant in the transferee court and the defendant is unwilling to waive those defenses. *See* §§ 6.2, 12.3 (discussing direct-filed cases).

Third, if a *Lexecon* waiver is not obtained, and the case was not filed directly in the transferee court, the transferee judge can hold the trial in the transferor district. *See* Bellwether Guide at 14–15 (providing examples of intercircuit or intracircuit assignments); Fallon, Grabill & Wynne at 2366 n.135 (noting that "the [New Orleans] transferee court in the *Vioxx* MDL . . . [held] the first bellwether trial in Houston, Texas, albeit fortuitously as a result of evacuating New Orleans for Hurricane Katrina"). This approach is not automatic. The MDL judge must apply to sit in the transferor court. One circuit has held that this can be done only upon a showing that there is a need for judges in the transferor district. *See In re Motor Fuel Temperature Sales Practices Litig.*, 711 F.3d 1050, 1053 (9th Cir. 2013); *see also* Sherman (Louisiana) at 459–62; MDL Standards at 18.

Fourth, after a case is remanded by the Panel, the MDL judge can ask the transferor judge to transfer the case back under 28 U.S.C. § 1404(a), thereby enabling the MDL judge to try it. That approach will only work, however, if the MDL court has personal jurisdiction and venue over the defendant or all parties consent to the transfer.

Finally, after a case is remanded by the Panel, the trial could take place before the transferor judge. Of course, that judge would need to get up to speed, and a trial by the transferor judge may not have as much influence over the other parties in the MDL as a trial conducted by the MDL judge.

Given these various options, *Lexecon* is by no means a fatal blow to the ability of transferee judges to conduct bellwether trials.

C. SELECTING THE CASES THAT WILL PROCEED TO TRIAL

After the completion of case-specific discovery within the pool of possible bellwether cases, the cases that will proceed as bellwether trials are chosen. As discussed above, the selection of the pool of cases is generally done by one of three methods—random selection, court selection, or selection by counsel.

Similarly, the selection of the actual trial cases from the pool is done by using one of those same three methods. *See* Fallon, Grabill & Wynne at 2360–65. In addition to using one of these three methods, the MDL judge can allow counsel for each side "to exercise a predetermined number of strikes or vetoes to eliminate cases in the pool from consideration prior to the actual selection." *Id.* at 2361.

§ 9.3 LEGAL AND PRACTICAL EFFECTS OF THE BELLWETHER TRIAL

A. APPLICABILITY (OR INAPPLICABILITY) OF PRECLUSION

Because a bellwether trial is not a class action trial, it is not normally binding on the other MDL cases absent express agreement of the parties. Both sides are entitled to their day in court, and they arguably would be denied a full and fair opportunity to litigate their claims if they were bound in other cases by the results of the bellwether trial. Savage at 446.

It might be possible in a given situation to argue that preclusion should apply. In *Parklane Hosiery Co. v. Shore*, 439 U.S. 322 (1979), the Supreme Court held that nonmutual issue preclusion can be used offensively if the defendant previously had a full and fair opportunity to litigate the common question. For example, if plaintiff A won a case against a defendant, that defendant might be precluded from litigating the identical dispositive issue against plaintiff B. But courts have "broad discretion" in whether to apply offensive collateral estoppel. *Flood v. Just Energy Mktg. Corp.*, 904 F.3d 219, 236 (2d Cir. 2018). Courts have been reluctant to invoke offensive collateral estoppel in the context of bellwether trials or similar settings.

For instance, in *In re Chevron U.S.A., Inc.*, 109 F.3d 1016 (5th Cir. 1997), which was not an MDL, the district court had approved a trial plan in which a group of 30 plaintiffs (15 selected by the plaintiffs and 15 selected by the defendants) would have their claims tried in what the district court characterized as a "unitary trial on the issues of general liability or causation" for all 3,000 plaintiffs in the litigation. *Id.* at 1019. The Fifth Circuit held that this procedure was an unconstitutional violation of the defendant's due process rights to a full and fair trial. *Id.* at 1020–21.

On the other hand, one commentator argues that if the plaintiffs win a *series* of bellwether trials, issue preclusion could arguably be fair and proper. Savage at 463–64.

Parties to the MDL may agree to be bound to the results of the bellwether trial by contract, but that is an agreed-upon result, not an application of issue preclusion. Of course, the actual litigants to the case are bound by the trial, unless it was clear that, in exchange for their consent to participate, the trial would not be binding. The parties may also agree to allow the bellwether plaintiffs to collect from any eventual aggregate settlement even if they lost their individual trials. Rubenstein (Newberg) § 11:19.

B. INFORMATIONAL APPROACH

Even if the results of bellwether trials are not legally binding on the other cases in the MDL, those trials still offer important information. Two of these benefits are: (1) the information provided by the bellwether trial might facilitate an overall settlement of all claims in the MDL; and (2) the bellwether trial can facilitate the creation of a "trial package," which can be used by other attorneys if the cases proceed to individual trials on remand. Fallon, Grabill & Wynne at 2325. Those benefits are discussed below.

(1) Information Provided from the Actual Trial

To be useful as a statistical matter, it is generally necessary to conduct "a significant number of trials[.]" Lahav at 197. For purposes of negotiating a settlement, however, "a small[er] number of trials" can provide both sides "with some sense of the strengths and weaknesses" of the cases overall. *Id.* For example, if plaintiffs won all of the bellwether cases, including those that were cherry-picked by defendants, that result would be very informative, even if there were only a handful of trials. Similarly, a string of defense verdicts, even in cases cherry-picked by plaintiffs' counsel, would be highly informative.

(2) Trial Packages

A trial package consists of the documents, discovery, background information, expert reports, depositions, trial testimony, transferee court rulings, and coordinated work product of the trial attorneys. Fallon, Grabill & Wynne at 2339. All of this information can be used on remand by the attorneys handling such cases, saving those attorneys time and expense. Bellwether trials can provide invaluable information to include in the trial packages.

§ 9.4 EXAMPLES OF BELLWETHER TRIALS

Below are examples of bellwether trials in several MDLs.

A. *IN RE VIOXX PRODUCTS LIABILITY LITIGATION*

In re Vioxx Products Liability Litigation was an MDL in the Eastern District of Louisiana. Vioxx is a prescription pain reliever manufactured by Merck & Company, Inc., and approved by the Federal Drug Administration in 1999. Between 1999 and 2004, Vioxx was prescribed approximately 105 million times. In 2005, after numerous lawsuits were filed alleging that Vioxx dramatically increased the risk of heart attacks and strokes, the Panel transferred over 4,000 federal court cases to a judge in the Eastern District of Louisiana. Fallon, Grabill & Wynne at 2334. Over time, the number of cases increased to 20,000 in the federal court and 30,000 in state courts. The claims were based on the laws of various states.

Six cases were chosen for bellwether trials. The first was a case applying Florida law, which involved the surviving spouse of a man who died of a heart attack in 2001 at age 53 after several weeks of using

Vioxx. The case resulted in a hung jury, so it was retried as the second bellwether trial. Although Merck won the second trial, one of Merck's expert witnesses misrepresented an important fact during trial. As a result, the verdict was vacated. Fallon, Grabill & Wynne at 2335.

The next trial involved a plaintiff who had used Vioxx for several years before he had a heart attack in 2002 at age 58. In a jury trial applying South Carolina law, the plaintiff won $50 million in compensatory damages and $1 million in punitive damages. The court adjusted the total award to $1.6 million and ordered that there would be a new trial if the plaintiff refused to accept the reduced amount. Despite the court's adjustment of the award, the defendant filed an appeal in the Fifth Circuit. The parties subsequently settled, and the appeal was dismissed. Fallon, Grabill & Wynne at 2336 n.63.

In the last three trials, the plaintiffs all suffered heart attacks in 2003. In one, the plaintiff used Vioxx for four months before having a heart attack at age 52. Kentucky law applied. Next was a case applying Utah law, in which the plaintiff suffered a heart attack at age 59 after using Vioxx for 10 months. The last one involved a plaintiff who used Vioxx for 6 months before having a heart attack at age 54. Tennessee law applied. In all three cases, the defendant won on liability. Fallon, Grabill & Wynne at 2336.

There were also state court trials, the results of which undoubtedly informed the parties' settlement negotiations. Merck prevailed in most of the state court trials, although one plaintiff in Texas won a $253 million jury verdict. Berenson at 1. *See also* Fallon, Grabill & Wynne at 2335 (during the time that the federal MDL court held six bellwether trials, "approximately 13 additional cases were tried before juries in state courts in New Jersey, California, Texas, Alabama, Illinois, and Florida"); *id.* at 2335 n.54 ("Parallel bellwether trials in the state courts serve essentially the same beneficial purposes as do bellwether trials in the federal MDL, and can also provide a wider geographic sampling of jury verdicts.").

These trials—even with their conflicting outcomes—encouraged the parties to reach an overall settlement. In November 2007, Vioxx offered a total of $4.85 billion to eligible claimants. The settlement was contingent on 85 percent of all federal and state plaintiffs joining the settlement. An independent claims administrator oversaw the administration of settlement claims. Ultimately, 95 percent of all plaintiffs joined the settlement. To encourage settlement, Vioxx required that plaintiffs' counsel enroll 100 percent of their clients in the settlement or drop the clients who refused to participate. That requirement ensured that plaintiffs' counsel did not settle only the weak claims and take the stronger claims to trial. Fallon, Grabill & Wynne at 2336–37; Sherman (Tulane) at 2213–15.

B. *IN RE PROPULSID PRODUCTS LIABILITY LITIGATION*

In re Propulsid Products Liability Litigation, MDL No. 135, 208 F.R.D. 133 (E.D. La. 2002), was also consolidated before a judge in the Eastern District of Louisiana. Propulsid is a prescription drug containing cisapride, approved by the Food and Drug Administration (FDA) in 1993 to treat heartburn and gastroesophageal reflux. It was manufactured by Janssen Pharmaceutica, Inc., a subsidiary of Johnson & Johnson. In 1998, the FDA ordered the warning label for Propulsid to reflect the link between the drug and irregular heart rhythm. Numerous lawsuits followed, alleging that the drug caused irregular heart rhythm. As in *Vioxx*, the MDL judge used bellwether trials to advance the litigation. Three cases were intended to be tried, although only one actually took place before the parties settled. Fallon, Grabill & Wynne at 2332.

The first case selected for trial involved a surviving spouse and children suing for the death of a man from cardiac arrhythmia. Louisiana law applied, and the defendant won. Fallon, Grabill & Wynne at 2333.

The second case involved a claim for damage to the plaintiff's intestinal track. Before trial, the court granted summary judgment to the defendant, because the plaintiff's medical problems predated her use of the drug, and the plaintiff therefore failed to state a claim. Fallon, Grabill & Wynne at 2333.

In the third case, the testimony of plaintiff's expert physician was excluded. Without the physician's testimony on causation, the court granted summary judgment to the defendant under Louisiana law. Fallon, Grabill & Wynne at 2333.

Although defendants won all of the bellwether cases, both sides learned information that facilitated a series of federal and state settlements. *See* Fallon, Grabill & Wynne at 2332–34. *See* § 17.6 (discussing controversy regarding the *Propulsid* settlement).

C. *IN RE TESTOSTERONE REPLACEMENT THERAPY PRODUCTS LIABILITY LITIGATION*

The *In re Testosterone Replacement Therapy Products Liability Litigation* MDL involved a complicated scenario of bellwether trials, anticipated bellwether trials, and settlements. The MDL involved thousands of cases relating to the side effects of testosterone replacement therapy drugs. The defendants included AbbVie, Endo Pharmaceuticals, and Eli Lilly & Co.

The parties initially selected eight cases to be tried as bellwethers. One plaintiff voluntarily dismissed his lawsuit, *see* 2017 WL 1833173 at *1 n.2. Another case was dismissed on summary judgment. *See* 2018 WL 4030585, at *1. The remaining six cases were tried before juries.

In the first bellwether case to be tried to a jury verdict, the jury found AbbVie not liable for compensatory damages but liable for $150 million in punitive damages on the theory that the company had misrepresented the risks of its drug. *In re Testosterone Replacement Therapy Prods. Liab.*

Litig., No. 14 C 1748, MDL No. 2545, 2017 WL 6569632, at *1 (N.D. Ill. Dec. 22, 2017). Ruling that the jury's findings were "logically incompatible," the transferee court vacated the verdict and damages and ordered a new trial. *Id.*

The second bellwether case tried to a jury verdict resulted in a finding for the plaintiff and an award of $140,000 in compensatory damages and $140 million in punitive damages. 2018 WL 3303269, at *1 (N.D. Ill. July 5, 2018). The court denied AbbVie's motion for judgment as a matter of law, but granted its motion for a new trial on all claims. *Id.* at *10.

In December 2017, approximately a month before the first of two scheduled bellwether trials against it, Eli Lilly agreed to settle all of the cases against it in the MDL. *See* CMO 92 (settlement of Eli Lilly cases), *In re Testosterone Replacement Therapy Prods. Liab. Litig.*, No. 1:14-cv-01748 (Doc. 2313) (N.D. Ill. Dec. 21, 2017).

In 2018, AbbVie and the plaintiffs selected six additional bellwether cases. *See* 2018 WL 4030585, at *1. In January 2018, a bellwether trial involving AbbVie resulted in a defense verdict. In March 2018, on the retrial for the plaintiff whose $150 million award against AbbVie had been thrown out, a jury awarded $3.2 million.

In June 2018, defendant Endo offered to settle about 1300 lawsuits for $200 million. *See* CMO 156—Order to Establish Endo TRT Qualified Settlement Fund, *In re Testosterone Replacement Therapy Prods.*

Liab. Litig., No. 1:14-cv-01748 (Doc. 2998) (N.D. Ill. June 21, 2019).

Also in June 2018, another bellwether trial against AbbVie ended in a defense verdict. AbbVie announced a tentative settlement of the cases against it in September 2018. *See* Notification of Docket Entry, *In re Testosterone Replacement Therapy Prods. Liab. Litig.*, No. 1:14-cv-01748 (Doc. 2927) (N.D. Ill. Nov. 27, 2018).

CHAPTER 10

ROLE OF TRANSFEREE JUDGE: FACILITATING SETTLEMENT

Centralization in MDL cases can often lead to aggregate settlements for all similarly situated claims. *See* Manual § 20.132 (MDL offers "a unique opportunity for the negotiation of a global settlement"). There is little doubt that settlements can achieve important objectives, such as quickly getting money into the hands of plaintiffs, "provid[ing] closure," and "clear[ing] dockets." Saack at 851.

In some instances, as in the *National Prescription Opiate Litigation* MDL, the MDL court has made known its desire to settle the cases early on. *See* § 1.1; Chapter 9 (introduction). In others, the MDL judge has referred the transferred cases to a special master for coordinated settlement efforts before resolving critical dispositive motions. *See* § 10.1.

As noted (*see* § 1.1), about 97 percent of all MDLs are resolved by the transferee court, either by settlement or other disposition. (Of course, the vast majority of non-MDL cases settle as well.) However, because many non-class settlement agreements are confidential, there is often no way to know conclusively whether the cases were resolved through dispositive pretrial motions, voluntary dismissals due to settlement, or some other basis. Nonetheless, "[a]necdotal evidence" indicates that a "large majority" of MDLs are terminated as a result of settlements. MDL Standards at xi. *Cf.* Burch

(Mass Tort Deals) at 15–22 (expressing concern about the large number of settlements in non-class MDLs).

If an MDL includes class actions, Federal Rule 23 can be used as the vehicle for settlement. In that situation, all of the protections of Rule 23 apply, including review by the district court to ensure that the settlement is "fair, reasonable, and adequate," Fed. R. Civ. P. 23(e)(2), and that the attorneys' fees awarded are "reasonable," Fed. R. Civ. P. 23(h). A number of the recent MDL settlements have occurred as class settlements under Rule 23, including *In re Deepwater Horizon*, 910 F. Supp. 2d 891 (E.D. La. 2012); *In re Volkswagen "Clean Diesel" Mktg., Sales Practices, & Products Liability Litigation*, No. 3:15-md-02672-CRB, 2016 WL 6248426 (N.D. Cal. Oct. 25, 2016); and *In re National Football League Players' Concussion Injury Litigation*, 307 F.R.D. 351 (E.D. Pa. 2015). In fact, "the largest class action settlements of late . . . all emerged from MDL consolidation[s] . . . ." Cabraser & Issacharoff at 850–51.

When no class action is involved in the MDL, Rule 23 does not apply. Even when an MDL includes class actions, Rule 23 does not apply to the non-class cases. No structural fairness protections similar to Rule 23 exist for non-class MDLs. As discussed below, some MDL judges view non-class MDL cases as "quasi-class actions." By analogy to Rule 23, such judges become heavily involved in overseeing and approving settlements. But the use of the quasi-class action approach is not the norm, and it raises problems of its own, including the absence of clear criteria similar to Rule 23.

This Chapter focuses on the MDL judge's role in settling both class and non-class cases.

§ 10.1 FUNDAMENTALS OF SETTLEMENT BY MDL JUDGES

This section addresses several issues that are important in understanding the role of the MDL judge in facilitating global settlements.

A. UNIQUE POSTURE OF MDL

MDL centralization provides unparalleled opportunities for global settlements. When large numbers of cases—involving numerous plaintiffs and plaintiffs' counsel—have been filed across the country, the mechanics of overseeing settlement talks can be daunting. For instance, a plaintiffs' attorney with a single non-class case in Oakland, California, will find it virtually impossible to take the lead on settling hundreds (or thousands) of similar cases against the defendant pending in multiple states. But the MDL leadership structure provides a mechanism for a small number of plaintiffs' attorneys to negotiate a global settlement with the defendant (or defendants). *See* §§ 7.1–7.5.

In *Volkswagen "Clean Diesel,"* for example, the settlement team on the plaintiffs' side consisted of only 22 attorneys, *see In re Volkswagen "Clean Diesel" Mktg., Sales Practices, & Prods. Liab. Litig.*, No. 3:15-md-02672-CRB (Doc. 1084) (N.D. Cal. Jan.

21, 2016) (order appointing plaintiffs' lead counsel and steering committee), even though about 500,000 vehicles (and approximately that number of class members) were involved, and even though the transfer motion applied to 63 actions in various federal districts and 451 potentially related actions in over 60 federal districts. *See In re Volkswagen "Clean Diesel" Mktg., Sales Practices, & Prods. Liab. Litig.*, 148 F. Supp. 3d 1367, 1368 (J.P.M.L. 2015).

To be sure, a defendant could try to settle cases one-by-one, with or without an MDL. But it is well understood that defendants prefer to reach global settlements, thus allowing them to resolve the problem once and for all, instead of litigating cases in a piecemeal fashion. Even in an aggregate settlement, a defendant may insist on a "walk-away" provision, allowing it to avoid the agreement if a specified percentage of all claimants do not join. Saack at 869. An MDL can help a defendant to secure global peace.

Global settlements can benefit plaintiffs as well. As one commentator has explained, plaintiffs who can offer global peace (or close to it) "may be able to command a premium" for the group. Rave at 2175.

Importantly, even though the Supreme Court in *Lexecon* has held that MDL proceedings are only for *pretrial* matters, *see* § 15.2, that limitation does not prevent MDL judges (and those appointed to assist them, such as special masters), from focusing on settlement while the cases are in the transferee court. Federal Rule of Civil Procedure 16(a)(5) makes clear that facilitating settlement is a pretrial proceeding. *See id.* ("[T]he court may order the attorneys and any unrepresented parties to appear for one or more pretrial conferences for such purposes as . . . facilitating settlement."). Because of this, the transferee court has the power to manage cases for settlement purposes.

For example, in an asbestos case, *In re Patenaude*, 210 F.3d 135 (3d Cir. 1999), three groups of plaintiffs, who had been in the MDL for seven years, wanted their cases remanded for trial. Those plaintiffs asserted that: (1) discovery was no longer pending; (2) their medical conditions were deteriorating; and (3) being forced to stay in the MDL was denying them access to justice. These plaintiffs petitioned the Third Circuit for a writ of mandamus to remand their cases for trial, but the Third Circuit refused, holding that because the transferee court was still working to facilitate settlement efforts, pretrial proceedings were still ongoing. *Id.* at 146. The Third Circuit explained that, although "the Panel has the discretion to remand a case when everything that remains to be done is case-specific," it is not required to do so at that point. *Id.* at 145.

B. ACTIVE ROLE OF THE MDL JUDGE

MDL judges frequently play an active role in promoting settlement. In addition to requiring the parties to engage in settlement discussions, the MDL judge can move the cases towards settlement in other ways. For instance, the court can focus initial discovery on information that is critical to the parties' assessments of whether to settle and for how much.

Moreover, the MDL judge can frontload important dispositive motions, thereby putting pressure on parties to settle before the court issues rulings that could be damaging to one side or the other. *See, e.g.*, *In re Nat'l Football League Players' Concussion Injury Litig.*, 307 F.R.D. 351, 390 (E.D. Pa. 2015) (noting that the unresolved, but potentially dispositive, issues of preemption and scientific causation weighed in favor of settlement), *aff'd*, 821 F.3d 410 (3d Cir. 2016), *cert. denied*, 137 S. Ct. 591 (2016). Alternatively, the MDL judge can render decisions on important motions and thereby encourage settlement in light of the clarity that such rulings provide. For instance, if a defendant was resisting settlement because it believed that it had a dispositive preemption motion, an unfavorable ruling on such a motion (and the defendant's inability to obtain interlocutory review) might bring that defendant to the bargaining table. More generally, MDL judges can suggest creative approaches to settlements that may not be apparent to the parties.

C. ROLE OF SPECIAL MASTERS IN SETTLEMENT NEGOTIATIONS

Many MDL judges choose not to get in the middle of settlement discussions, fearing that they might be perceived as advocating for one side or another, making it difficult to later rule on motions or otherwise oversee the proceedings. *See* Pocket Guide at 11 (noting that "recusal" might be necessary" if an MDL judge oversees settlement discussions and a "settlement does not occur"). A common approach is to use a federal magistrate judge or special master to conduct settlement negotiations, often while the MDL judge is overseeing discovery, conducting other pretrial proceedings, or even trying bellwether cases. *See id.*

MDL judges often turn to prominent lawyers or retired judges to serve as special masters in complex cases. For instance, although Robert Mueller, the former Director of the Federal Bureau of Investigation, is best known for his role as special prosecutor investigating President Trump and others in the Trump campaign, his immediate task before taking on that role was to serve as special master in the *VW Clean Diesel* MDL. *In re Volkswagen "Clean Diesel" Mktg., Sales Practices, & Products Liability Litigation*, No. 3:15-md-02672-CRB (Doc. 973) (N.D. Cal. Jan. 19, 2016) (order appointing Robert S. Mueller III as Settlement Master). Similarly, noted mediator Ken Feinberg, who gained fame as the special master of the September 11 Victim Compensation Fund, has served as a mediator in numerous high-profile MDLs, including *In re Roundup Products Liability Litigation*, No. 3:16-md-02741-VC (Doc. 3873) (N.D. Cal. May 22, 2019); and *In re Chrysler-Dodge-Jeep Ecodiesel Mktg., Sales Practices, & Products Liability Litigation*, No. 17-md-02777-EMC (Doc. 184) (N.D. Cal. July 13, 2017). Other MDL judges turn to retired federal judges to serve as special masters for settlement negotiations. For example, retired Judge Layn Phillips has served as a special master in numerous of MDL settlement negotiations, including the *National Football League Concussion* MDL.

When the MDL judge decides to use a special master, the judge will often designate that person. In other instances, however, the judge will allow the parties to jointly select someone or offer suggestions. *See, e.g.*, *In re Nat'l Prescription Opiate Litig.*, No. 1:17-md-02804-DAP (Doc. 69) (N.D. Ohio Jan. 11, 2018) at 1 (noting that the MDL judge "requested from the parties suggestions for appointment of one or more Special Masters in this extremely complex litigation").

Plaintiffs' counsel and defendants often share the cost of a special master. *See In re Nat'l Prescription Opiate Litig.*, No. 1:17-md-02804-DAP (Doc. 69) (N.D. Ohio Jan. 11, 2018) at 5–6 (stating that defendants and plaintiffs are each responsible for 50% of the three special masters' compensation). Such costs can be large when prominent individuals (such as retired judges or high-profile attorneys) charge high hourly rates and devote weeks or months to settlement negotiations. Of course, magistrate judges can perform similar functions without requiring the parties to spend additional money.

D. SETTLEMENT OF STATE CASES

The transferee court has jurisdiction only over the federal cases. The code of conduct for judges normally does not allow a judge to mediate cases in other jurisdictions without the agreement of the judges and parties involved in those cases. *See* Code of Conduct for U.S. Judges, Commentary to Canon 4A(4) at 17 ("[t]his Canon generally prohibits a [federal] judge from mediating a state court matter, except in unusual circumstances[,]" such as "when a judge is mediating a federal matter that cannot be resolved effectively without addressing the related state court matter"). To achieve a global settlement, the parties may encourage the plaintiffs' attorneys in state court to participate in the federal settlement discussions. Alternatively, the MDL judge can coordinate with state judges who are overseeing related state claims. *See* § 16.1; *see also* Sherman (Tulane) at 2214–15 (describing coordination between federal and state courts in the *Vioxx* litigation). Indeed, when similar cases are pending in state court, the MDL court might find it advantageous to select a special master who can help broker a settlement of both the federal and the state cases. MDL Standards at 85.

If the state court actions are progressing at a rate different from that of the MDL, the transferee court (in limited circumstances) may have the power under the All Writs Act, 28 U.S.C. § 1651, to enjoin the related state actions that are interfering with the MDL judge's jurisdiction over the federal cases. Sherman (Tulane) at 2220–21. *See, e.g.*, *In re Jimmy John's Overtime Litig.*, 877 F.3d 756, 767 (7th Cir. 2017) (recognizing that the All Writs Act has been applied in the MDL context because of "the unique nature of such proceedings"). However, under the Anti-Injunction Act, 28 U.S.C. § 2283, this power is available only when "the state court action threatens to frustrate proceedings and disrupt the orderly resolution of the federal litigation." *In re Diet Drugs*, 282 F.3d 220, 234 (3d Cir. 2002) (upholding district court injunction against mass opt-out in state court that would have interfered with an impending settlement in the MDL court).

§ 10.2 DIFFERENT POSTURES OF MDL CASES WITH AND WITHOUT CLASS ACTIONS

As noted, when a case is settled in an MDL class action, the settlement must be conducted under Rule 23. By contrast, when the MDL involves only individual actions, it is unclear whether—and how—the MDL judge can oversee and approve a global settlement. These issues are addressed below. First, the class action approach is briefly discussed. Then, in the non-class approach, two scenarios are considered: (1) the MDL judge has no role in overseeing or approving the settlement, and (2) the judge takes an active role by analogizing the MDL aggregation to a class action (often referred to as a "quasi-class action").

A. CLASS ACTION SETTLEMENTS

In a class action settlement in federal court, a case must first satisfy the Rule 23 requirements for a class action. All federal class actions under Rule 23 must satisfy a host of requirements, including an objective definition, numerous claimants, one or more common issues of law or fact, at least one representative who is typical of the class, and adequacy of both the class representatives and class counsel. Fed. R. Civ. P. 23(a); Klonoff (Class Action Nutshell) §§ 3.1–3.7. The class must also satisfy one of the four types of class actions specified in Rule 23(b). Class actions involving money damages (as opposed to injunctive or declaratory relief) are normally brought under Federal Rule of Civil Procedure 23(b)(3). Rule 23(b)(3) imposes two requirements (in addition to those under Rule 23(a)): that common issues of law and fact predominate over individual issues, and that a class action is the superior mechanism for resolving the case. *See* Fed. R. Civ. P. 23(b)(3); Klonoff (Class Action Nutshell) § 4.4.

When the parties propose a settlement at the same time that they raise the issue of class certification (a procedure known as a settlement class), the court must give even closer scrutiny to the class certification requirements than for a contested class action. The only caveat is that the issue of trial manageability (a component of superiority) need not be satisfied because there will be no trial. *See Amchem Prods., Inc. v. Windsor*, 521 U.S. 591, 593 (1997) ("Whether trial would present intractable management problems, *see* Rule 23(b)(3)(D), is not a consideration when settlement-only certification is requested, for the proposal is that there be no trial."); Klonoff (Class Action Nutshell) § 9.1.

Under Rule 23(e), the court may approve a class settlement only after finding that it is "fair, reasonable, and adequate." Fed. R. Civ. P. 23(e)(2). Courts look at numerous criteria; indeed, Rule 23(e) was amended (effective Dec. 1, 2018) to specify criteria that the court must consider in reviewing a settlement, including the adequacy of representation, whether negotiations were conducted at arm's length, and whether the relief obtained for the class is adequate, taking into account the "costs, risks, and delay of trial and appeal." Rule 23(e)(2). The Rule also requires that notice be sent to the class, describing the terms of the settlement. *Id.* Before giving notice, a court first conducts a preliminary review to determine whether there is a likelihood that the settlement will ultimately be approved, and that the requirements for class certification will be met. Rule 23(e)(1)(A), (B).

In some instances, a settlement may fail even preliminary review. For instance, in *In re National Football League Players' Concussion Injury Litigation*, 961 F. Supp. 2d 708 (E.D. Pa. 2014), the first proposed settlement was for a fixed $765 million, but the MDL judge was uncertain that that amount would cover all retired NFL players who suffered injuries. She therefore denied preliminary approval. She later granted preliminary (and ultimately final) approval once the NFL agreed to make the settlement uncapped. *See* 301 F.R.D. 191 (E.D. Pa. 2014) (granting preliminary settlement approval); 307 F.R.D. 351 (E.D. Pa. 2015) (granting final approval); 821 F.3d 410 (3d Cir. 2016) (affirming district court's class certification and settlement approval), *cert. denied*, 137 S. Ct. 591 (2016).

After preliminary approval, notice of the proposed settlement terms, and a period for objections (and, in Rule 23(b)(3) classes, a period for opt outs), the court is required to conduct a hearing before deciding whether the settlement is "fair, reasonable, and adequate." Fed. R. Civ. P. 23(e)(2). The court will take into consideration any objections filed, as well as the number of class members who have opted out of the settlement (assuming an opt-out right is available). In reviewing the settlement, the court is acting as a fiduciary for the class. The court cannot rewrite the settlement for the parties; it must either approve or disapprove the settlement. Klonoff (Class Action Nutshell) § 9.1. However, upon disapproval the court may make suggestions for changes that would make the court more likely to approve a future settlement proposal, as the MDL judge did in the *NFL Concussion* MDL.

A class member whose objection is overruled is allowed to appeal on the ground that the settlement is not "fair, reasonable, and adequate," or that the requirements for class certification have not been met. *See Devlin v. Scardelletti*, 536 U.S. 1, 14 (2002) (unnamed class members who timely objected to a class settlement have a right to appeal without first intervening).

Many prominent MDL settlements have used the class action device and its procedures. *See, e.g.*, *In re Deepwater Horizon*, 739 F.3d 790 (5th Cir. 2014) (affirming district court's class certification and settlement approval); *In re Nat'l Football League Players' Concussion Injury Litig.*, 821 F.3d 410 (3d Cir. 2016) (same), *cert. denied*, 137 S. Ct. 591 (2016); *In re Volkswagen "Clean Diesel" Mktg., Sales Practices, & Prods. Liab. Litig.*, 895 F.3d 597 (9th Cir. 2018) (same), *cert. denied sub nom. Fleshman v. Volkswagen, AG*, 139 S. Ct. 2645 (2019). In a class settlement, Rule 23 also requires the court to determine reasonable attorneys' fees for class counsel, Fed. R. Civ. P. 23(h), and class members who dispute a fee award may object and (if unsuccessful) may appeal the fee award. Examples of objections to fee awards in MDLs include *In re Volkswagen "Clean Diesel" Mktg., Sales Practices, & Products Liability Litigation*, 914 F.3d 623 (9th Cir. 2019), *cert. denied sub nom. Nagel Rice, LLP v. Volkswagen Group of America, Inc.*, No. 18-1503, ___ S. Ct. ___, 2019 WL 4923470 (Oct. 7, 2019); and *In re National Football League Players' Concussion Injury Litigation*, No. 2:12-02323-AB, 2018 WL 1635648 (E.D. Pa. Apr. 5, 2018), *appeal docketed*, No. 18-2281 (3d Cir. June 12, 2018). *See* § 11.1.

B. NON-CLASS SETTLEMENTS

Many MDLs do not include class actions. This is particularly true in many (if not most) mass tort MDLs. *See* § 1.4. Rule 23 does not govern, and its protections do not apply to non-class cases. Moreover, protections similar to those under Rule 23 do not exist under either the MDL statute, the JPML Rules, or the Federal Rules of Civil Procedure. This gap for non-class cases has raised concern among judges and scholars. As one prominent federal appellate judge has noted, "outside the federal rules governing class actions, there is no prescribed independent review of the structural and substantive fairness of a settlement including evaluation of attorneys' fees, potential conflicts of interest, and counsel's allocation of settlement funds among class members." *Sullivan v. DB Investments, Inc.*, 667 F.3d 273, 334 (3d Cir. 2011) (Scirica, J., concurring); *see also* Erichson

(Vanderbilt), at 36 (also noting that Rule 23 protections are not available in non-class MDLs).

Given this gap, some MDL judges have allowed cases to settle without active involvement, and without any sort of fairness review. Other judges have analogized non-class MDLs to class actions and have taken an active role, similar to what a judge does in a class action. These approaches are discussed below.

(1) Hands-Off Approach

Some courts in non-class MDLs do not become involved in the settlement process, either by overseeing settlement discussions or reviewing the ultimate agreements or attorneys' fees. For example, in *In re Welding Fume Products Liability Litigation*, MDL No. 1535 (N.D. Ohio 2012), the court named an administrator to determine how to disperse the $21.5 million in settlement funds to the plaintiffs. Arguably, the case presented a conflict of interest between injured parties and those with claims of exposure but no injury. Also, there was no guarantee of any recovery above $100. However, because the case was not a class action, the court did not make a determination of fairness. Saack at 869–76 (discussing *Welding Fume* and other similar examples).

With rare exceptions, it is difficult to identify cases falling into the "hands-off" approach. Unlike class action proceedings, which are public and transparent, settlement discussions and resolutions in non-class cases often remain confidential. One commentator has argued that, because most MDL judges addressing non-class MDLs do not treat them as quasi-class actions, most cases fall into the hands-off category. Mullenix (Litigation) at 152, 162. If that is true, then in most non-class MDLs, "there is relatively no judicial oversight as attorneys labor to cut a deal," and no review of the fairness of the settlement or magnitude of attorneys' fees. *Id.* at 156. In those situations, "the actions of attorneys negotiating and accomplishing non-class aggregate settlements are relatively unconstrained." *Id.* at 155. *But see* Burch (Mass Tort Deals) at 104 (providing statistics showing that the percentage of MDL judges who are truly "hands off" is small).

(2) Hands-On Approach

Other MDL courts take an active role in settlements even when no class action is involved. As noted, some courts have labeled non-class MDLs quasi-class actions.

This approach was used, for example, in *In re Zyprexa Products Liability Litigation,* 424 F. Supp. 2d 488, 491 (E.D.N.Y. 2006) (calling the litigation a quasi-class action); *In re Vioxx Products Liability Litigation*, 650 F. Supp. 2d 549, 554 (E.D. La. 2009) (same); and *In re Guidant Corp. Implantable Defibrillators Products Liability Litigation*, MDL No. 05-1708, 2008 WL 682174, at *6 (D. Minn. Mar. 7, 2008) (same). In all three cases, the court approved global settlements, appointed attorneys to committees to manage the litigation, administered the settlements, and established common-benefit funds to compensate the lead lawyers. *See Zyprexa*, 424 F. Supp. 2d at 490–91; *Vioxx*, 650 F. Supp. 2d at 551–53; *Guidant*, 2008 WL 682174, at **1–3.

Some scholars have attacked the quasi-class action approach, arguing that the settlements adopting that approach are unfair and unethical in ways that do not apply to class actions. Concerns identified by such scholars include the use of coercive terms that are designed to ensure maximum participation by plaintiffs. *See, e.g.*, Erichson & Zipursky, at 266–68 (criticizing the *Vioxx* settlement, including the requirement that counsel for any plaintiff unwilling to agree to the settlement terms must withdraw); Burch (NYU) at 118 (criticizing the quasi-class action approach). Merely invoking the quasi-class action concept does not mean that the MDL judge will follow every requirement of Rule 23. And it is anything but clear whether a claimant in a non-class settlement will have appellate rights comparable to those available to class members in a class settlement, even if the MDL judge has called the procedure a quasi-class action. As discussed in Chapter 17, reform proposals have been made to codify specific requirements for review of non-class settlements in MDLs. *See* § 17.7.

(3) Intermediate Approach

In addition to the two general approaches described above, two commentators have identified an intermediate position. They argue that, instead of asserting the authority to review and potentially reject a non-class settlement, MDL judges "should use the MDL process to force the disclosure of information to allow the parties in MDL cases to make informed decisions about whether to accept proposed settlements." Bradt & Rave I at 1264. "[O]ften, the single most useful piece of information that the MDL judge can communicate to claimants will be a simple and frank assessment of the fairness of [the] deal, even if that assessment will have no binding force." *Id.*

§ 10.3 PARTIAL SETTLEMENTS

Settlements in an MDL are not an all or nothing proposition. It is not uncommon for some individual cases in an MDL to settle, while other cases continue through discovery and motion practice. It is also common for settlements to go forward with respect to some causes of action but not others. *See* Manual § 13.21. Such settlements, of course, do not resolve the MDL as a whole, but they can narrow the cases and claims that are returned to transferor courts. The Manual for Complex Litigation cautions, however, that partial settlements "present a number of potential problems," especially if the settlements leave many claims and parties without a resolution. *Id.*; *see also* § 21.651 (discussing partial settlements in class actions); *see generally* Baker at 1944 n.3 ("A partial settlement can leave a plaintiff's firm or consortium with ongoing expenditures of time and money as it continues to prosecute the unsettled claims against the defendant.").

CHAPTER 11

ROLE OF TRANSFEREE JUDGE: ATTORNEYS' FEES, EXPENSES, AND INCENTIVE PAYMENTS

§ 11.1 INTRODUCTION

No discussion of multidistrict litigation would be complete without an examination of attorneys' fees. Attorneys' fees are what drive plaintiffs' attorneys to spend thousands of hours and enormous sums of money in MDL cases. In many of these cases, the attorneys take the significant risk of recovering no attorneys' fees or expenses. Defendants often will devote major resources to MDL cases, leaving no stone unturned. If the defendants succeed—for example, by winning dispositive motions—plaintiffs' attorneys may end up with no fees and no recoupment of their out-of-pocket expenses.

Nonetheless, attorneys compete strenuously for leadership roles in MDLs, even though such a role means substantial up-front investments by the designated attorneys and their law firms. They do this because the payoff can be enormous. For instance, in one recent MDL, *In re Syngenta AG MIR 162 Corn Litig.*, 357 F. Supp. 3d 1094 (D. Kan. 2018), *appeals docketed*, Nos. 19-3008, 19-3005, 19-3006, 19-3009 (10th Cir. Jan. 8, 2019), a settlement of $1.51 billion resulted in a fee award (currently on appeal) of more than $503 million. *Id.* at 1110. In *BP Deepwater Horizon*, fees awarded to class counsel were approximately $555.2 million. *In re Deepwater*

Horizon, MDL No. 2179, 2016 WL 6215974, at *1 (E.D. La. Oct. 25, 2016). And in the *NFL Concussion* MDL, fees awarded to class counsel (again, currently on appeal) were approximately $106.8 million. *In re National Football League Players' Concussion Injury Litigation*, No. 2:12-02323-AB, 2018 WL 1635648, at *1 (E.D. Pa. Apr. 5, 2018), *appeal docketed*, No. 18-2281 (3d Cir. June 12, 2018).

Complicated attorneys' fees issues arise in the MDL context. Unlike a class action involving small claims, in which class counsel usually act alone, MDLs involve numerous individual plaintiffs represented by attorneys, usually under contingent-fee agreements. When individual cases are transferred to an MDL, the laboring oar shifts from the many attorneys handling individual cases to a small leadership team selected by the MDL judge, and others who contribute to the MDL cases as a whole (by performing "common-benefit" work). *See* §§ 7.1–7.5. Because the attorneys doing common-benefit work want to be paid for that work, and attorneys with contingent-fee agreements (known as individually retained private attorneys or "IRPAs") want to recover their agreed-upon percentages, a conflict often arises. A question in those MDLs is whether the court has the authority to limit or cap private contractual contingent-fee agreements to reflect that the IRPAs were relieved from having to perform difficult litigation tasks that were taken over by common-benefit counsel.

Important distinctions arise depending on whether the underlying MDL includes class actions. A class action provides a framework not only for adequacy of representation and review of the fairness of class settlements, but also for awarding attorneys' fees. Under Federal Rule of Civil Procedure 23(h), the court is responsible for setting "reasonable" attorneys' fees, and class members have a right to object to the fees proposed by class counsel. For MDLs that do not involve class actions, there are no guiding principles. No standards for setting fees are provided in the MDL statute, the JPML Rules, or the Federal Rules of Civil Procedure. Many major fee awards in MDLs have been in non-class action settlements, but Rule 23(h) does not apply in such cases.

As is true in the settlement process, some courts have essentially applied attorneys' fees procedures akin to those used for class actions. In other situations, it is not entirely clear how attorneys' fees are awarded. When a class action is not involved, the MDL settlement terms are often confidential. *See, e.g.*, Saack at 857; Erichson & Zipursky at 279.

Some MDL judges address attorneys' fees issues in the process of selecting leadership attorneys. For example, an appointment order or case management order may direct any attorney claiming common benefit fees to keep contemporaneous records or to submit periodic (monthly or quarterly) billing records to the court. *See, e.g.*, PTO 11: Protocol for Common Benefit Work and Expenses, *In re Volkswagen "Clean Diesel" Mktg., Sales Practices, & Products Liability Litigation*, No. 3:15-md-02672-CRB (Doc. 1254) (N.D. Cal. Feb. 25, 2016); PTO No. 9, *In re Chinese-*

Manufactured Drywall Products Liability Litigation, No. 2:09-md-02047-EEF-JCW (Doc. 147) (E.D. La. July 28, 2009).

This Chapter addresses the attorneys' fees issues described above. In addition to attorneys' fees, however, issues also arise with respect to the awarding of expenses to plaintiffs' counsel and the awarding of incentive payments to plaintiffs (usually class representatives) who have played a major role in the litigation. Expenses and incentive payments are also addressed in this Chapter.

§ 11.2 ATTORNEYS' FEES

A. ATTORNEYS' FEES IN MDL CASES INVOLVING CLASS ACTIONS

As noted (§ 10.2), many recent MDL settlements have been class action settlements. This means that the MDL judge is tasked under Rule 23(e)(2) with determining whether the settlement is "fair, reasonable, and adequate." It also means that the award of attorneys' fees is governed by Rule 23(h). (As will be discussed below, there may also be a question, even in class actions, regarding how the attorneys' fees are allocated among common-benefit counsel and to IRPAs.)

(1) Methods for Calculating Fees

Courts have used four approaches for determining the reasonableness of attorneys' fees in class actions, including class actions within MDLs: the percentage method; the lodestar method; a blended method (the percentage method, but with the lodestar used as a "cross check"); and a multi-factor test based on case law.

Using the percentage method, the court determines the appropriate attorneys' fee award in light of the size of the recovery. This method is derived from the common fund doctrine. *See Boeing Co. v. Van Gemert*, 444 U.S. 472, 478 (1980) ("[A] litigant or lawyer who recovers a common fund for the benefit of persons other than himself or his client is entitled to a reasonable attorney's fee from the fund as a whole.") While the applied percentage is based on the specifics of each case, "benchmark" percentages sometimes operate as a starting point. For example, in the Ninth Circuit, the benchmark percentage is 25 percent. *See, e.g., In re Bluetooth Headset Prods. Liab. Litig.*, 654 F.3d 935, 942 (9th Cir. 2011). Use of the benchmark, or any other percentage adopted by the court, must be supported by case-specific facts. *In re Volkswagen "Clean Diesel" Mktg., Sales Practices, & Prods. Liab. Litig.*, No. 3:15-md-02672-CRB (Doc. 3231), at 2 (N.D. Cal. May 17, 2017).

Percentage awards vary from case to case, depending on a variety of facts and circumstances. Fee awards can be under 20 percent, but can also be 30 percent or more. While some courts have indicated that percentages should be lower in so-called mega-fund cases (those involving settlements of $100 million or more), other courts disagree, noting that reduced percentages for large settlements undercut attorneys' incentives to maximize recoveries for their clients. *See, e.g.*, *In re Syngenta AG MIR 162 Corn Litig.*, 357 F. Supp. 3d 1094, 1114–15 (D. Kan. 2018) (discussing both approaches and declining to apply a lower percentage to a mega-fund case). Dozens of cases can be found in which courts in mega-fund class actions have awarded fees of 30 percent or more of the common funds. *Id.* at 1115 (citing expert declaration listing over 40 settlements of $100 million or more with fee awards of 30 percent or greater).

Under the lodestar method, the court determines: (1) the reasonable number of hours expended by attorneys for the common benefit of the class; and (2) the reasonable hourly rates for those attorneys. The court multiplies those numbers to determine the lodestar. For example, assume 2,000 common-benefit hours at a reasonable hourly rate of $500. The lodestar would be $1 million. The lodestar may be enhanced based on the specific circumstances. This enhancement is known as a multiplier. Assume, for example, the $1 million lodestar discussed above. A fee award of $1.5 million would mean that a multiplier of 1.5 was applied. *See generally* Fallon at 382–83.

Courts usually use customary hourly rates for lawyers with comparable experience and expertise in the court's local area, although the use of "a national hourly rate" is sometimes appropriate, MDL Standards at 64, such as when lawyers from various parts of the country are involved or the work is highly specialized. Courts may choose to use current rates instead of historical rates to "adjust for inflation and loss of use of [the] funds." *Id.* at 65.

The blended method combines both the lodestar and percentage methods. Courts determine a reasonable percentage but then cross-check the award by using the lodestar method (although generally not as rigorously as an award based entirely on the lodestar method). If the two figures are wildly out of sync, the court might make adjustments. For example, it might reduce the percentage if the lodestar figure is much lower than the figure based on the percentage method. Or it might increase the percentage if the lodestar reveals the need to do so. Fallon at 385–86. (Some courts also apply the lodestar and then use the percentage method as a cross-check.)

Also, several federal circuits have developed lists of factors for assessing fees. Because such factors are derived from case law, they may differ from circuit to circuit. Some circuits utilize the so-called *Johnson* factors, developed in *Johnson v. Georgia Hwy. Expr., Inc.,* 488 F.2d 714 (5th Cir. 1974). These are:

(1) the time and labor involved;

(2) the novelty and difficulty of the questions;

(3) the skill requisite to perform the legal service properly;

(4) the preclusion of other employment by the attorney due to acceptance of the case;

(5) the customary fee;

(6) whether the fee is fixed or contingent;

(7) time limitations imposed by the client or the circumstances;

(8) the amount involved and the results obtained;

(9) the experience, reputation, and ability of the attorneys;

(10) the "undesirability" of the case;

(11) the nature and length of the professional relationship with the client; and

(12) awards in similar cases.

488 F.2d at 717–19. For somewhat different criteria, *see, e.g.*, *Wal-Mart Stores, Inc. v. Visa U.S.A., Inc.*, 396 F.3d 96, 117 (2d Cir. 2005) (considering nine factors). The applicability of these factors, individually and collectively, varies by case and is within the discretion of the court. Fallon at 383. Typically, these factors are applied along with the percentage or lodestar method.

(2) Example of a Fee Award in an MDL Involving a Class Action

The various approaches discussed above are exemplified in *In re Syngenta AG MIR 162 Corn Litigation*, 357 F. Supp. 3d 1094 (D. Kan. 2018), *appeal docketed*, No. 19-3009 (10th Cir. Jan. 8, 2019). There, the MDL judge had to determine the attorneys' fees to be awarded out of a settlement fund of $1.51 billion. Plaintiffs' counsel argued that the award should be one-third of the settlement fund. The court agreed, and awarded $503 million in fees.

In addition to using the percentage method, the court applied the *Johnson* factors and found that virtually all of them supported counsel's request for one-third of the settlement fund. The litigation was time consuming (more than 1.2 million hours spent), with thousands of suits and, ultimately, a federal MDL. Many complicated tasks were required for successful prosecution, including massive discovery, extensive and difficult motions practice, and a completed trial (and two partial trials). Great skill was required to complete these tasks, and the resulting settlement was impressive. The court also found that a one-third fee was justified based on awards in other class actions. *Id.* at 1114–15. Finally, the court conducted a lodestar cross-check, finding that the total lodestar (number of hours times a reasonable hourly rate) was about $357 million, resulting in a multiplier of only 1.4 to achieve an award of $503 million. The court found that a multiplier of 1.4 was "extremely modest in light of the great risk undertaken in pursuing these claims on a contingent-fee basis." *Id.* at 1115. The court withheld for later decision the proportion of that $503 million that would be used to pay IRPAs. *See In re Syngenta AG MIR 162 Corn Litig.*, No. 2:14-md-02591-JWL-JPO, 2018 WL 6839380 (D. Kan. Dec. 31, 2018) (awarding fees to IRPAs from the $503 million), *appeal docketed*, No. 19-3082 (10th Cir. Apr. 23, 2019). *See* subsection D(2)(b).

B. ATTORNEYS' FEES IN NON-CLASS MDL CASES

Just as there are no criteria for approval of a non-class MDL settlement, *see* § 10.2, there are no standards—in the MDL statute, the JPML Rules, or the Federal Rules of Civil Procedure—with respect to how (if at all) an MDL judge should determine attorneys' fees. Some courts have concluded that they have no role to play in reviewing non-class MDL attorneys' fee awards, while other courts engage in active review by characterizing the proceedings as a quasi-class action.

(1) No Court Involvement in Setting Fees

As noted (§ 10.2), in a non-class MDL settlement, when the court is not treating the case as a quasi-class action, the court may end up not reviewing settlement fairness or awarding attorneys' fees at all. And because the settlements and fee awards are not public (unlike in a class action), it is difficult to know what role, if any, the MDL court played in these cases. Because many non-class MDLs are not treated as quasi-class actions (*see* § 10.2), it is likely that, in many cases, MDL judges do not play a hands-on role in the determination of attorneys' fees.

(2) Court Involvement by Analogy to a Class Action

Some courts set fees in non-class MDLs using essentially the same approach as in the class action context. A prominent example is *In re Vioxx Products Liability Litigation*, 760 F. Supp. 2d 640 (E.D. La.

2010). In *Vioxx*, the MDL judge applied a multi-step approach in determining attorneys' fees based on a settlement fund.

First, the court determined the value of the benefit obtained for the clients—a settlement of $4.85 billion. The court then set the "initial benchmark percentage" for common-benefit fees that would apply to the $4.85 billion. The plaintiffs' leadership committee had initially requested 8 percent for common-benefit fees, but later requested 7.5 percent. Although the court considered this proposal, it exercised its independent judgment. After reviewing empirical studies and comparable MDL fee awards, the court found 6 percent of the settlement ($291 million) to be an appropriate initial benchmark for the common-benefit fees. This amount was in addition to fees going to IRPAs under their contingent-fee contracts. 760 F. Supp. 2d at 652–55.

The court next applied the *Johnson* factors to determine whether a departure from the initial 6 percent figure was warranted. The court noted the "intensive and sustained efforts" of the attorneys providing the common-benefit work. 760 F. Supp. 2d at 656. It further noted that the MDL involved product liability claims that posed significant challenges for plaintiffs and raised complex issues involving causation and medical knowledge. *Id.* And the court noted that the settlement itself was a "fair and adequate bargain" for claimants. *Id.* at 658. The court further recognized the skill and talent of the common-benefit attorneys. The court concluded that the *Johnson* factors warranted a 0.5 percent increase of the benchmark percentage to 6.5 percent, an increase of $24.25 million. Finally, the court conducted a lodestar cross-check. After determining the number of hours and the reasonable average hourly rate, the court determined that a 6.5 percent award would result in a multiplier of 1.2633, which the court deemed reasonable (noting that prior courts had accepted multipliers between 1.19 and 4.45). Accordingly, the court found that 6.5 percent was a reasonable fee award. 760 F. Supp. 2d at 661–62.

C. ALLOCATION OF FEE AWARDS AMONG COMMON-BENEFIT COUNSEL

The relatively few attorneys who are appointed to leadership committees cannot always handle all of the common-benefit work. In many instances, dozens (or even hundreds) of non-leadership attorneys may have contributed to the overall result. The court will frequently be faced with the question of how to allocate the common-benefit fees. (This assumes that the court is overseeing the fee award, either because the case is a class action or is being treated as a quasi-class action.) Ultimately, the court's task is to examine the hours, work performed, and the value of the contribution of each attorney seeking common-benefit fees.

One source urges MDL judges to seek input from the plaintiffs' steering committee "or some subset thereof," because those attorneys "have observed the common benefit efforts of [non-leadership attorneys] throughout the arc of the litigation." MDL Standards at 66. The use of a special master to oversee the allocation process may also be appropriate. *Id.* But even when a special master or the leadership team makes an allocation recommendation, the decision on how to allocate fees rests with the MDL judge. *Id.* at 68.

Although there is no cookie-cutter approach, an instructive case is *In re Chinese-Manufactured Drywall Products Liability Litigation*, No. 2:09-md-02047-EEF-JCW (Doc. 22089) (E.D. La. Feb. 4, 2019). That MDL involved homeowners who sued manufacturers, distributors, and others in connection with allegedly defective drywall manufactured in China and used in the construction of plaintiffs' homes. A series of related class settlements were reached that included attorneys' fees of approximately $200 million. Having determined that 52 percent of the fees should go to common-benefit counsel and 48 percent should go to IRPAs, the court had to divide up the 52 percent.

Early in the litigation, the MDL judge ordered attorneys doing common-benefit work to report, on a monthly basis, the hours worked and tasks performed. After the settlement was agreed to, the court designated a Fee Allocation Committee consisting of both members and non-members of the Plaintiffs' Steering Committee. The Fee Allocation Committee's task was to review the fee requests, meet with the relevant attorneys, and ultimately make recommendations on allocating fees among the common-benefit attorneys who submitted fee requests.

In making the ultimate allocation decisions, the MDL judge had to divide the common-benefit funds among 61 law firms and individual attorneys who did common-benefit work. For each of those 61 firms/attorneys, the court examined the nature of work performed, hours spent, and the recommendation of the Fee Allocation Committee (as well as the recommendation of the court-appointed special master, who was designated to make allocation recommendations). Because the Fee Allocation Committee's recommendation was not unanimous, the judge also considered the views expressed in a minority report submitted by the dissenting members. The judge conducted a lengthy analysis of the individual fee requests, ultimately setting a wide range of fee amounts—between $0 and $23.2 million. Slip Op. at 10–71.

D. ALLOCATION BETWEEN COMMON-BENEFIT ATTORNEYS AND INDIVIDUALLY RETAINED PRIVATE ATTORNEYS

In addition to allocating fees among common-benefit attorneys, courts have taken it upon themselves to allocate funds between common-benefit attorneys and IRPAs. Rather than simply letting IRPAs seek their fees directly from their clients under their contingent-fee contracts, these courts have overseen and determined attorneys' fees for both common-benefit attorneys and IRPAs.

Common-benefit work is work that benefits all of the cases, while non-common-benefit work is work that benefits only a particular client. The following tasks are generally considered common-benefit work:

- conducting bellwether trials, including related discovery;
- working on significant overarching issues, such as class certification;
- briefing issues related to classwide or MDL-wide discovery, such as the admissibility of expert testimony under *Daubert*; and
- participating in global settlement negotiations.

By contrast, the following tasks are generally considered non-common-benefit work:

- filing individual complaints, including class action complaints;
- consulting with individual clients;
- monitoring proceedings and informing clients on developments; and
- advising individual clients on settlement terms.

See, e.g., In re Volkswagen "Clean Diesel" Mktg., Sales Practices, & Prods. Liab. Litig., No. 3:15-md-02672-CRB (Doc. 3178) (N.D. Cal. Apr. 24, 2017), at 5–7 (distinguishing between common-benefit work and work benefiting only individual plaintiffs). This list is not exhaustive, and courts maintain flexibility in determining whether particular tasks are common-benefit work.

To understand the allocation methods, it is first necessary to examine the concept of "common-benefit funds." After discussing those funds, this section discusses the two allocation approaches that courts use: (1) awarding only common-benefit fees and relegating IRPAs to enforcing their contingent-fee contracts separately; or (2) imposing a fee cap on IRPAs and permitting IRPAs to receive those lower amounts from the common fund.

(1) Common-Benefit Funds

MDL judges have long recognized that IRPAs derive valuable benefits from the assistance of common-benefit counsel. Were it not for common-benefit attorneys, the IRPAs would have to do all pretrial motions, discovery, and other tasks themselves. Common-benefit attorneys serve to alleviate much (or in some instances, most) of that work. Recognizing this situation, many MDL judges set up "common-benefit funds," under which IRPAs who try or settle cases in an MDL pay a fixed percentage of the judgment or settlement into the fund (generally between 4 and 8 percent) for common-benefit counsel. Coordinating Multijurisdiction Litigation at 7; *see* § 7.2. Common-benefit attorneys can then ask the judge to award fees to them from the fund. Rubenstein (Attorney Fee Digest) at 89. For instance, if an IRPA has a fee agreement for 30 percent, and the court orders that 6 percent of the proceeds be paid into the common-benefit fund, the IRPA's net fee will be 24 percent (assuming no referral fees or other fees, such as hiring local counsel).

This fund is usually set up by the MDL judge early in the case, although "it will usually remain unfunded until much later in the litigation process, when cases are resolved through trial or settlement." MDL Standards at 52–53. This money is paid by the IRPAs out of their contingent fees. *Id.* at 57–58.

(2) Allocation Approaches

The common-benefit fund does not address the more basic question of whether IRPAs are entitled to their full contractually agreed-upon amount when common-benefit counsel are performing major functions. Courts have taken two basic approaches, discussed below.

(a) IRPAs Must Enforce Their Fee Agreements Separately

Under the first approach, the court will set a fee award for common-benefit counsel, leaving IRPAs to enforce their contingent-fee contracts separately. Of course, IRPAs may have also performed common-benefit work, and they can petition the court for fees for that work. But under this first approach, they cannot ask for their contractual fees to be paid out of a common settlement fund.

An illustration of this approach is *In re Volkswagen "Clean Diesel" Marketing, Sales Practices, & Products Liability Litigation* 914 F.3d 623 (9th Cir. 2019), *cert. denied sub nom. Nagel Rice, LLP v. Volkswagen Group of America, Inc.,* No. 18-1503, ___ S. Ct. ___, 2019 WL 4923470 (Oct. 7, 2019). In that case, in addition to agreeing to compensate class members, Volkswagen agreed to pay $175 million in attorneys' fees and expenses, amounts deemed reasonable by the MDL judge. That amount was to be paid to class counsel and other attorneys who did common-benefit work, roughly 100 law firms. The judge also received and reviewed an additional 244 fee applications from IRPAs. The judge denied those requests for payment out of the $175 million fund, finding that the work performed benefited only the attorneys' individual clients, and "not the class as a whole." *Id.* at 639. The judge recognized, however, that "[w]hile Non-Class Counsel are not entitled to fees from Volkswagen as part of this class action, [they] may be entitled to payment of certain fees and costs pursuant to attorney-client fee agreements." *Id.* at 639–40. In other words, IRPAs could recover their contingent fees only by seeking recovery from their clients. The Ninth Circuit affirmed, finding that "the district court did not abuse its discretion when it determined that the efforts of non-Class Counsel for which they sought fees did not benefit the class such that they would be entitled to compensation" from the common fund. *Id.* at 642.

(b) IRPA Fees Are Paid from the Settlement Fund but Are Capped

Other courts have taken a different approach. They have permitted IRPAs to recover fees from the settlement fund, but have capped the recovery at a certain percentage, recognizing that the work of common-benefit attorneys made the IRPAs' tasks much easier. This approach has generated controversy, with IRPAs sometimes challenging the legitimacy of fee caps.

For instance, in *In re National Football League Players' Concussion Injury Litigation*, No. 2:12-md-02323-AB, 2018 WL 1635648 (E.D. Pa. Apr. 5, 2018), *appeal docketed*, No. 18-2281 (3d Cir. June 12, 2018), the MDL judge first concluded that the common-benefit attorneys were entitled to just over $106 million in attorneys' fees, the amount that the lead attorneys requested. This was approximately 11 percent of the settlement value. *Id.* at *1. In a separate order, the MDL judge focused on the fees that could be recovered by IRPAs. Concluding that the fee percentage for class members should not exceed 33 percent, and given her award of 11 percent to the common-benefit attorneys, the judge ruled that the percentage available for IRPAs was 22 percent, with the opportunity to seek a deviation in extraordinary circumstances. 2018 WL 1658808, at *3. The judge cited numerous MDL cases imposing fee caps and concluded that she had the power to impose such a cap as part of her inherent authority to review fee agreements. She noted that fee caps were necessary to avoid "free rider" problems of IRPAs receiving vast assistance from common-benefit attorneys, yet recovering the full percentages designated in their contracts. *Id.* at *2. Thus, even IRPAs who had negotiated fee percentages as high as 40 percent were limited to the 22 percent fee cap, unless they could show extraordinary circumstances supporting an upward deviation.

Similarly, in *In re Syngenta AG MIR 162 Corn Litigation*, MDL No. 2591, 2018 WL 6839380 (D. Kan. Dec. 31, 2018), *appeal docketed*, No. 19-3082 (10th Cir. Apr. 23, 2019), the MDL judge first determined the total attorneys' fees to be approximately $503 million (*see* § 11.2). He then held that attorneys' fees for IRPAs should be capped at 12 percent. *Id.* at *10. Like the MDL judge in *NFL Concussion*, the MDL judge in *Syngenta* concluded that he had the authority to review the reasonableness of contingent fees and impose fee caps. The MDL judge rejected the position of five law professor experts, who questioned whether the court had authority to impose caps on private fee agreements. *Id.* at *4. The MDL judge concluded that he "may exercise [his] inherent authority to supervise attorneys appearing before [him], to act as a fiduciary for and protect the interests of the settlement class members, and to ensure that the integrity of the judicial process is not undermined by the recovery of unreasonable attorney fees." *Id.*

Both rulings have been appealed (the former to the Third Circuit, the latter to the Tenth Circuit). *See NFL Concussion*, No. 18-2281 (appeal filed June 12, 2018); *Syngenta*, No. 19-3082 (appeal filed Apr. 23, 2019). As of the date this text was submitted for publication, neither circuit had ruled.

§ 11.3 EXPENSES

MDL courts also routinely review and award out-of-pocket expenses to plaintiffs' counsel in MDL cases. These expenses can be considerable, particularly when cases are settled on a class-wide basis. For example, in *In re Syngenta AG MIR 162 Corn Litigation*, MDL No. 2591, 2018 WL 6839380 (D. Kan. Dec. 31, 2018), the MDL court reviewed a request by class counsel for more than $48 million in expenses (on top of attorneys' fees). A special master had reviewed counsel's request, but the court ordered the special master to "perform an additional review of expenses," and noted the need for "the submission by applicants of supplemental documentation (particularly with respect to miscellaneous expenses, air travel, and meal expenses)." *Id.* at *15.

In *In re National Football League Players' Concussion Injury Litigation*, No. 2:12-02323-AB, 2018 WL 1635648 (E.D. Pa. Apr. 5, 2018), the court awarded approximately $5.7 million in expenses, the amount requested by class counsel. The court found that the expenses sought were reasonable. *Id.* at *3.

Courts have also awarded expenses in so-called quasi-class actions. For example, in *Vioxx*, the MDL judge awarded over $40 million in expenses. *In re Vioxx Prods. Liab. Litig.*, 760 F. Supp. 2d 640, 642 n.1 (E.D. La. 2010). The court explained that the "requests for reimbursement of common benefit costs were vetted first by the Court-appointed CPA, then by a sub-committee of the Fee Allocation Committee, and finally by the entire Fee Allocation Committee." *Id.*

§ 11.4 INCENTIVE PAYMENTS

MDL judges overseeing class action settlements sometimes award "incentive payments" to plaintiffs (usually class representatives) who play a significant role in the litigation. Such awards (also known as "service awards") may come from amounts awarded to attorneys as fees, or may come separately from a settlement fund. The notion is that these plaintiffs have performed an important service to the court and the other claimants and should be compensated. For instance, plaintiffs may have given deposition testimony, responded to written discovery, provided documents, participated in bellwether trials, provided input during settlement discussions, or performed other tasks that benefited the claimants as a whole. *See, e.g.*, *In re Checking Account Overdraft Litig.*, 830 F. Supp. 2d 1330, 1357 (S.D. Fla. 2011) ("Service awards compensate named plaintiffs for the services they provided and the risks they incurred during the course of the class action litigation.").

Awards in the $5,000 range are not uncommon. *See, e.g.*, *In re AT&T Mobility Wireless Data Services Sales Tax Litig.*, 792 F. Supp. 2d 1028, 1042 (N.D. Ill. 2011) (awarding incentive payments of $5,000 to each of the class representatives in an MDL settled on a classwide basis, in view of the representatives' "role in reviewing, considering, and approving the Settlement Agreement"). Indeed, much higher amounts have been awarded. *See, e.g.*, *In re Nat'l Football League Players' Concussion Injury Litig.*, No. 2:12-02323-AB, 2018 WL 1635648, at **10–11 (E.D. Pa. Apr. 5, 2018) (awarding $100,000 to each of three class representatives); *In re Domestic Drywall Antitrust Litig.*, MDL No. 2437, 2018 WL 3439454, at

*20 (E.D. Pa. July 17, 2018) (awarding $50,000 to each of four class representatives).

No instance has been found in which incentive payments have been awarded in MDL cases outside of the class action context.

CHAPTER 12

ROLE OF THE TRANSFEREE JUDGE: CHOICE-OF-LAW ISSUES

When a case is transferred for pretrial proceedings under 28 U.S.C. § 1407, the transferee court must decide what law to apply on various issues. The MDL context creates a choice-of-law conundrum. The case is filed in one district, yet the Panel has exercised its authority to transfer the case to another district. In many instances, that transfer will be to a district within a different circuit than the transferor court's circuit. By statute, the transfer is only for pretrial proceedings, and in theory (but not usually in practice, *see* § 1.1), the cases are supposed to be returned to the transferor courts. An additional complication in the choice-of-law analysis is that some MDL cases are in federal court based on federal question jurisdiction (28 U.S.C. § 1331), while other cases are based on state law, and are in federal court based on diversity jurisdiction (28 U.S.C. § 1332). The analysis is not necessarily the same for these two categories. This Chapter addresses these choice-of-law issues.

§ 12.1 DIVERSITY ACTIONS

There is a consensus among MDL judges that in diversity actions, the transferee court applies the state substantive law of the transferor court's state, including that state's choice-of-law rules. For example, in a case transferred from the Southern District of California to the District of Iowa, the MDL judge in Iowa would apply California's choice-of-law rules to determine what law governs the case. In taking this approach, MDL judges have relied on *Van Dusen v. Barrack*, 376 U.S. 612 (1964). In *Van Dusen*, the Supreme Court held that for transfers pursuant to 28 U.S.C. § 1404(a)—when personal jurisdiction and venue are proper in the original court but the transfer is made for the convenience of the parties—the law of the transferor court applies. *See* 376 U.S. at 639 ("A change of venue under § 1404(a) generally should be, with respect to state law, but a change of courtrooms.").

Courts have extended the *Van Dusen* holding to suits transferred under section 1407. Under both sections 1404(a) and 1407, the plaintiffs chose a proper venue for their complaint, but for reasons of judicial efficiency, the cases were transferred to an alternative district. Rensberger at 855. Moreover, in a diversity case, the suit is in federal rather than state court only because the litigants are residents of different states. No federal question is involved. As in *Van Dusen*, the transfer is "but a change of courtrooms."

Examples of courts adopting this approach include *In re Air Crash Disaster at Boston, Mass., July 31, 1973*, 399 F. Supp. 1106, 1108 (D. Mass. 1975); *In re Nucorp Energy Securities Litigation*, MDL No. 514, 1983 WL 1298, at *1 (S.D. Cal. Mar. 24, 1983); and *In re Cessna 208 Series Aircraft Products Liability Litigation*, MDL No. 1721, 2007 WL 2172764, at *4 (D. Kan. July 25, 2007); *see also* Rensberger at 850 (discussing examples).

As these authorities have recognized, in MDL cases, applying the state law that governed when the suit was originally filed preserves the plaintiff's "venue privilege," which *Van Dusen* held was worthy of protection. Rensberger at 856. Applying the law of the transferor court also protects the goals of *Erie Railroad Co. v. Tompkins*, 304 U.S. 64 (1938), by ensuring that the same state law will apply whether the case is in federal or state court—a result that should not change in an MDL. Rensberger at 856.

For the MDL judge, it is less convenient to apply the choice-of-law rules of the transferor court in this situation. If an MDL involves cases transferred from multiple jurisdictions, the determination of legal issues will be much more complicated than if the MDL court could simply apply one set of choice-of-law rules to all of the cases. Nonetheless, MDL courts have applied the choice-of-law rules of the transferor courts despite the inconvenience. *See* Rensberger at 856.

Some commentators have suggested that the application of choice-of-law rules in MDL cases "inevitably leads to some smoothing out of differences in the applicable law." Bradt & Rave III at 1307. Although MDL judges endeavor to apply various states' laws, "MDLs are often resolved without fine-grained attention to state law." *Id.* In particular, "when cases are resolved by global settlement agreement, those agreements—at least those made public—do not typically value the claims based on differences in the applicable state law[s]." *Id.* at 1307–08.

§ 12.2 FEDERAL QUESTION

There is a circuit split as to what law a transferee court should apply in an MDL when the case arises under federal question jurisdiction. In federal question cases, the law that applies is federal law, but the interpretation and understanding of that law may vary depending on the circuit. Most courts have concluded that for federal questions, the law of the circuit where the transferee court is based should apply. *See* Marcus (Yale) at 721 (concluding that "the transferee court must be free to decide a federal claim in the manner it views as correct without deferring to the interpretation of the transferor circuit"). Some transferee courts, however, apply the law of the transferor court's circuit in some circumstances. Rensberger at 858–59. These approaches are discussed below.

A. APPLYING THE LAW OF THE TRANSFEREE COURT

Most courts apply the federal law interpretations of the transferee court's circuit. The seminal case on this issue is *In re Korean Air Lines Disaster of Sept. 1, 1983*, 829 F.2d 1171 (D.C. Cir. 1987). *See* Rensberger at 861.

Korean Air Lines involved a civilian airplane that was shot down by the Soviet Union over the Sea of Japan during the Cold War. The families of deceased passengers sued the airliner for wrongful death to recover damages. Under the Warsaw Convention and its amendment (the Montreal Agreement), recovery for international passengers was limited to $75,000.

The Montreal Agreement required airline tickets to specify the liability limitation in 10-point type, but the airline printed the notification in 8-point type. The plaintiffs sought recovery in excess of the $75,000, claiming that they were not bound by the Montreal Agreement's limitation on liability because the font used on the tickets was smaller than required. The Second Circuit, where some of the lawsuits originated, had previously ruled that similar violations of the Montreal Agreement voided the liability limitation. The district court for the District of Columbia—where all of the cases were centralized under section 1407—nonetheless held that the inadequate font size did not void the limitation on liability, even with respect to the cases in which the transferor court was within the Second Circuit. *Korean Air Lines*, 829 F.2d at 1172; Rensberger at 861.

On appeal, the D.C. Circuit affirmed. First, the court found that *Van Dusen* was not controlling because federal law, not state law, was involved. Second, the court reasoned that all federal courts are equal, and all are competent to apply federal law. "Federal courts have not only the power but the duty to decide issues of federal law correctly." *Korean Air Lines* at 1175. A lower court's duty is to apply the precedent from its circuit, even if it conflicts with the precedent of another circuit. It is up to the Supreme Court to fix circuit splits. As the D.C. Circuit noted:

> The federal courts spread across the country owe respect to each other's efforts and should strive to avoid conflicts, but each has an obligation to

> engage independently in reasoned analysis. Binding precedent for all is set only by the Supreme Court, and for the district courts within a circuit, only by the court of appeals for that circuit.

Id. at 1176. Because the D.C. Circuit agreed with the district court that the inadequate font size did not void the limitation on liability, it affirmed the district court.

Many other circuits apply the federal law of the transferee court. *See, e.g.*, *In re Temporomandibular Joint (TMJ) Implants Products Liability Litigation*, 97 F.3d 1050, 1055 (8th Cir. 1996) ("When analyzing questions of federal law [in an MDL], the transferee court should apply the law of the circuit in which it is located."); *U.S. ex rel. Hockett v. Columbia/HCA Healthcare Corp.*, 498 F. Supp. 2d 25, 39–40 (D.D.C. 2007) (same).

B. APPLYING THE LAW OF THE TRANSFEROR COURT

Some circuits apply *Korean Air Lines* in all situations involving federal law. Others apply the case in most situations, but apply the law of the transferor court's circuit when Congress has created non-uniform federal law that is tied to venue. Rensberger at 869.

For example, in *Eckstein v. Balcor Film Investors*, 8 F.3d 1121 (7th Cir. 1993), plaintiffs brought a securities fraud suit under the Securities Exchange Act of 1934. Two groups of cases (one group from

Wisconsin, the other from California) were centralized in the Eastern District of Wisconsin under section 1407. Under a federal statute, the statute of limitations for the suits depended on the law of the circuit in which the suit was filed. Under Seventh Circuit law, the actions were time-barred when filed. Under Ninth Circuit law, the actions were not time-barred. The MDL judge, relying on *Korean Air Lines*, applied Seventh Circuit law, even in the suits filed in California, and dismissed the suits.

The Seventh Circuit rejected the MDL judge's approach. It reasoned that, because applicable federal law was "geographically non-uniform," *Korean Air Lines*' approach to a unitary federal law did not apply. *Eckstein*, 8 F.3d at 1127. Rather, the court held that *Van Dusen* applied because the federal courts were instructed to use different laws depending on where the claim originated. Thus, the situation was more analogous to a suit in diversity. For ordinary federal question cases, however, the Seventh Circuit court agreed with the Second Circuit that the law of the transferee court's circuit was controlling. *Id.* at 1126. *See also Olcott v. Delaware Flood Co.*, 76 F.3d 1538, 1546–47 (10th Cir. 2009) (agreeing with *Eckstein*'s approach).

At least one legal commentator would go even further than the Seventh Circuit and apply the law of the transferor court's circuit on all issues of federal law. That commentator notes that, if the federal law of the transferee court's circuit is applied to pretrial rulings, then when the case is remanded to the transferor court for trial (as required by *Lexecon* and the MDL statute), confusion would result if, at the moment of remand, the law of the transferor court's circuit suddenly applied. Rensberger at 894–95. Applying the law of the transferor court's circuit in all instances avoids that problem. Yet no circuit has embraced that view, apart from the narrow exception in *Eckstein*. *See, e.g.*, *AER Advisors, Inc. v. Fidelity Brokerage Services, LLC*, 921 F.3d 282, 288 (1st Cir. 2019) (noting that every circuit to consider the issue "has concluded that when one district court transfers a case to another, the norm is that the transferee court applies its own Circuit's cases on the meaning of federal law").

§ 12.3 CONSIDERATIONS FOR DIRECT-FILED CASES

Direct-filed cases raise complicated choice-of-law issues. In some instances, plaintiffs file in the MDL court even though personal jurisdiction and venue in the MDL court are lacking. Parties do this to avoid the cumbersome transfer process, achieve efficiencies, and respond to MDL judges' expressed preference for direct-filed actions when possible. *See* § 6.2. In many of the cases, the parties will enter into a stipulation whereby the defendant agrees to waive personal jurisdiction and venue to facilitate direct filing but the parties also agree that if the transferee court completes pretrial proceedings, the case will be transferred to a court that has personal jurisdiction and venue. Bradt (Notre Dame) at 799. *See* § 6.2. Despite the fact that defendants do not waive personal jurisdiction or venue for the case as a whole, courts generally apply the choice-of-law rules of the state where the MDL judge is located. *Id.* at 800–01 (citing examples). One commentator disagrees with that approach, arguing that when the transferee court lacks personal jurisdiction or venue, choice-of-law should be "governed by the choice-of-law rules of an otherwise proper forum that the plaintiff selects at the outset of her case." *Id.* at 765, 816. Research has uncovered no case that has adopted this commentator's approach.

CHAPTER 13

PERSONAL JURISDICTION AND VENUE ISSUES IN MDL CASES

Personal jurisdiction and venue are core topics in every first-year civil procedure course. Students learn that these requirements—based on due process (personal jurisdiction) and 28 U.S.C. § 1391 (venue)—are threshold requirements that plaintiffs must satisfy, unless the defendant waives them. As noted repeatedly in this text, few cases transferred under section 1407 return to their transferor courts. Thus, even if there was personal jurisdiction and venue over the defendant where the suit was filed, the question is whether personal jurisdiction and venue must also be satisfied in the transferee district. In other words, does the defendant have the right to contest personal jurisdiction and venue (and thereby seek dismissal from the MDL) by treating the transferee district as the actual district for the litigation? Or is it irrelevant whether there is personal jurisdiction and venue in the transferee court?

This is not just an issue for defendants. Plaintiffs may also want to argue that they should not be forced to litigate in a forum that: (1) they did not choose; and (2) would not have satisfied personal jurisdiction and venue had the case been filed there originally.

Even if there are significant arguments for looking at personal jurisdiction and venue in the transferee court, the downside is that doing so would severely constrain the Panel in selecting a transferee district.

In a case involving multiple plaintiffs and defendants, it would be all but impossible to find a transferee district that could satisfy personal jurisdiction and venue for all of the cases. And even if there is only a single defendant, the likelihood is that only a small number of districts will satisfy personal jurisdiction for all of the cases. In either scenario, the Panel's choices of district would be extremely limited. Indeed, the difficulty of finding a single federal district that would qualify as a proper venue under the ordinary venue statute was a principal motivation for enacting the MDL statute. *See* Bradt & Rave III at 1296.

Scholars have begun focusing seriously on personal jurisdiction and venue concerns in MDL cases, and those issues could ultimately reach the Supreme Court. In any event, any student or practitioner looking at MDL practice should be familiar with how personal jurisdiction and venue play out in MDL cases.

As discussed below, no doubt influenced by the potentially devastating impact on MDL practice, the Panel, federal district courts, and the federal circuits have uniformly held that personal jurisdiction and venue in the transferee court are irrelevant. The courts, however, have taken different analytical approaches in reaching that result.

§ 13.1 PRACTICAL CONSEQUENCES OF MDL TRANSFER

As suggested above, issues of personal jurisdiction and venue in MDL are not merely academic; MDL transfer can have profound practical consequences for both plaintiffs and defendants.

Assume, for example, that a case is filed in federal district court in San Francisco, California (the Northern District of California), the defendant's principal place of business and state of incorporation, and also plaintiff's home town. There is both personal jurisdiction and venue over the defendant. Now assume that the case is transferred under section 1407 to the district court in Maryland, where there is no personal jurisdiction or venue over the defendant. This transfer dramatically impacts both the plaintiff and the defendant.

The plaintiff is unhappy: her case is now far away from her home, and her California attorney may end up with no role if she is not selected to serve in a leadership role. The seminal case of *Phillips Petroleum v. Shutts*, 472 U.S. 797 (1985), held (in the circumstances of that case) that unnamed class members in a class action could not raise personal jurisdiction issues because, as unnamed class members, they were passive. *Id.* at 810. But it is not at all clear that *Shutts* is controlling when the plaintiff is named and has filed an individual lawsuit. *See* Dodson at 1479 (arguing that "[t]he principles animating *Shutts* do not apply to nonclass plaintiffs"). In short, the plaintiff's unhappiness is far from academic, and her personal jurisdiction concerns are not necessarily foreclosed by *Shutts*.

The defendant is also unhappy litigating in a distant forum, in which it is not subject to either personal jurisdiction or venue. And defendants are traditionally the ones to raise personal jurisdiction and venue concerns.

Given that it is all but certain that the hypothetical case will be conclusively resolved by the federal judge in Maryland, *see* § 1.1, both the plaintiff and the defendant have reason to complain. Yet, as explained below, under existing law, neither plaintiff nor defendant can mount any sort of personal jurisdiction or venue attack involving the transferee court.

§ 13.2 THE PANEL'S INTERPRETATION OF PERSONAL JURISDICTION AND VENUE UNDER SECTION 1407

Early in its existence, the Panel addressed personal jurisdiction and venue under section 1407. Those cases (discussed in subsection A below) held that as long as there is personal jurisdiction and venue in the transferor court, those requirements are satisfied in the transferee court as well. As discussed in subsection B, this is usually true even if the defendant was not served with process when the Panel ordered transfer. This issue does not arise for cases filed directly in the MDL court, assuming that there is personal jurisdiction and venue, or that the defendant waives them.

A. PERSONAL JURISDICTION AND VENUE ISSUES INVOLVING THE TRANSFEREE COURT

The Panel has frequently noted, with little explanation, that "[t]ransfers . . . are simply not encumbered by considerations of in personam jurisdiction and venue." *In re RAH Color Techs. LLC*

Patent Litig., 347 F. Supp. 3d 1359, 1360 n.5 (J.P.M.L. 2018). *Accord, e.g., In re Helicopter Crash Near Wendle Creek, British Columbia, on Aug. 8, 2002*, 542 F. Supp. 2d 1362, 1363 (J.P.M.L. 2008). According to the above authorities, the only issue is whether the transferor court (not the transferee court) has jurisdiction and venue.

A seminal Panel decision on personal jurisdiction and venue is *In re Plumbing Fixture Cases*, 298 F. Supp. 484 (J.P.M.L. 1968). There, 37 actions were transferred to the Eastern District of Pennsylvania. The plaintiff in one of the actions argued that, under section 1407, the transferee court lacked the authority to rule on a motion for class certification. The Panel disagreed, ruling that a class certification determination fell under section 1407(a)'s reference to "pretrial proceedings." *Id.* at 495. The Panel held that "[a] transferee court may make any order to render any judgment that might have been rendered by the transferor court in the absence of transfer" because "*the jurisdiction and powers of the transferee court are coextensive with that of the transferor court*[.]" *Id.* at 495 (emphasis added). That situation applies "from the time of entry of the order of transfer until the time of entry of an order to remand." *Id.* at 496. The Panel analogized a section 1407 transfer to a change of venue under 28 U.S.C. § 1404(a), *id.* at 495–96, even though "[t]o transfer a case [under section 1404], the transferor court must find that the intended transferee court has personal jurisdiction and is an appropriate venue." *Intelect Corp. v. Cellco P'Ship GP*, 160 F. Supp. 3d 157, 172 (D.D.C. 2016).

Four years later, in *In re Kauffman Mutual Fund Actions*, 337 F. Supp. 1337 (J.P.M.L. 1972), 12 antitrust and securities actions were transferred to the District of Massachusetts. The defendants resisted transfer, arguing that the plaintiff "should not be able to secure from the Panel, under . . . § 1407, what the venue provisions of federal law otherwise prohibit." *Id.* at 1339. The Panel rejected that argument, stating that "the Panel's discretion under Section 1407 is not limited by venue considerations[.]" *Id.* Moreover, "the fact that defendants may not all be amenable to suit in the same jurisdiction does not prevent their transfer . . . for pretrial proceedings where the prerequisites of Section 1407 are otherwise satisfied." *Id.*

In *In re Sugar Industry Antitrust Litigation*, 399 F. Supp. 1397 (J.P.M.L. 1975), the Panel reiterated its position. Although denying transfer for a potential tag-along action, the Panel addressed and rejected the defendants' personal jurisdiction arguments for opposing transfer. The defendants argued that a transfer to a district in California, the venue urged by the plaintiffs, would "unconstitutionally deprive [the defendants] of the protection guaranteed by the [D]ue [P]rocess [C]lause of the Fifth Amendment," because "they d[id] not have the requisite minimal contacts with California to give the California court in personam jurisdiction over them." *Id.* at 1400. The Panel summarily rejected the defendants' argument, stating that it "ha[d] considered that constitutional argument and [found] it without merit." *Id.*

Likewise, in *In re FMC Corp. Patent Litigation*, 422 F. Supp. 1163 (J.P.M.L. 1976), the Panel rejected a defendant's personal jurisdiction and venue arguments against a proposed transfer. In advocating for a transfer to the Northern District of Ohio, not the District of Kansas, the defendant argued that the "lack of jurisdiction and venue makes the District of Kansas an inappropriate transferee forum because that court would lack authority to enforce its rulings on discovery matters . . . unless [defendants] voluntarily waive their objections to venue." *Id.* at 1165. The Panel found those arguments "unpersuasive[,]" and "based on a total misconception of Section 1407." *Id.* The Panel concluded that "transfer under Section 1407 is, in essence, a change of venue for pretrial purposes." *Id.* According to the Panel, "[f]ollowing a transfer, the transferee judge has all the jurisdiction and powers over pretrial proceedings in the actions transferred to him that the transferor judge would have had in the absence of transfer." *Id.*

Under these decisions, parties seeking to raise personal jurisdiction and venue challenges must focus on the personal jurisdiction and venue of the transferor court, as opposed to the transferee court. For example, if the Panel transfers a case from the Northern District of California to the District of Maryland, as in the hypothetical above, parties challenging personal jurisdiction must focus on the personal jurisdiction of the Northern District of California, despite arguing the issue before the MDL judge in the District of Maryland. *See Parthasarathy* *v. RS Inv. Mgmt., LP*, No. JFM 04-3798, 2005 WL 4146020, at *1 (D. Md. Nov. 5, 2005).

B. RELEVANCE OF LACK OF SERVICE OF PROCESS

The Panel has expressed little concern about personal jurisdiction even when transfer occurs before the defendant has been served in the transferor court. In *In re Library Editions of Children's Books*, 299 F. Supp. 1139 (J.P.M.L. 1969), 19 antitrust cases were transferred to the Northern District of Illinois. The County of Los Angeles, the plaintiff in one of the cases, opposed the transfer because some defendants had not yet been served. The Panel rejected the County's position, holding that "the power of the Panel and the courts to effectuate a transfer under [Section] 1407 is not vitiated by the transferor court's lack of personal jurisdiction over a defendant." *Id.* at 1142.

To reach this conclusion, the Panel relied on *Goldlawr, Inc. v. Heiman,* 369 U.S. 463 (1962), which held that a court without personal jurisdiction could transfer a case under 28 U.S.C. § 1406(a) to a court that had personal jurisdiction. *Library Editions,* 299 F. Supp. at 1141–42. Similarly, the Panel reasoned, a transfer could take place under section 1407, even though service of process had not occurred in the transferor court. *Id.*

Although the Panel held that service on all defendants is not required before transfer, it did hold that transfer in those circumstances would depend on several factors, including: "(1) the strength of the showing that transfer is desirable, (2) the presence or absence of plaintiff's good faith in naming the unserved defendants, (3) the extent of plaintiff's effort to serve each defendant with process, (4) the degree to which the unserved defendant's interests appear to be the same as those of the defendants coming before the Panel, (5) the number of unserved defendants, and (6) the importance of their presence before the Panel in aiding its decision." *Id.* at 1143.

Most Panel decisions, however, have not found those factors to be a constraint. *See, e.g.*, *In re Sugar Industry Antitrust Litig.*, 427 F. Supp. 1018, 1027 n.11 (J.P.M.L. 1977) (rejecting a defendant's argument that transfer was improper because it had not been served with process; the Panel did not examine the factors from *Library Editions*); *In re Gypsum Wallboard*, 302 F. Supp. 794, 794 (J.P.M.L. 1969) (same).

§ 13.3 FEDERAL DISTRICT AND CIRCUIT COURT INTERPRETATIONS

The issues of personal jurisdiction and venue in MDLs have been addressed not only by the Panel but also by federal district and circuit courts. Those courts have sometimes differed from the Panel in their reasoning, although the bottom line is still the same: personal jurisdiction and venue in the transferee court are not a concern.

Two circuits, the Second and the Sixth, have held that personal jurisdiction and venue are established nationwide under section 1407. In *In re Agent Orange Products Liability Litigation MDL No. 381*, 818 F.2d

145 (2d Cir. 1987), the Second Circuit rejected the appellants' Fifth Amendment due process challenge to the transferee court's exercise of jurisdiction over them. *Id.* at 163. Although the Second Circuit cited the Panel's decisions in *Sugar Industry* and *FMC Corp.,* it took a very different analytical approach. The Second Circuit explained that "Congress may, consistent with the due process clause, enact legislation authorizing the federal courts to exercise nationwide jurisdiction," and found that section 1407 is "[o]ne such piece of legislation[.]" *Id.* Thus, the Second Circuit found the answer in section 1407 itself and reached the same result as the Panel's decisions (that personal jurisdiction and venue in the transferee court were irrelevant), but did so through different reasoning.

The Sixth Circuit subsequently adopted the "nationwide personal jurisdiction" rationale in *Howard v. Sulzer Orthopedics*, 382 Fed. Appx. 436 (6th Cir. 2010). There, the plaintiff argued that "the [transferee] court's refusal to transfer the case back" to the transferor court "violated due process." *Id.* at 442. In rejecting that argument, the Sixth Circuit stated that, under section 1407, "[c]ontacts with the United States, and not a particular state, are what matters in federal court." *Id.* Consequently, "the transferor court . . . had personal jurisdiction over [plaintiff], and through § 1407 the [transferee court] did as well." *Id.* at 442. *Accord, e.g., In re Chinese-Manufactured Drywall Prods. Liab. Litig.*, No. 09-2047, 2017 WL 5971622, at *19 (E.D. La. Nov. 30, 2017) ("[I]t is clear and beyond dispute that Congress has constitutional authority to shape federal court's jurisdiction beyond state lines to encompass nonresident parties. And Congress has done so repeatedly—with Rule 4, MDLs, and class actions.").

Some federal courts, however, have adopted the reasoning of the Panel (that the focus is on personal jurisdiction and venue in the transferor court). For example, in *In re Testosterone Replacement Therapy Products Liability Litigation Coordinated Pretrial Proceedings*, 136 F. Supp. 3d 968 (N.D. Ill. 2015), the court stated that "[i]n an MDL proceeding, the [transferee] court . . . has jurisdiction over cases transferred to it under 28 U.S.C. § 1407 if the originating, transferor courts would have jurisdiction." *Id.* at 973. *Accord, e.g., In re Takata Airbag Prods. Liab. Litig.*, MDL No. 2599, 2019 WL 2570616, at *19 (S.D. Fla. June 21, 2019).

Finally, as noted (§ 6.2), there is one situation in which personal jurisdiction and venue in the MDL court are critical: when the plaintiff files directly in that court. As one commentator explains, "plaintiffs cannot file directly in the MDL court if the MDL court would lack personal jurisdiction over the defendant . . . unless the defendant consents." Dodson at 1475. *See* § 6.2.

§ 13.4 SCHOLARLY REACTION

Scholars have taken conflicting views on the issue of personal jurisdiction and venue in MDLs. One commentator disagrees with the federal court of appeals cases relying on nationwide personal jurisdiction, arguing that "Congress did not authorize nationwide personal jurisdiction in

MDL[.]" Bradt (William & Mary) at 1214. He also disagrees with the Panel's view that "the parties' rights are not affected by limited transfer," in light of the reality that "cases are rarely remanded for trial." *Id.* at 1215. Nonetheless, he agrees for the most part with the results reached by those courts, noting that "[p]laintiffs are likely to be scattered around the country," and multiple defendants may be as well. *Id.* at 1220. He concludes that "considerations of convenience for any single party must take a backseat." *Id.* In his view, given the unique purposes of MDL and the dispersed location of the parties, personal jurisdiction and venue concerns should not eviscerate the MDL statute's purpose of achieving efficiency for the lawsuits as a whole. In his view, while it is proper to focus on personal jurisdiction in the transferee court, the question of whether jurisdiction exists should be determined by balancing the "national interest in dispute resolution" against the "individual interest in meaningful participation." *Id.* at 1228. *See also* Bradt & Rave III at 1298 (arguing that "the benefits of MDL on all sides will typically outweigh the costs in terms of centralizing nationwide litigation in a single geographic location," but that "the Fifth Amendment imposes some limitations on where an MDL can be located to ensure that the parties have a reasonable opportunity to be heard").

Another commentator takes a different approach. Agreeing with the Second and Sixth Circuits, he argues that section 1407 can reasonably be interpreted to establish nationwide personal jurisdiction and venue, and that Congress can constitutionally do so. Nelson at 61–72. Alternatively, he argues that if the Panel is correct that personal jurisdiction and venue in the transferee court depend on whether the transferor court has personal jurisdiction and venue, then those issues must be resolved in the transferor court before transfer can be finalized. *Id.* at 43. That commentator also argues that, even under the Panel's analytical approach, transfer should not be allowed unless and until service of process has been effectuated in the transferor court. *Id.* at 41–43.

Research has revealed virtually no authority for the argument that, under due process and the federal venue statute, personal jurisdiction and venue must independently exist in the transferee court. *But see* Dodson at 1482–83 (arguing that plaintiffs should be able to object to transfer to a court that lacks personal jurisdiction over them); *cf.* Bradt (William & Mary) at 1228 (discussed above). Presumably, scholars understand that such an approach would cripple the MDL statute. But the dearth of scholarly support does not mean that the issue is dead. A litigant in an MDL could well decide to challenge personal jurisdiction and venue in the transferee court, with the plan of pursuing the arguments all the way to the Supreme Court. In recent years, the Supreme Court has been receptive to arguments cutting back on personal jurisdiction over defendants. *See, e.g.*, *Bristol-Myers Squibb v. Superior Court*, 137 S. Ct. 1773 (2017); *Daimler AG v. Bauman*, 571 U.S. 117 (2014).

On the other hand, in *Bristol-Myers Squibb*, the Court stated that the due process analysis may work differently under the Fifth Amendment than under the Fourteenth Amendment. 137 S. Ct. at 1783–84 ("[S]ince our decision concerns the due process limits on the exercise of specific jurisdiction by a State, we leave open the question whether the Fifth Amendment imposes the same restrictions on the exercise of personal jurisdiction by a federal court."). That statement could signal the Court's receptiveness to a more expansive view of personal jurisdiction in the federal courts—both generally and in the MDL context specifically. But that remains to be seen. In any event, the issue of whether there must be personal jurisdiction and venue in the transferee court is still in play until the Supreme Court rules on the issue.

CHAPTER 14

APPEALS OF RULINGS BY MDL JUDGES

The scope of appellate review of rulings by MDL judges has been a subject of heated debate in recent years. Defendants and defense-oriented organizations, such as the U.S. Chamber of Commerce and Lawyers for Civil Justice, have been advocating for an amendment to section 1407 or to the Federal Rules of Civil Procedure to expand the opportunities for interlocutory review of MDL court rulings. Those proposals are discussed in Chapter 17, *see* § 17.1.

As explained below, the limited scope of appellate review stems from the final judgment rule and the fact that only narrow exceptions to that rule exist. Moreover, because many MDLs are resolved by voluntary settlement before trial, there is frequently never a contested final judgment from which to appeal important legal rulings.

This Chapter addresses the contours of appellate remedies available in MDLs. First, it discusses the final judgment rule, the limited exceptions to that rule, and the types of important rulings in MDLs that, in many instances, cannot be appealed. It then discusses the Supreme Court's opinion in *Gelboim v. Bank of America,* 135 S. Ct. 897 (2015), which holds that a dispositive ruling that completely disposes of an individual case within an MDL is appealable without waiting for the completion of the entire MDL proceedings. Finally, this Chapter discusses various issues that are frequently appealed in MDL cases.

§ 14.1 THE FINAL JUDGMENT RULE AS A LIMIT ON APPEALABILITY

A. SCOPE OF THE FINAL JUDGMENT RULE AND ITS IMPLICATION FOR MDL CASES

Under 28 U.S.C. § 1291, federal courts of appeals have jurisdiction over appeals from all "final decisions" of federal district courts. Other than in the limited situations described below, appeals of interlocutory rulings are not allowed. "A 'final decision' generally is one which ends the litigation on the merits and leaves nothing for the court to do but execute the judgment." *Catlin v. United States,* 324 U.S. 229, 233 (1945). The Supreme Court has explained that the final judgment rule "emphasizes the deference that appellate courts owe to the trial court as the individual initially called upon to decide the many questions of law and fact that occur in the course of a trial," while avoiding "the harassment and cost of a succession of separate appeals" from multiple rulings. *Firestone Tire & Rubber Co. v. Risjord*, 449 U.S. 368, 374 (1981).

Many crucial rulings by an MDL judge are interlocutory because they do not "end[ ] the litigation on the merits." *Catlin*, 324 U.S. at 233. For instance, most discovery rulings are interlocutory. Similarly, rulings on motions to exclude expert testimony on *Daubert* grounds (*see* § 8.5) are interlocutory. The denial of a motion for summary judgment—whether on legal or factual grounds—is interlocutory. The denial of a motion to dismiss on preemption grounds is interlocutory. Such rulings can substantially impact the course of the litigation, but absent one of the narrow exceptions discussed below, they cannot be challenged during an ongoing MDL.

B. LIMITED EXCEPTIONS TO THE FINAL JUDGMENT RULE

There are several exceptions to the final judgment rule, but for the most part they offer no basis for an interlocutory appeal of the types of orders discussed above.

(1) Collateral Order Doctrine

Under the "collateral order" doctrine of *Cohen v. Beneficial Industrial Loan Corp.*, 337 U.S. 541 (1949), review of a non-final order may be allowed if it: (1) conclusively determines disputed questions; (2) resolves an important issue completely separate from the merits of the action; and (3) cannot be effectively reviewed on appeal from a final judgment. *See, e.g.*, *Firestone Tire & Rubber Co.*, 449 U.S. at 375 (holding that a denial of a motion to disqualify counsel was not an immediately appealable collateral order). Those criteria are hard to satisfy, and generally do not apply to discovery rulings or rulings refusing to grant dispositive motions. *See, e.g.*, *Mohawk Indus., Inc. v. Carpenter,* 558 U.S. 100 (2009) (unanimously holding that a trial court's order requiring production of information allegedly protected by the attorney-client privilege was not a collateral order).

(2) Death Knell Doctrine

Before 1978, some federal circuits had allowed appeal when an interlocutory ruling, as a practical matter, ended the case. But that avenue for appeal was invalidated in *Coopers & Lybrand v. Livesay,* 437 U.S. 463 (1978). In that case, the Supreme Court held that an order denying class certification was not immediately appealable and that the death knell exception was based on policy considerations more properly left to Congress. Even if an adverse interlocutory ruling (such as the denial of summary judgment) would, as a practical matter, force the defendant to settle, the discredited death knell doctrine would not provide a ground for immediate appeal.

(3) Certification Under 28 U.S.C. § 1292(b)

Section 1292(b) permits a district court to certify an otherwise non-appealable order for appellate review when three criteria are met: (1) the "order involves a controlling question of law"; (2) there is "substantial ground for difference of opinion" regarding the order; and (3) "an immediate appeal from the order may materially advance the ultimate termination of the litigation." The district court must state in writing that those criteria are satisfied, and application for an appeal must be made within 10 days after entry of the certification order. If the district court refuses to certify the case for appeal, the court of appeals cannot hear the case unless another legal basis exists for interlocutory review. And even if the district court certifies an order for appeal under section 1292(b), the court of appeals has unreviewable discretion to decline the appeal for any reason (including docket congestion).

As a practical matter, it is difficult to convince any judge—particularly an MDL judge—to certify an issue for immediate appeal, especially when the judge must find that "there is a substantial ground for difference of opinion." One study of 127 mass tort MDLs by a prominent defense firm found only 15 attempts to seek section 1292(b) certification (presumably reflecting the view of MDL attorneys that section 1292(b) certification is an uphill battle). The study found no instance in which a defendant's section 1292(b) motion was granted on an issue that impacted a large number of claims. Beisner & Schwartz at 6. A different study, however, found no cases in which an MDL judge, after denying interlocutory review of an issue, was later reversed after final judgment on that issue. Devine at 2. In any event, section 1292(b) is available in the infrequent situation in which both the MDL judge and the circuit believe that the MDL proceeding would benefit from an early appellate court ruling on an important legal issue.

(4) Injunction Orders Under 28 U.S.C. § 1292(a)(1)

Section 1292(a)(1) grants appellate courts jurisdiction over interlocutory orders of district courts "granting, continuing, modifying, refusing or dissolving injunctions, or refusing to dissolve or modify injunctions." Most of the orders discussed above (discovery orders, *Daubert* rulings, denials of dispositive motions) do not implicate section 1292(a)(1). And the Supreme Court has not been persuaded by creative arguments to extend the scope of section 1292(a)(1).

For instance, in *Gardner v. Westinghouse Broadcasting Company*, 437 U.S. 478 (1978), the Court narrowly interpreted 28 U.S.C. § 1292(a)(1) in connection with the review of orders denying class certification. Even though the plaintiff's underlying complaint sought equitable relief for the entire class, the Court reasoned that the order denying class certification did not entirely dispose of the relief sought, but merely limited its scope. Accordingly, the order was not appealable under section 1292(a)(1). 437 U.S. at 480–81.

(5) Mandamus

The All Writs Act, 28 U.S.C. § 1651, permits an appellate court to grant a petition for mandamus in extraordinary circumstances. Under the mandamus power, the courts of appeals may take jurisdiction and intervene to prevent or correct fundamental abuses of power by a district court. Use of the mandamus power, however, is rarely warranted. A writ of mandamus is justified only when there is irreparable harm and a clear usurpation of judicial power by the district court. *See* § 5.5. In the context of the types of orders discussed here, it is rare that an appellant could satisfy the stringent standards for mandamus.

It is conceivable that, even if a party's mandamus petition is denied by a court of appeals, that party may still benefit. For instance, in *In re Depuy Orthopaedics, Inc.*, 870 F.3d 345 (5th Cir. 2017), the defendants sought mandamus after the MDL court denied their personal jurisdiction challenges in certain cases scheduled for trial. The defendants had waived personal jurisdiction and venue objections for certain bellwether trials, but argued that the MDL court erred in finding that they had waived such objections for all cases pending in the MDL. In a fractured opinion, a majority of the Fifth Circuit panel held that the MDL court had erred in finding that the defendants' waiver applied to all cases in the MDL. *Id.* at 348. A different majority found that petitioners had shown a clear and indisputable right to a writ of mandamus, but nonetheless denied the petition, concluding that petitioners had not shown that they had no other adequate means to obtain relief, because they could appeal after trial. *Id.* In lieu of a writ of mandamus, the Fifth Circuit majority "request[ed] the district court to vacate its ruling on waiver and to withdraw its order for [the forthcoming] trial[.]" *Id.* Thus, although the defendants were denied the writ of mandamus, they obtained a beneficial outcome. Despite this unusual case, however, mandamus is rarely a viable option for achieving relief.

(6) Appeal Under Rule 23(f)

Under Federal Rule of Civil Procedure 23(f), a party can seek permission from the court of appeals to appeal "an order granting or denying class action certification[.]" Unlike section 1292(b), Rule 23(f) does not require permission of the district court. Rule 23(f) contains no specific criteria. The Advisory Committee Notes accompanying Rule 23(f) state that the courts of appeals have "unfettered discretion whether to permit the appeal, akin to the discretion exercised by the Supreme Court in acting on a petition for certiorari." Rule 23(f) facilitates the appeal of rulings granting or denying class certification, even in the MDL context. It does not, however, apply to other types of interlocutory orders.

(7) Appeal Under Rule 54(b)

Federal Rule of Civil Procedure 54(b) provides for "the entry of a final judgment as to one or more, but fewer than all, claims or parties" in a lawsuit when the district court determines that "there is no just reason for delay." As discussed immediately below, this Rule provides a mechanism for immediate appeal of orders granting dispositive motions. It does not, however, provide a mechanism for appealing discovery rulings or orders denying dispositive motions.

§ 14.2 THE *GELBOIM* OPINION

The Supreme Court's decision in *Gelboim v. Bank of America*, 135 S. Ct. 897 (2015), is one of two Supreme Court cases addressing issues specific to

MDL (the other being *Lexecon* (*see* §§ 9.2, 15.2)). The Court in *Gelboim* held that when an MDL judge, in ruling on a dispositive motion, dismisses an individual case within an MDL, that order is immediately appealable, even though the MDL is still ongoing.

The case involved an MDL consisting of more than 60 actions alleging that certain banks understated their borrowing costs, causing the London InterBank Offered Rate to be depressed and thus enabling the banks to pay lower interest rates on financial instruments sold to investors. One of the complaints (the Gelboim-Zacher complaint) alleged only an antitrust claim, and the MDL judge dismissed the claim on the ground that plaintiffs could not show antitrust injury. The Second Circuit dismissed the plaintiffs' appeal on the ground that other claims remained pending in the MDL, so that there was no final judgment. The Supreme Court reversed, holding that "the order dismissing [plaintiffs'] case in its entirety removed [plaintiffs] from the consolidated proceeding, thereby triggering their right to appeal under § 1291." 135 S. Ct. at 904. Because the Gelboim-Zacher plaintiffs' case had been disposed of in its entirety, there was a final judgment.

Importantly, the Court made clear that, even when only some claims in a multi-claim complaint are dismissed, an immediate appeal may be possible under Federal Rule of Civil Procedure 54(b):

> District courts may grant certifications under [Rule 54(b) when only some claims are dismissed], thereby enabling plaintiffs in actions

> that have not been dismissed in their entirety to pursue immediate appellate review.

135 S. Ct. at 906. Thus, under *Gelboim,* there is a clear avenue for appeal when an MDL judge grants a dispositive motion in part and dismisses one or more claims in a case. But *Gelboim* does not solve the defense bar's concern that there is no immediate right to appeal when the MDL judge *denies* a dispositive motion (or makes another important interlocutory ruling). *See* § 17.1.

§ 14.3 APPEALS IN MDL CASES AFTER FINAL JUDGMENT

Notwithstanding the final judgment rule, there are many appeals in MDL cases. It is beyond the scope of this text to cover all situations in which MDL cases have resulted in appeals. Instead, this text provides a few illustrations to show that, notwithstanding the final judgment rule, the federal appellate courts are still active participants in the MDL process. As discussed below, two types of district court orders that are subject to appellate review are orders granting dispositive motions and orders in connection with class action settlements.

A. APPEALS OF MDL RULINGS GRANTING DISPOSITIVE MOTIONS

In a number of cases, the federal courts of appeals have reviewed orders by MDL judges granting dispositive motions. The most recent and prominent example is *Merck Sharp & Dohme Corp. v. Albrecht*, 139 S. Ct. 1668 (2019). As discussed in detail in § 8.7,

Merck illustrates a preemption issue that arose in an MDL court and was litigated all the way to the U.S. Supreme Court.

Another example of an appeal in an MDL is *Alexander v. FedEx Ground Package System, Inc.*, 765 F.3d 981 (9th Cir. 2014). In that case, an MDL judge in the Northern District of Indiana granted summary judgment in a case alleging unpaid wages. A critical issue was whether the plaintiffs were employees (as they alleged) or independent contractors. The district court held that the plaintiffs were independent contractors. The cases were subsequently remanded so that the transferor court could address certain other claims, and the parties later settled the claims that were remanded. Plaintiffs then appealed the MDL judge's ruling to the Ninth Circuit, which reversed, finding that the plaintiffs were employees as a matter of law. *Id.* at 997.

And in *In re Donald J. Trump Casino Securities Litigation*, 7 F.3d 357 (3d Cir. 1993), the Third Circuit heard an appeal from an MDL transferee court's dismissal of the plaintiffs' claims under Rule 12(b)(6) for failure to state a claim upon which relief could be granted. The plaintiffs alleged that the prospectus accompanying the defendants' bonds contained misleading statements and material omissions, in violation of the federal securities laws. The district court dismissed plaintiffs' claims under the "bespeaks caution" doctrine, under which "a court may determine that the inclusion of sufficient cautionary statements in a prospectus renders misrepresentations and omissions contained therein nonactionable." *Id.* at 364. The Third Circuit affirmed, holding that "the bespeaks caution doctrine is both viable and applicable to the facts of this appeal." *Id.* The Third Circuit also took the "opportunity to make clear that § 1407 empowers transferee courts to enter a dispositive pre-trial order terminating a case." *Id.* at 367.

B. APPEALS AFTER CLASS ACTION SETTLEMENTS

Many federal courts have ruled on appeals after class action settlements. Numerous examples are discussed below. (Citations to the many appeals discussed herein are omitted.)

For instance, in the *BP Deepwater Horizon* MDL, there have been dozens of appeals to the Fifth Circuit on such issues as whether the district court correctly applied Rule 23 in approving settlement classes; whether the claims administrator properly interpreted the settlement agreement; whether a certain plaintiff fraudulently induced BP to enter into a settlement agreement; and whether certain plaintiffs' claims were properly dismissed as a sanction for unethical conduct.

In the *Diet Drugs* MDL, there were multiple appeals to the Third Circuit on issues such as whether the district court abused its discretion by suspending claims-processing deadlines due to an unexpectedly high volume of claims; whether the defendant was required to show that a plaintiff received actual notice of the settlement in order for that plaintiff to be bound by the settlement agreement; whether the district court erred in approving an amendment to the settlement agreement that allowed claimants to opt out if the settlement fund became insolvent; whether the court of appeals had jurisdiction to hear a challenge to an interim award of attorneys' fees; whether the district court had the power under the All Writs Act to limit the actions of opt-out plaintiffs pursuing their claims in state courts; and whether certain plaintiffs could collaterally challenge the adequacy of their representation in the class settlement.

Similarly, in the *NFL Concussion* MDL, several appeals involving the settlement have been decided by the Third Circuit (and in a number of instances are pending). For instance, the Third Circuit has decided issues such as the appealability of preliminary and conditional approval of a proposed settlement class; whether the district court correctly followed Rule 23 in certifying the class action for settlement purposes and approving the settlement; and whether the district court had the authority to void cash advancement agreements between class members and third-party litigation funders.

In sum, the federal appellate courts have been actively involved in reviewing rulings of MDL judges. *See generally* Gluck at 1707 (finding in a Westlaw search "at least 100 MDL cases that reached the circuit courts on direct review" during a recent 5-year period and noting that this figure excludes "cases that relate to MDLs but do not arise directly from them," such as law of the case issues in the transferor court).

§ 14.4 PROPER CIRCUIT COURT FOR APPEAL

In virtually all circumstances, appeals of rulings by the MDL judge are filed in the federal circuit where the MDL judge is based, not in the circuit where the transferor court is based. For example, if the MDL is centralized in Richmond, Virginia, appeals would be filed in the U.S. Court of Appeals for the Fourth Circuit. There are exceptions, however. As the *Alexander* case discussed in § 14.3 reveals, if a judgment becomes final only after a case is remanded, then the appeal must be filed in the transferor court's circuit. In *Alexander*, for example, even though the MDL was in Indiana, the appeal went to the Ninth Circuit, not the Seventh Circuit.

There is also another narrow exception to the rule that appeals go to the MDL judge's circuit. Under section 1407(b), an MDL judge "may exercise the powers of a district judge in any district for the purpose of conducting pretrial depositions in such coordinated or consolidated pretrial proceedings." 28 U.S.C. § 1407(b). In *In re Corrugated Container Antitrust Litigation,* 662 F.2d 875 (D.C. Cir. 1981), an MDL judge in the Southern District of Texas issued a contempt order (by telephone from Texas) to a witness in the District of Columbia for refusing to answer questions. On appeal to the D.C. Circuit, the court of appeals summarized the general rule that "[o]rdinarily, . . . appeals from the orders of the judge appointed to preside over the transferred case go to the appellate court which normally rules over the district court"—in that case, the Fifth Circuit. *Id.* at 880. The appeal in *Corrugated Container*, however, was properly brought in the D.C. Circuit because the district judge was exercising the "powers of a district judge in the District of Columbia." *Id.* at 879.

One final point should be noted. The Panel never has appellate authority to review the rulings of the MDL judge. The Panel has no appellate authority, either over the transferor court or the transferee court. Herr (MDL) § 11:5.

CHAPTER 15

REMAND

In some ways, this Chapter is largely theoretical. It provides a detailed discussion of the remand process—whereby the Panel remands cases from the transferee court to the transferor court. As noted repeatedly in this text, however, MDL cases are almost always resolved by the transferee court and are rarely remanded to the transferor court. The Supreme Court has recognized this reality. *See Gelboim v. Bank of America*, 135 S. Ct. 897, 905 n.6 (2015) (quoting the Manual for Complex Litigation for the proposition that "[f]ew cases . . . are remanded for trial," and that "most multidistrict litigation is settled in the transferee court").

One source contends that, even if the parties seek remand, a court should generally not remand the cases if continued MDL treatment can streamline discovery, prevent inconsistent legal rulings, facilitate settlement, or achieve other efficiencies. MDL Standards at 83. *But see* Burch (Mass Tort Deals) at 210–14 (raising concerns about the fact that most MDL cases are never remanded).

As a practical matter, few attorneys in MDL cases will have to deal with the intricacies of the remand process. But there is no way of knowing in advance whether cases in a particular MDL will end up being remanded to the transferor court. Consequently, all MDL practitioners must understand the parameters of remand—and, in particular, the rule under

Lexecon that normally cases that are ready for trial must be remanded.

The Chapter begins with a slight detour, discussing one type of remand that may occur early in an MDL. It then focuses on the traditional remand, which may occur much later in the litigation. In discussing the traditional remand context, the Chapter addresses *Lexecon* in detail, along with ways for an MDL judge to retain cases for trial.

§ 15.1 REMAND OF PARTICULAR CLAIMS

Under 28 U.S.C. § 1407(a), the Panel is permitted to "separate any claim, crossclaim, counter-claim, or third-party claim and remand any of such claims before the remainder of the action is remanded." As one authority notes, this provision enables the Panel "to refine the somewhat blunt 'transfer/no transfer' decision it must otherwise make." Herr (MDL) § 5:57. This approach may be used when an action has claims, crossclaims, counterclaims, or third-party claims that are not suitable for, or relevant to, the overall MDL. *Id.* § 5:59. The Panel, however, rarely orders remand of such claims.

Section 1407(a) refers only to claims and does not allow the Panel to remand particular issues to the transferor court. Herr (MDL) § 5:58; Manual § 20.133.

§ 15.2 REMAND AT THE CONCLUSION OF THE MDL

The more common remand procedure occurs much later in the litigation, when the MDL judge has completed all of the pretrial work in the cases. As discussed below, the Supreme Court in *Lexecon* places significant limitations on a transferee court's ability to try MDL cases (although, as discussed in Chapter 9, MDL judges frequently conduct bellwether trials). After addressing *Lexecon,* this Chapter addresses the mechanics of remand.

A. THE *LEXECON* RULE AND WAYS TO CIRCUMVENT IT

Before the Supreme Court's opinion in *Lexecon Inc. v. Milberg Weiss Bershad Hynes & Lerach,* 523 U.S. 26 (1998), it was common for MDL judges to transfer cases to themselves for trial under the change of venue statute, 28 U.S.C. § 1404(a). Those courts reasoned that granting a motion to transfer venue was a pretrial ruling that MDL judges could decide. MDL judges relied on self-transfer early on, and the Panel's own rules permitted it. *See* Herrmann (NY Law Journal) at 58. But the Supreme Court unanimously repudiated that approach in *Lexecon.*

The *Lexecon* case has a complicated procedural background. Lexecon, a law and economics consulting firm, brought a diversity suit against two law firms, alleging various intentional torts, including malicious prosecution. The law firms had been plaintiffs' counsel in class action litigation involving a large savings and loan institution.

Lexecon was a defendant in that litigation. The various cases involving the savings and loan, including the suit against Lexecon, were transferred to the District of Arizona under the MDL statute. Lexecon and the class action plaintiffs reached what they called a "resolution," and the claims against Lexecon were dismissed. Lexecon then sued the law firms in the Northern District of Illinois, alleging that the firms had maliciously brought the claims knowing that they lacked merit.

The law firms asked the Panel to transfer the case to the MDL. The Panel agreed but transferred the case to a different judge in the District of Arizona, because the MDL judge had recused himself from the case. The parties in the MDL (other than in the *Lexecon* suit) reached a settlement, and Lexecon asked the Panel to remand its case against the two law firms to the Northern District of Illinois. The law firms opposed remand and asked the judge in the District of Arizona to transfer the case to himself for trial under section 1404(a). Ultimately, the MDL judge granted the section 1404(a) request. Lexecon unsuccessfully sought mandamus from the Ninth Circuit. The case went to trial in the District of Arizona (with most claims having been previously dismissed). After a judgment for the law firms, Lexecon appealed to the Ninth Circuit, which upheld the self-assignment. The Supreme Court granted certiorari and reversed.

The Supreme Court relied on the language of section 1407(a), which provides that transferred actions "shall" be remanded at the conclusion of pretrial proceedings. As the Court noted, the statute "places an obligation on the Panel to remand no later than the conclusion of pretrial proceedings in the transferee court[.]" *Lexecon*, 523 U.S. at 36–37. Although the Panel had authorized self-transfer by rule, "no exercise in rulemaking can read that obligation out of the statute." *Id.* at 37 (citing section 1407(f), which requires that rules be consistent with the statute). Moreover, the fact that the statute contained a narrow exception authorizing transfer *for trial* of an action under section 4C of the Clayton Act (section 1407(h)) showed that "Congress knew how to distinguish between trial assignments and pretrial proceedings in cases subject to § 1407." 523 U.S. at 38. And the Court found nothing to support the law firms' argument that the legislative history of section 1407 supported self-transfer for trial. 523 U.S. at 39–40. As a result, the Court held that the federal court in Arizona lacked authority under section 1407 to conduct the trial.

Lexecon does not end trials by transferee courts. As noted above, bellwether trials are frequent. In addition, commentators have suggested several ways to avoid the *Lexecon* limitation even at the conclusion of pretrial proceedings. Such techniques, discussed in § 9.2, include the execution of *Lexecon* waivers by all parties and holding the trial in the transferor district (with the MDL judge presiding). And, of course, the MDL judge can try cases that were originally filed in the transferee court, provided that personal jurisdiction and venue exist (or have been waived). In addition, after remand to the transferor court, the transferor judge can transfer the case back to the

MDL judge for trial under 28 U.S.C. § 1404(a). That approach, however, works only if the transferee court has both personal jurisdiction and venue. In short, while *Lexecon* imposes restrictions on the ability of the transferee court to try cases, there are several ways to circumvent the case.

B. REMAND PROCEDURES AND REQUIREMENTS

When remand is appropriate, the cases are remanded to their respective transferor courts. The transferee judge usually recommends remand "by filing a suggestion of remand with the Panel." JPML Rule 10.1(b). However, the Panel can also remand a case based on a party's motion or on its "own initiative by entry of an order to show cause, a conditional remand order or other appropriate order." *Id. See* Manual § 20.133.

When the Panel enters a conditional remand order, a party opposing remand must file an opposition within seven days or that party will be deemed to have acquiesced to remand. JPML Rule 10.2(b) and (c). Within 14 days of filing its notice of opposition, the party opposing remand must file its supporting brief. Failure to do so is deemed a withdrawal of the opposition. JPML Rule 10.2(e).

The JPML rules note that "the Panel is reluctant to order a remand absent the suggestion of the transferee judge." JPML Rule 10.3(a). And, in practice, the absence of a suggestion (or the judge's express refusal to issue one) "creates a difficult burden for the party seeking remand to overcome."

Herr (MDL) § 10:6. By the same token, if the transferee judge *has* suggested remand, the party opposing remand will have a hard time persuading the Panel not to do so. *Id.* Because the MDL judge's view is so important, when a party moves to remand, the JPML rules require the party to state whether it has requested a suggestion of remand from the MDL judge (and, if so, how the judge responded). JPML Rule 10.3(a)(i). That party must also provide the Panel with a copy of the transferee court's final pretrial order, if one has been filed. JPML Rule 10.3(a)(ii).

When the parties receive a remand order from the Clerk of the Panel, they "shall furnish forthwith to the transferee district clerk a stipulation or designation of the contents of the record or part thereof to be remanded." JPML Rule 10.4(a). When the transferee court's clerk receives the remand notice, the clerk shall transmit to the clerk of the transferor district a copy of the docket sheet for each remanded case, a copy of the master docket, the entire file for each case remanded, a copy of the final pretrial order (if any), and the record on remand. JPML Rule 10.4(b). *See* DeGaris at 187. The Manual for Complex Litigation notes the importance of having the transferee judge prepare a final pretrial order that outlines the proceedings and rulings, identifies "issues remaining for discovery and trial, and indicates the nature and expected duration of further pretrial proceedings." Manual § 20.133; *see also* MDL Standards at 93.

Remand is not automatic merely because the parties or transferee judge deem it appropriate. As one authority notes, if cases are not ready for trial, "remand is unlikely." Herr (MDL) § 10:6.

The decision to remand rests solely with the Panel. Conceivably, a party that disagrees with the Panel's approach could seek mandamus, but it is highly unlikely that a federal appellate court would intervene. *See* §§ 5.3, 5.6. And remand is not an all or nothing proposition. The Panel has the authority to remand some cases in an MDL but not others (for example, if only certain cases are ready for trial). Herr (MDL) § 10:15. Regardless of whether the remand is in whole or in part, the Panel does not attach conditions to its order or require the parties to undertake particular actions as conditions for remand. *Id.* § 10:6.

Before remand, the MDL judge might wish to take action to ensure that only cases with plausible claims are sent back. One source suggests the use of *Lone Pine* orders (*see* § 8.3) "at or near the end of the MDL" for the purpose of "weed[ing] out truly meritless cases" and "ensur[ing] that the transferor courts receive only viable cases." MDL Standards at 89. *But see* Burch (Mass Tort Deals) at 118–19 (arguing that *Lone Pine* orders are often used to coerce plaintiffs to settle).

Finally, it should be noted that even after all of the cases are remanded, the MDL may remain open for a period of time for "clean-up," even "long after significant action in it has been completed." MDL

Standards at 93. The Panel decides when to end the MDL. *Id.*

C. LEGAL EFFECT OF A REMAND ORDER

Once the Panel enters a remand order, the transferee court loses jurisdiction over the transferred cases. Manual § 20.133. The transferor court receives the cases with all of the rulings by the transferee court. The rulings of the transferee court are the "law of the case," Herr (MDL) § 10:5; Manual § 20.133, but the transferor court has authority to modify those rulings (in the limited circumstances permitted by law of the case), just as it would have the authority to do so had it entered the orders initially. *See, e.g., In re Ford Motor Co.,* 591 F.3d 406, 411–12 (5th Cir. 2009) (discussed in § 8.1). Nonetheless, "[t]ransferor courts should deviate from rulings of transferee courts only rarely[.]" MDL Standards at 93.

It is not uncommon for the MDL court to rule on expert issues that impact an entire class or a large group of plaintiffs, but not to rule on issues involving individual plaintiffs. As such, if the case is ultimately remanded to the transferor court for trial, it may not be ready for trial because there are case-specific issues to address. *See* Cox & Walker at 3 ("[T]he MDL court may have deferred several case-specific issues to the remand court, such as expert and evidentiary issues that are best addressed by the trial judge."). On remand, the attorneys should be prepared to identify to the transferor court the plaintiff-specific issues that have not been adjudicated.

CHAPTER 16

FEDERAL/STATE COORDINATION AND STATE MINI-MDL PROCEDURES

As noted throughout this text, section 1407 applies only to cases within the federal court system. The same is true for transfers of venue under 28 U.S.C. § 1404(a). Consolidation under Rule 42 is even more restrictive; it is limited to cases pending before the same federal court. Apart from bankruptcy, there is no legal mechanism for formally consolidating related federal and state cases.

This is a serious gap. Many of the leading multiparty cases over the last several decades have involved numerous lawsuits pending in both federal and state courts. Examples of federal MDLs in which there were myriad state court cases include *Vioxx, see* Sherman (Tulane) at 2213–14; *In re Syngenta AG MIR 162 Corn Litigation,* 131 F. Supp. 3d 1177, 1186 (D. Kan. 2015); *In re Chinese-Manufactured Drywall Products Liability Litigation*, 680 F. Supp. 2d 780, 782 (E.D. La. 2010); and *In re Diet Drugs*, 582 F.3d 524, 529 (3d Cir. 2009).

There are several reasons why related cases may be pending in both federal and state courts. First, many plaintiffs' lawyers deliberately select state court over federal court whenever possible, believing that a state venue may be more plaintiff-friendly. Also, some cases may not qualify for diversity jurisdiction. Second, depending on the residence of the parties, the nature of the pleadings, and the particular federal court's attitude regarding removal, some removed cases will be remanded, while others will remain in federal court. Finally, some plaintiffs' lawyers may choose to file suit in federal court (for instance, because they have chosen to assert federal law as well as state law claims).

Control of all of the federal cases—without the ability to coordinate with the overlapping state cases—can make it very difficult for the MDL judge to achieve overall efficiency for all related litigation. When cases are also pending in state courts, it is important for the MDL judge to coordinate with the state judges (or at least with the attorneys who have the state court matters). Coordination is important not only for settlement, but also to achieve efficiencies in discovery and to avoid conflicting legal rulings. This Chapter addresses issues surrounding federal/state coordination.

Although the focus of this book is on federal MDL law and practice, many states have their own MDL procedures. This Chapter examines MDL procedures at the state level. This topic is important not only for those working on cases that are exclusively in state court, but also for those working on a federal MDL that involves related state court cases. If the cases within a particular state can themselves be coordinated before one judge, the process of federal/state coordination can be simplified, because the federal MDL judge will not need to coordinate with as many state court judges. *See* Sherman (Tulane) at 2214 (noting that federal/state coordination in *Vioxx* was enhanced because all of the New Jersey state cases had been consolidated before one state court judge).

§ 16.1 INFORMAL FEDERAL/STATE COORDINATION

Although MDL centralization is limited to cases in federal court, federal and state judges sometimes coordinate their related cases on an informal basis, particularly when the judges are within the same state. Matters for coordination may include discovery, motions practice, coordinated appointment of lead counsel, and scheduling trials and other proceedings. *See* Manual §§ 20.31–20.313 (discussing various types of informal coordination); *see generally* Coordinating Multijurisdiction Litigation at 8–13. Indeed, to facilitate such coordination, the MDL Panel sometimes transfers federal cases to the district where similar state cases are pending. *See* § 4.2.

One commentator suggests anecdotally that the opportunity for federal/state coordination is a "frequently overlooked" benefit of MDL centralization. "Without an MDL proceeding, there is no obvious leader among the federal judges handling federal cases." Herrmann (Litigation) at 46. "Once an MDL proceeding is in place, however, [the MDL judge] will be seen by some state court judges as having weighty authority." *Id.* When a federal MDL exists, "state court judges are more likely" to coordinate with related federal litigation. *Id.*

Coordination is least difficult when common counsel are involved and when the federal and state cases are centered in one state (or relatively few states). MDL coordination with state cases is much more difficult when the state cases are geographically dispersed throughout the country and many lawyers are involved. Manual § 20.311.

A. IDENTIFYING THE UNIVERSE OF CASES

In focusing on federal/state coordination, an important initial step for federal MDL judges is to direct the parties to identify all related cases in various jurisdictions, and to establish early communication networks with the judges and attorneys in the parallel state proceedings. Setting up communication and collaboration networks early in the MDL provides dividends down the road. When state judges are informed about the federal MDL and the possibility of collaboration, informal coordination becomes more likely. Dodge at 342.

B. ESTABLISHING AN INFRASTRUCTURE

In addition to starting federal/state communications soon after the MDL is established, the federal transferee judge often begins by establishing the court's internal framework to handle the cases efficiently. Dodge at 342–43. Looking at the MDL as a whole, the federal and parallel state courts should consider ways to share information to avoid duplicative discovery. Tools like joint scheduling, joint discovery plans, and joint settlement initiatives can help drive down costs and promote efficiency. MDL Standards at 71. By coordinating discovery, the courts can often avoid inconsistent federal and state rulings on discovery disputes and legal issues. *Id.*

In federal MDLs in which there are also related cases in state courts, a federal/state liaison attorney can be appointed. The purpose of a federal/state liaison attorney is to help update the federal MDL court, state judges, and state attorneys on the status of the federal and state cases. MDL Standards at 75. MDL judges can also appoint a magistrate judge to help coordinate with the state court litigation. Alternatively, special masters can be appointed to handle such coordination, although that approach is more costly. Hanks at 46–47; MDL Standards at 75, 78–79 (providing examples). *See* §§ 8.9–8.10 (discussing magistrate judges and special masters). MDL judges can also ask the parties in state cases to contribute to the common-benefit fund in the federal court, although that approach "often creates tension." Gluck at 1704.

C. COORDINATING DISCOVERY, COURT FILINGS, AND COURT PROCEEDINGS

To reduce discovery costs, the federal transferee judge often attempts to coordinate discovery between the federal and state cases. Federal MDL judges can begin this process by creating a joint discovery plan, or, with the parties' agreement, designating one case as the lead case and having its discovery plan act as the plan for the other cases. Manual § 20.14.

The federal MDL judge can also create a joint document depository and have parties share their discovery. Manual § 20:14. Other discovery can be coordinated as well. When the litigants in state or federal court file or cross-file deposition notices, interrogatories, and requests for production, the resulting fruits of discovery can be used in all of the cases in the MDL and the state courts. Allowing other parties to review the discovery prevents duplicative work. *Id.* § 11.423.

Federal and state judges "have jointly presided over hearings on pretrial motions, based on a joint motions schedule, sometimes alternating between state and federal courthouses." Manual § 20.313. Other suitable areas for joint hearings include status conferences and *Daubert* hearings. MDL Standards at 77. *See also* Manual § 20.14.

Coordination can also improve the discovery process. For example, by cross-noticing depositions and allowing all parties to be present either in person or by video conference or telephone, parties can ensure that all of their questions are answered without having to re-depose the witnesses. Manual § 11.423. Coordinated depositions are also suitable when witnesses are called to identify, explain, or authenticate documents. And they are valuable when depositions of high-level corporate officials are sought. This coordination minimizes the likelihood that the same officials will have to be deposed multiple times.

D. FEDERALISM ISSUES

Although federal/state coordination is highly desirable, it can raise federalism concerns. Too much federal court deference to proceedings in state court can delay the administration of the federal MDL. On the other hand, comity concerns can be created if state courts are not treated as equal players. *See* MDL Standards at 74.

E. CASE EXAMPLES

Several examples illustrate how federal MDL judges can effectively coordinate with state courts to manage related litigation.

In *In re Vioxx Products Liability Litigation*, 360 F. Supp. 2d 1352 (J.P.M.L. 2005), discussed in § 9.4, the plaintiffs alleged that the pain medication Vioxx increased the risks of suffering heart attacks and strokes. The litigation was consolidated in the Eastern District of Louisiana.

In the initial transfer order, the Panel centralized 4,000 cases. This number later increased to 20,000 in federal court. There were also 30,000 cases in state court. Sherman (Tulane) at 2213–14. The federal MDL judge had a meeting with representatives of all counsel, state and federal, and set up an administrative framework to handle the cases. This included special masters, hiring a private claims consultant to handle the claims process, and designating six bellwether trials. *Id.* at 2214. From the meetings, the federal MDL judge learned about discovery that had already taken place in the related New Jersey state court litigation, thereby accelerating the timeline for the bellwether trials. The bellwether trials facilitated early settlement discussions, and ultimately led to a $4.85 billion settlement that resolved both the federal and state cases. *Id.* Coordination was made easier because all of the New Jersey state cases were consolidated before a single judge.

Similarly, *In re Syngenta AG MIR 162 Corn Litigation,* 131 F. Supp. 3d 1177 (D. Kan. 2015), involved claims by corn growers and other plaintiffs who suffered damages as a result of China's refusal to accept certain genetically modified corn. The plaintiffs' corn had allegedly become cross-pollinated with genetically modified corn produced by Syngenta. The MDL was consolidated in the District Court of Kansas.

Soon after the MDL was established, the MDL judge issued a lengthy coordination order to establish coordination with various state courts in which related cases had been filed. Coordination Order, *In re Syngenta AG MIR 162 Corn Litig.*, No. 14-md-02591-JWL-JPO (Doc. 1099) (D. Kan. Oct. 21, 2015). The order noted that the federal MDL encompassed more than 300 cases, but that thousands of related state court actions were pending in Minnesota, and some were pending in Louisiana. The order stated that "[t]he MDL Court has and will continue to encourage coordination with courts presiding over Related Actions to coordinate discovery activities and other pretrial activities whenever it is practicable and desired by a given court or courts." *Id.* at 2. The major goals of the coordination were to "minimize undue duplication of discovery and undue burden on courts, parties, and non-parties in responding to discovery requests, save substantial expense by the parties and non-parties, and produce substantial savings in judicial resources." *Id.* The plan involved coordinated discovery, creation of a single document depository, and sharing of discovery (including expert and other depositions). *Id.* at 3–18.

As the plan was implemented, discovery "was coordinated across multiple jurisdictions pursuant to orders issued by [the MDL] Court and courts in Minnesota and Illinois." *In re Syngenta AG MIR 162 Corn Litig.*, 357 F. Supp. 3d 1094, 1100 (D. Kan. 2018). Also, the federal and state courts frequently coordinated on motions. *See id.* at 1100–01 (describing proceedings in state courts). And settlement negotiations encompassed both the federal MDL and state cases. *See id.* at 1101. The result was a $1.51 billion settlement involving Syngenta, a federal nationwide class, and eight statewide class actions. *Id.* at 1100–01.

§ 16.2 STATE MDL STATUTES

There is no state mechanism analogous to MDL that allows for coordination of state cases across state lines. Nonetheless, a number of states have their own MDL procedures that allow for centralization before one judge of cases within a single state. If state cases relating to a federal MDL are heavily concentrated within one state, or a small number of states, a statewide centralization process can significantly enhance the ability of the federal MDL judge to coordinate with related state court litigation.

The state MDLs vary significantly. Some are established by statute, some are by rule, and some are informal. Some are for pretrial purposes only, while others encompass trial as well. In some states, a separate judicial panel (similar to the federal MDL Panel) orders centralization, while in others that is done by the state supreme court or another designated judge. And in many of the states, coordination focuses on common questions of fact or law, not just common questions of fact, as in the federal statute. Herrmann, Ritts & Ray at 40–41.

The discussion below briefly summarizes various types of state MDLs. It is not exhaustive. The focus is on 10 states: California, Colorado, Illinois, Maryland, Massachusetts, New Jersey, New York, Pennsylvania, Texas, and West Virginia.

California. Under California's Code of Civil Procedure, § 404–404.9, when there are related cases in different counties, coordination may be requested by the presiding judge, by any party (with permission of the presiding judge), or by all of the parties. CA Civ. Proc. § 404. The actions must be complex and must qualify under standards listed in section 404.1. Those standards include whether the common question of fact or law is "predominating and significant"; convenience to parties, witnesses, and counsel; relative development of actions and work product of counsel; judicial efficiency; court calendars; disadvantages of duplication and inconsistency in rulings, orders, or judgments; and, likelihood of settlement in the absence of coordination. The request is reviewed by the Chairperson of the Judicial Council, who may assign—or authorize the presiding judge to assign—a judge to consider whether coordination is appropriate, § 404, and if so, which appellate court will have jurisdiction for review. § 404.2. Once an appointed judge decides that coordination of cases is appropriate, the Chairperson of the Judicial Council assigns (or authorizes the presiding judge of a court to assign) a judge to hear and determine the coordinated actions. § 404.3. A pending action (an add-on case) that shares a common question of fact or law with an existing coordinated action can be added after coordination is ordered, using the same § 404.1 criteria. § 404.4. California permits actions to remain coordinated for trial. Herrmann, Ritts & Ray at 41.

Colorado. Colorado's Rules of Civil Procedure (Colo. Rules) establish a Panel on Consolidated Multidistrict Litigation, made up of three to seven judges from different state judicial districts. Colo. Rule 42.1(a)(1). When multiple actions involving a common question of law or fact are pending in different judicial districts, the Panel—on its own initiative, by request of any court, or by request of any party to the actions—may recommend transfer of related actions to a single judge for resolution of any or all of the matters at issue. Colo. Rule 42.1(b). "Upon the determination by the Panel that the actions should be transferred under this rule, the Panel shall certify the actions to the Chief Justice [of the Colorado Supreme Court] and recommend the assignment of a specific judge to hear the actions." Colo. Rule 42.1(h). "If no original proceedings are commenced in the Supreme Court or a show cause order is not issued by the Supreme Court within 21 days after entry of the certification order by the Panel, the Chief Justice shall assign the actions to a judge." Colo. Rule 42.1(i). The criteria are the same as those under California Civ. Proc. § 404. Colo. Rule 42.1(g). For consolidated actions that proceed to jury trial, proper venue is required, which means that the court hearing the consolidated actions may need to remand transferred actions to their original districts for trial, unless venue also lies in the district to which they were transferred. Colo. Rule 42.1(b).

Illinois. The Illinois Supreme Court Rules set out the procedures for consolidating civil actions pending in different judicial circuits that involve one or more common questions of fact or law. Ill. S. Ct. Rule 384(a). The Supreme Court determines, on its own motion or on the motion of any party, whether consolidation of actions for pretrial, trial, or post-trial proceedings would serve the convenience of the parties and witnesses and would promote the just and efficient conduct of the actions. Ill. S. Ct. Rule 384(a). In contrast to the federal MDL statute, the Illinois Rule does not provide for the designation of a specific transferee judge, but only for the designation of a judicial circuit to which the cases may be transferred. Ill. S. Ct. Rule 384(a).

Maryland. Maryland's Rules of Civil Procedure (Md. Rules) permit transfer and consolidation of actions pending in different judicial circuits for pretrial or trial proceedings when they involve a common question of law or fact. Md. Rule 2–327(d)(1). There is no separate panel or judicial body making that determination. Instead, a motion to transfer is made (by a party or on the transferor court's own initiative) to the circuit administrative judge having authority over the transferor court. Md. Rule 2–327(d)(2). The actions may be transferred only to a circuit court where they might have been brought, and where similar actions are pending. Md. Rule 2–327(d)(1). In addition, the transfer must promote the just and efficient conduct of the actions to be consolidated, not unduly inconvenience the parties and witnesses in the actions proposed for transfer, and be accepted by the transferee court. Md. Rule 2–327(d)(3).

Massachusetts. Rule 42 of the Massachusetts Rule of Civil Procedure (Mass. Rules) closely follows Federal Rule of Civil Procedure 42 in that it permits a court to consolidate actions involving a common question of law or fact. Unlike in federal court, however, where consolidation must be within a single district, Massachusetts permits consolidation of actions pending "in the same county or in different counties." Mass. Rule 42(a). A motion to consolidate actions must be filed and decided in the court of the earliest-filed case. Mass. Super. Ct. Rule 31. If consolidation is granted, the cases are heard in the court of the earliest-filed case, and the order of consolidation is also an order of transfer with respect to all related cases filed in other counties. Mass. Super. Ct. Rule 31. However, the judge deciding a motion to consolidate may order, "in the interest of justice or with the consent of all parties," that cases will be heard in the court of a later-filed action, provided that the transferee judge agrees. Mass. Super. Ct. Rule 31. The court hearing the cases has discretion to determine whether the actions will be tried together. Mass. Rule 42.

New Jersey. New Jersey permits consolidation of actions pending in Superior Court involving a common question of law or fact arising out of the same transaction or series of transactions. N.J. Ct. R. 4–38:1(a). The Rule empowers the Assignment Judge of the county "in which the venue is laid in the action first instituted" to hear a motion for consolidation if the actions proposed for inclusion are "not triable in the same county or vicinage." N.J. Ct. R. 4:38–1(a). The motion for consolidation may be on a party's motion, the judge's own initiative, or on certification of the matter to the judge by a judge of the Law or Chancery Division. N.J. Ct. R. 4:38–1(a). The Assignment Judge may apply to the New Jersey Supreme Court "to have the case(s) classified as multicounty litigation, and assigned to a designated judge for centralized management." *Multicounty Litigation Guidelines and Criteria for Designation (Revised),* NJ Directives Dir. 02-19 (Feb. 22, 2019), at 1. Notice of the application for multicounty litigation (MCL) designation is given, and the parties, the state bar, and the public are given an opportunity to object or comment. *Id.* Once the period for objections or comments closes, the application and any objections or comments that were received are presented to "the Supreme Court for its review and determination." *Id.*

Numerous factors are considered in determining whether cases should be consolidated. They include, among others, whether large numbers of claims are involved and associated with a single product, mass disaster, or complex environmental or toxic tort; whether centralization may increase delay or expense, or otherwise prejudice a party; and whether the cases require "specialized expertise and case processing" by the dedicated multicounty judge and staff. *Multicounty Litigation Guidelines and Criteria for Designation (Revised),* NJ Directives Dir. 02-19 (Feb. 22, 2019), at 1–2. If the case is designated as MCL, the New Jersey Supreme Court assigns the case to a judge for centralized management. *Id.* at 1.

New York. Coordination of related actions in New York is managed by a Litigation Coordinating Panel composed of "one justice of the [New York] Supreme Court from each judicial department of the state." N.Y. Ct. R. § 202.69(b)(1). The Panel itself, a justice, administrative judge, or party may apply for coordination of actions. N.Y. Ct. R. § 202.69(b)(2). In determining coordination, the Panel considers a list of factors, including (among others), complexity of actions; whether common questions of fact or law exist, and their importance; risk of delay, increased expense, complication, or other prejudice to a party; risk of duplicative or inconsistent outcomes; convenience; "whether coordinated discovery would be advantageous"; judicial efficiency; manageability; and the pendency of related matters in federal or other state courts. N.Y. Ct. R. § 202.69(b)(3).

If the Panel determines that actions will be coordinated, the order will specify the number of Coordinating Justices and the county or counties in which coordinated cases will proceed. N.Y. Ct. R. § 202.69(b)(4). The selected Coordinating Justice overseeing a coordinated proceeding must "consult" with the judge(s) presiding over related actions pending in federal or other state courts "in an effort to advance the purposes of this section." N.Y. Ct. R. § 202.69(c)(3). The Coordinating Justice may terminate coordination, on his or her own initiative or upon motion by any party, and remand actions to their counties of origin for trial, unless the parties consent to trial before the Coordinating Justice. N.Y. Ct. R. § 202.69(d).

Pennsylvania. Under the Pennsylvania Rules of Civil Procedure (Pa. Rules), when actions pending in different counties involve a common question of law or fact, or arise from the same transaction or occurrence, any party may file a motion for coordination of the actions in the court in which a complaint was first filed. Pa. Rule 213.1(a). That court determines whether to order coordination and an appropriate location for the coordinated proceedings. Pa. Rule 213.1(c). As in other jurisdictions, Pennsylvania sets out factors for the determination, focusing on the predominance and significance of the common questions, convenience and efficiency, avoiding prejudice to parties, as well as "duplicative and inconsistent" outcomes, and the likelihood of settlement if the cases are left uncoordinated. Pa. Rule 213.1(c). The ultimate question is whether coordination is "a fair and efficient method of adjudicating the controversy." Explanatory Comment to Pa. Rule 213.1 (1990).

Texas. In Texas, a Multidistrict Litigation Panel (Texas MDL Panel) appointed by the Texas Supreme Court may oversee pretrial proceedings in civil actions involving one or more common questions of fact filed after September 1, 2003 (or those filed before that date that involve claims for asbestos- or silica-related injuries to the extent permitted under other state law). Tex. R. Jud. Admin. 13.1. A party in a related case, a judge, or the Texas MDL Panel itself may request transfer of related cases to a single court for pretrial proceedings. Tex. R. Jud. Admin. 13.3. The Texas MDL Panel reviews the request, along with any evidence submitted, and may conduct a hearing to determine whether to order the proposed transfer. Tex. R. Jud. Admin. 13.3. If three of the five Panel members find that the cases involve one or more common questions of fact, and that transfer "will be for the convenience of the parties and witnesses and will promote the just and efficient conduct of the related cases," then the Panel may order transfer. Tex. R. Jud. Admin. 13.3(*l*). *See, e.g.*, *In re Volkswagen Clean Diesel Litig.*, 516 S.W.3d 704 (Tex. J.P.M.L. 2016) (Texas MDL pretrial proceeding involving over 60 lawsuits in ten different Texas counties).

West Virginia. In its Trial Court Rules (W. Va. Rules), West Virginia adopted "a process for efficiently managing and resolving mass litigation," including establishment of a Mass Litigation Panel. W.V. Rule 26.01. The Panel, consisting of seven judges appointed by the Chief Justice with the West Virginia Supreme Court's approval (*see* W. Va. Rule 26.02), is charged with, among other things, the central organization and case management of any Mass Litigation referred to it by the Chief Justice. W. Va. Rule 26.05. "Any party, judge, or the Administrative Director of the Courts may seek a referral of actions" to the Panel by filing a motion "in any circuit court in which an action is pending." W. Va. Rule 26.06(a)(1). The request is reviewed by the Chief Justice, who may rule on the motion directly or defer ruling until after directing the Panel to hold a hearing and receiving their findings of fact and a recommendation. W. Va. Rule 26.06(c). The rules define "Mass Litigation" as any two or more actions pending in one or more circuit courts involving common questions of law or fact pertaining to: (1) mass accidents or single catastrophic events; (2) personal injury mass torts involving products; (3) property damage mass torts involving product failure; (4) consumer fraud or warranty actions involving a product defect without actual personal injury or property damage; or (5) actions alleging harm or injury caused to numerous claimants by multiple defendants under nuisance or other property damage causes of action. W. Va. Rule 26.04(a).

CHAPTER 17

REFORM ISSUES

A limited survey of federal and state judges found little enthusiasm for reforming the federal MDL process. Gluck at 1689. The judges surveyed agreed that every case is different and that MDL judges need flexibility to adapt broad rules to the specific cases. *Id.* The *only* area for reform suggested by any of the judges surveyed was the possible establishment of a uniform rule governing attorneys' fees in MDLs. *Id.* Apart from that, the consensus was that the process is working well and that new rules or statutory requirements would undermine the flexibility that has made MDLs so successful. Although the number of judges surveyed (20) was small, the degree of unanimity is striking. And putting aside the survey, there has been no outcry among federal MDL judges urging reform.

For the most part, plaintiffs' attorneys likewise have not urged MDL reform. As with the judges surveyed, plaintiffs' attorneys emphasize the need for flexibility and oppose a "one size fits all" approach to MDL cases. *See, e.g.*, Devine at 2–3 (noting that MDL judges need broad discretion to manage complex litigation).

By contrast, the defense bar—and defense-oriented organizations, such as the U.S. Chamber of Commerce—have been outspoken about their desire for significant reform. The defense bar's efforts have led to proposed legislation focusing on federal MDLs, *see* H.R. 985, 115th Cong. § 105 (2017). (H.R. 985

passed the House in 2017 but made no headway in the Senate.) Many in the plaintiffs' bar view the defense bar's criticisms of MDL to be hyperbolic and unfounded.

In addition, the Federal Rules Civil Advisory Committee has designated a subcommittee (the Rules Subcommittee) to study possible rule changes for federal MDLs. *See* Advisory Committee April 2019 Agenda Book at 207–74. Again, most of the proposals submitted to the Committee have come from the defense bar.

In addition to the reform efforts noted above, scholars have suggested a host of reform proposals. One of the earliest efforts was by the American Law Institute, which focused in the 1990s on more formal ways to coordinate federal and state cases. And, in recent years, scholars have focused on several areas of MDL practice that they believe are in need of reform.

An exhaustive discussion of all of the reform proposals that have been offered is beyond the scope of this text. The sections below discuss some of the more highly publicized proposals, without taking a position on the merits of any particular proposal. The proposals discussed include:

- expanded interlocutory appeal;
- more stringent proof requirements;
- requiring consent for bellwether trials;

- specifying that master complaints be subject to the same pleading requirements as individual complaints;
- requiring disclosure of third-party funders;
- strengthening the requirements for selection of MDL leadership appointments;
- adding provisions (by rule or statute) enabling MDL judges to oversee settlements and attorneys' fees in non-class situations; and
- increasing coordination of federal/state cases by encompassing state cases within federal MDLs.

It is not clear (at the time this text went to press) whether any of these proposals will make headway. As noted, MDL judges are not urging reform, and no one can doubt that the MDL process has led to the resolution of many thousands of cases that otherwise would have clogged the federal courts. Thus, it is likely that Congress and the Rules Subcommittee will proceed with caution. Although some focused reforms might be adopted, fundamental changes to the MDL process are unlikely.

§ 17.1 EXPANDED INTERLOCUTORY REVIEW

Perhaps the most prominent reform proposal is for enhanced interlocutory review. As explained (§ 14.1), many important MDL decisions, such as rulings on *Daubert* motions and denials of dispositive motions, are interlocutory and, in general, are not immediately appealable. The existing exceptions to the final judgment rule are narrow and difficult to satisfy. Several approaches have been offered for expanding interlocutory appellate review in MDLs.

One approach appears in H.R. 985, 115th Cong. § 105 (2017), which would add a new subsection to section 1407:

> (1) IN GENERAL. The Court of Appeals having jurisdiction over the transferee district shall permit an appeal to be taken from any order issued in the conduct of coordinated or consolidated pretrial proceedings conducted pursuant to [§ 1407(b)], provided that the order is applicable to one or more civil actions seeking redress for personal injury and that an immediate appeal from the order may materially advance the ultimate termination of one or more civil actions in the proceedings.

Id.

There are several notable features of this proposal. First, it provides for mandatory review if the criteria are met (unlike, for example, Rule 23(f), which allows appellate review of a decision granting or denying class certification at the discretion of the appellate court). And, unlike 28 U.S.C. § 1292(b), certification of the issue for appeal by the district judge is not required. Second, the requirement that the appeal "materially advance" the litigation is not onerous because the appeal must only materially advance "the ultimate termination of one or more civil actions or proceedings," without necessarily impacting a substantial number of cases. Third, the proposed amendment is limited to "actions seeking redress for personal injury," reflecting the defense bar's concern that the need for appellate guidance is greatest in mass tort personal injury cases (which make up the majority of individual cases in MDLs, *see* § 1.4).

A somewhat different approach has been urged by Lawyers for Civil Justice (LCJ), a coalition of defense trial lawyer organizations, law firms, and corporations. LCJ's proposal is as follows:

> A court of appeals shall permit an appeal from an order granting or denying a motion under Rule 12(b)(2) or Rule 56 in the course of coordinated or consolidated pretrial proceedings conducted pursuant to 28 U.S.C. § 1407(b), provided that the outcome of such appeals may be dispositive of claims in [50] or more actions in the coordinated or consolidated pretrial proceedings. An appeal of an order granting or denying a motion under Rule 56 shall encompass any rulings on expert evidentiary challenges on which the Rule 56 motion was based.

LCJ Proposals at 6.

Unlike H.R. 985, the LCJ proposal is not limited to personal injury actions, but it would require an impact on 50 or more claims (as opposed to H.R. 985, which requires an impact on only a single claim). The grounds for interlocutory review are limited to rulings on summary judgment motions and motions to dismiss for lack of personal jurisdiction. The summary judgment interlocutory appeal, however, can encompass rulings on expert evidentiary challenges, to the extent that the summary judgment motion was based in part on purported deficiencies in the opposing party's experts. If the criteria of the proposed statute are met, the right to appeal shall exist and is not discretionary (unlike, for example, Rule 23(f)).

Still another variation (proposed by a scholar) would authorize an appeal as of right in an MDL when "(1) the order . . . raise[s] an issue of law; (2) there [is] no controlling law on point, or the district court . . . elected not to follow it; and (3) appellate review [is] potentially dispositive of a significant number of the cases consolidated in the MDL proceeding." Pollis at 1685. Like the LCJ proposal, and unlike H.R. 985, this proposal is not limited to personal injury actions. Unlike the LCJ proposal, this proposal is not limited to rulings on motions under Rule 12(b)(2) or Rule 56. And while the LCJ proposal specifies a precise number of cases that, at a minimum, must be impacted, this proposal refers more vaguely to an impact on a "significant number" of cases. Pollis at 1685.

Proponents of these proposals argue that under the current system, numerous important rulings are never reviewed on appeal, and defendants are pressured to settle rather than risk proceeding to a potentially adverse final judgment with no assurance of success on appeal. As the House Report accompanying H.R. 985 states, "Given the high stakes of these cases, and the likelihood of a coerced settlement based on incorrect legal rulings, interlocutory review is critical." H.R. Rep. No. 115-25, at 36 (2017). LCJ asserts that existing appellate devices are deficient. It argues that the approach of 28 U.S.C. § 1292(b)—requiring certification for appeal by the district court—is flawed because "[s]ome parties are reluctant to seek certification for interlocutory review even when there are good reasons for it," and because "some judges are reluctant to grant such review because they view it as needless delay of cases that might otherwise get resolved." LCJ Proposals at 5. Moreover, LCJ maintains that mandamus "is an imperfect mechanism for the purpose of seeking review of a key decision." *Id.*

Critics of these proposals to expand appellate review argue that it would lead to harmful consequences for appellate courts. As the dissenting statement in the House Report accompanying H.R. 985 notes, the proposed legislation "would strain already-limited judicial resources"; "foster extensive litigation" to interpret "the bill's numerous new and vaguely-worded standards"; and "substantially increase the burdens on appellate courts possibly by as much as five-fold[.]" *Id.* at 61. Another critic argues that such a statute or rule would "strip[ ] [MDL judges] of [their] critical discretion over such appeals[.]" Devine at 3.

§ 17.2 MORE STRINGENT PROOF REQUIREMENTS

One of the chief complaints emphasized in various reform proposals (albeit without empirical studies) is that "[m]any claims filed in MDL proceedings are bogus: there is no apparent evidence of injury or exposure to the alleged risk." H.R. Rep. No. 115-25, at 33 (2017). A similar concern was expressed by an MDL judge overseeing a product liability case, who stated that "MDL consolidation for products liability actions [has] the unintended consequence of producing more new case filings of marginal merit[,] . . . many of which would not have been filed otherwise." *In re Mentor Corp. Obtape Transobturator Sling Prods. Liab. Litig.*, MDL No. 2004, 2016 WL 4705807, at *2 (M.D. Ga. Sept. 7, 2016). Various proposals have been offered to address this perceived problem.

H.R. 985, § 105(i), offers an approach directed specifically at personal injury actions. Under that proposal, a new subsection would be added to section 1407:

> In any coordinated or consolidated pretrial proceedings conducted pursuant to [§ 1407(b)], counsel for a plaintiff asserting a claim seeking redress for personal injury whose civil action is assigned to or directly filed in the proceedings shall make a submission sufficient to demonstrate that there is evidentiary support (including but not limited to medical records) for the factual contentions in plaintiff's complaint regarding the alleged injury, the exposure to the risk that allegedly caused the injury, and the alleged cause of the injury. The submission must be made within the first 45 days after the civil action is transferred to or directly filed in the

> proceedings. That deadline shall not be extended. Within 90 days after the submission deadline, the judge or judges to whom the action is assigned shall enter an order determining whether the submission is sufficient and shall dismiss the action without prejudice if the submission is found to be insufficient. If a plaintiff in an action dismissed without prejudice fails to tender a sufficient submission within the following 30 days, the action shall be dismissed with prejudice.

Id.

This proposal, which is limited to personal injury actions, requires evidentiary proof to support a plaintiff's claims of injury, exposure, and causation. It imposes strict timelines. If the judge finds that the submission is insufficient, the suit must be dismissed without prejudice (which will become a dismissal with prejudice if the plaintiff does not submit sufficient evidence within 30 days following the ruling).

LCJ addresses the same issue, again with a focus on personal injury cases, but its proposal calls for a rule change rather than a statutory change. Thus, LCJ's proposal would amend Federal Rule of Civil Procedure 26 as follows:

> Within sixty (60) days of the filing of a civil action in, or the removal or transfer of any civil action to, a multidistrict proceeding under 28 U.S.C. § 1407 in which a plaintiff alleges

personal injury, plaintiff in each such action shall make an initial disclosure which:

(i) identifies with particularity any product, service, or exposure at issue in the action, and provides documents or electronically stored information evidencing same; and

(ii) identifies with particularity the specific injury at issue in the action, including the date of the injury, and provides documents or electronically stored information evidencing same. For civil actions filed in the transferee district prior to the establishment of a multidistrict proceeding under 28 U.S.C. § 1407, the initial disclosure shall be made within sixty (60) days of the Order of the Judicial Panel on Multidistrict Litigation establishing such proceeding.

LCJ Proposals at 4.

Like H.R. 985, the LCJ proposal is focused solely on MDLs relating to personal injuries. The proposed disclosures would be required in every personal injury MDL. The proposal (like H.R. 985) provides no avenue for seeking to extend the time limit to provide such information.

The House Report accompanying H.R. 985 states that "[w]hen a mass tort MDL proceeding is created, a helter-skelter 'gold rush' ensues." H.R. Rep. No. 115-25, at 33 (2017). According to the Report, "[o]pportunistic lawyers launch advertising campaigns that result in the rapid filing of poorly investigated—and often frivolous or fraudulent—

claims that never would have been filed." *Id.* The House proposal is designed to remedy "the lack of screening of these mass tort claims." *Id.*

LCJ similarly argues that the Federal Rules "are failing to provide sufficient procedures for early vetting, and the *ad hoc* use of mechanisms such as fact sheets and *Lone Pine* orders varies wildly and is inherently inconsistent with the fundamental idea of the [Federal Rules of Civil Procedure] that procedures should be uniform, clear and accessible." LCJ Proposals at 3. The LCJ further contends that MDL dockets are being "overloaded with meritless claims" that "distort perceptions of the value and complexity of MDL cases." *Id.* Finally, the disclosures are required so that defendants can "understand the claims made against them." *Id.*

Critics maintain that the defense bar offers a distorted view of MDL practice. They argue, moreover, that mandatory fact statements early in the case "place[ ] a significant burden on plaintiffs to prove their allegations to a considerable degree at the beginning of their case, denying them the ability to further develop their claims through the discovery process." H.R. Rep. No. 115-25 (dissenting views), at 60. Critics also argue that many MDL judges already require fact sheets when they think it helpful. *Id. See, e.g., In re Nat'l Prescription Opiate Litig.*, No. 1:17-md-02804-DAP (Doc. 638) (N.D. Ohio June 19, 2018) (fact sheet implementation order). And critics contend that a mandatory approach "den[ies] courts the necessary flexibility to adapt case management orders to specific circumstances[.]" H.R. Rep. No. 115-25, at 60 n.39 (citing letter by Professor Burch).

§ 17.3 BELLWETHER TRIALS

H.R. 985 and LCJ also offer proposals to address bellwether trials. According to LCJ, bellwether trials are used even when they are not representative, and "parties often feel unduly pressured to participate" in them. LCJ Proposals at 6. According to LCJ, bellwether trials "often appear to be used for both the expense and the *in terrorem* effect of large jury verdicts to spur global settlement discussions," as opposed to being a source for "generating useful information for the parties." *Id.* LCJ further argues that "plaintiffs will often voluntarily dismiss proposed bellwethers that might prove adverse to them, thus skewing any sample towards greater recoveries than average." *Id.* In addition, LCJ maintains that, to avoid *Lexecon* concerns, MDL judges "are trying cases [that were] filed in the court's jurisdiction, exacerbating the non-representativeness problem." *Id.* at 7. And, according to LCJ, a plaintiffs' verdict "is more likely to be interpreted as proof of the merits," while a defense verdict "is seen as a reason that more trials are needed." *Id.*

The report accompanying H.R. 985 makes similar points. It notes that while the statute authorizes MDL judges to conduct only pretrial proceedings, some judges "pressure defendants to agree to . . . pseudo-trials that supposedly test a claim's suitability for settlement—in order to pressure a settlement in the case." H.R. Rep. No. 115-25, at 35. The report argues that "those trials are not fair tests of the plaintiffs' claims because they consist of claims hand-picked by plaintiffs' attorneys that do not fairly represent the claims of all the plaintiffs in the MDL proceedings." *Id.*

To address these concerns, LCJ proposes an amendment to Rule 23 (Rule 23.3) for MDLs. The proposed rule amendment provides that:

> In any coordinated or consolidated pretrial proceedings conducted pursuant to 28 U.S. Code § 1407, the judge or judges to whom actions are assigned by the Judicial Panel on Multidistrict Litigation shall not conduct a trial in any action in those consolidated or coordinated proceedings unless all parties to that action consent.

Id. The proposed language in H.R. No. 985, § 105(j), is identical to LCJ's language, with minor stylistic changes. Under these proposals, the MDL judge could not conduct a bellwether trial—even of a case that was filed in the transferee court—without the explicit consent of all parties.

Critics of these proposals argue that adopting a statutory or rule amendment would mean no bellwether trials at all. As the dissenting report to H.R. 985 states, "[t]he requirement that all parties consent to trial means that it is unlikely that any such cases would go to trial, meaning further cost and delay for plaintiffs." H.R. No. 115-25, at 60. Critics of the proposals claim that the defense bar paints a distorted picture of bellwether trials. According to the critics, the courts and parties have given careful consideration to selecting representative cases, and bellwether trials in fact shed light on the strengths and weaknesses of the claims, serving as a catalyst for settlement. These critics argue that bellwether trials should be encouraged, not reduced or eliminated. Moreover, the defense bar's argument that plaintiffs are the ones who are manipulating bellwether trials has been vigorously disputed. As one commentator argues, "defendants . . . selectively settle the best cases before they ever go before a bellwether jury," thus enabling defendants to "manipulate and distort the information that results from this process[.]" Sekula at 860, 863. Critics also dispute the defense bar's assertion that defendants are somehow uniquely disadvantaged by bellwether trials. *Cf.* Bradt & Rave II at 22 ("Because they care about the bottom line across all of the cases against them, not the outcome of any individual case, repeat-player defendants can rationally take gambles on individual cases that are calculated to maximize gain over the whole series of cases.")

§ 17.4 MASTER COMPLAINTS

LCJ notes that in MDLs, it is common for "a 'master complaint' to function as the pleading that guides the proceedings (particularly discovery)[.]" LCJ Proposals at 11. According to LCJ, many courts "have refused to decide motions to dismiss consolidated or 'master' complaints." LCJ Proposals at 11. Moreover, LCJ claims that plaintiffs' attorneys in MDLs "have often used master complaints as parking lots for claims, saving a space for a named individual without providing even the minimal information—such as product bought or harm encountered—required by Rule 8." *Id.* LCJ's proposed solution is to amend Federal Rule of Civil Procedure 7 to specify that master complaints in MDLs are among the pleadings that are allowed, subjecting such complaints to the pleading requirements of Rules 8, 9, 11, and 12, and allowing defendants to challenge them by motion.

Critics of the LCJ's proposal argue that its concerns are unsubstantiated, and the remedy it proposes is unnecessary. According to these critics, MDL judges routinely allow defendants to file dispositive motions in response to master complaints, and cases holding to the contrary are outliers. *See, e.g.*, *In re Zimmer Nexgen Knee Implant Prods. Liab. Litig.*, MDL No. 2272, 2012 WL 3582708, at *1 (N.D. Ill. Aug. 16, 2012) (denying defendants' motion to dismiss master complaint in knee implant product liability MDL); *In re FEMA Trailer Formaldehyde Prods. Liab. Litig.*, MDL No. 07-1873, 2008 WL 5217594, at *1, *20 (E.D. La. Dec. 12, 2008) (granting in part and denying in part motions to dismiss master complaint involving breach-of-warranty claims for heightened formaldehyde levels in government-supplied trailers); *but see In re Nuvaring Prods. Liab. Litig.*, No. 4:08MD1964, 2009 WL 2425391, at *2 (E.D. Mo. Aug. 6, 2009) (refusing to allow motion to dismiss a master complaint). Indeed, as the Rules Subcommittee noted in 2018, if master complaints "are pleadings in the Rule 7 sense, they are presumably subject to Rule 12(b) motions to dismiss and Rule 12(f) motions to strike." Advisory

Committee April 2018 Agenda Book at 149. Critics of the LCJ proposal argue that, because master complaints are clearly pleadings, a rule change is unnecessary.

§ 17.5 DISCLOSURE OF THIRD-PARTY LITIGATION FUNDERS

Third-party funding (*see* § 7.2) is not unique to MDL practice. LCJ asserts, however, that it raises particularly serious concerns in the context of MDL (and other aggregate litigation). According to LCJ, "the existence of third-party litigation funding correlates strongly with inventories of junk cases, because funds are used for mass media recruitment without sufficient due diligence into the merits of the claims." LCJ Proposals at 8. LCJ also argues that "[p]arties . . . need to understand third-party litigation funding agreements because they can affect the efficient administration of mass settlements." *Id.* LCJ's solution is mandatory disclosure of third-party funders (not just in MDLs but in all civil cases). Parties would be required to disclose:

> any agreement under which any person, other than an attorney permitted to charge a contingent fee representing a party, has a right to receive compensation that is contingent on, and sourced from, any proceeds of the civil action, by settlement, judgment or otherwise.

Id. at 9. This approach, according to LCJ, "allows the parties in the litigation to identify the real parties interest, which is important in developing both litigation and settlement strategies." *Id.* at 8.

One response to LCJ's proposal is that a number of courts already require disclosure of third-party funders (some by local rule). *See* Tighe at 1 (study revealed that, as of November 2017, about half of all federal circuit courts and a quarter of all federal district courts required the disclosure of the identity of litigation funders for recusal purposes). This trend may demonstrate that rule reform is unnecessary. On the other hand, it may support the wisdom of codifying mandatory disclosure nationwide.

§ 17.6 CHANGES TO THE LEADERSHIP SELECTION PROCESS

In recent years, several criticisms have been leveled against the MDL committee structure system. Two principal ones are that: (1) the repeat player aspect of the appointment process undermines the interests of plaintiffs; and (2) leadership attorneys do not reflect a broad ethnic and gender makeup but instead tend to consist primarily of white males. Those criticisms (and reform suggestions) are summarized in subsections A and B. Subsection C provides an analysis of those criticisms.

A. REPEAT PLAYERS CRITICISM

One critic of the leadership appointment process argues that the process favors repeat players, who may be more concerned about pleasing the court and maximizing attorneys' fees than in adequately representing all of the plaintiffs in the MDL. Burch (NYU) at 95–101. One argument is that "the systematic lack of checks and balances" in MDLs "may benefit everyone but the plaintiffs." Burch (Mass Tort Deals) at 2. As a result, plaintiffs' attorneys recover "hefty common-benefit fees," corporations "resolve litigation with what may be relatively minimal expense," and third-party funders benefit, but in the process plaintiffs' lawyers "sell [their clients] out[.]" *Id.* The study offers data from 72 product liability and sales practices MDLs pending as of May 14, 2013, *id.* at 95, revealing that 50 attorneys "claimed 30% of all leadership roles." *Id.* at 95–96.

This critic argues that judges should defer appointing permanent lead attorneys "until they have sufficient information on conflicts of interest." Burch (NYU) at 138. And when permanent lead attorneys are selected, the selection should be based on the "clients' different interests," likely "creat[ing] a cognitively diverse committee." *Id.* at 122. Third-party funders can be used to ensure that attorneys are not selected because of their resources to fund large-scale MDL litigation. *Id.* at 123. This critic also argues that lead attorneys' fees should be based on quantum-meruit assessments, and not set "through the backdoor of settlement." *Id.* at 128, 138; Burch (Mass Tort Deals) at 189–200. Finally, this critic argues that lead attorneys should be encouraged "to entertain input from non-lead attorneys on critical motions and strategy." Burch (NYU) at 138. This critic does not contend that courts should invariably avoid appointing repeat players, but rather that strict checks and balances are necessary.

B. LACK OF DIVERSITY CRITICISM

A number of commentators assert that the "repeat player" phenomenon has the effect of stifling diversity among MDL leadership. Numerous articles have focused on that concern. *See, e.g.*, Bronstad (Gender Diversity) at 1 (reporting that the percentage of MDL leadership appointments going to female attorneys has increased in recent years, but still remained below 30 percent as of 2018). Those raising concerns about the lack of diversity among MDL leadership look to MDL judges to pay more attention to diversity in appointing leadership attorneys.

C. ANALYSIS OF REPEAT PLAYER AND LACK OF DIVERSITY CRITICISMS

No one disputes that a relatively small number of prominent attorneys frequently appear in leadership positions in MDL cases. Why that happens is complicated. MDL judges interviewed for a survey indicated that their goal is simply to select the best lawyers who can work well together, and who have the expertise needed to manage and oversee the extremely complex MDL proceedings. Gluck at 1701–02. These MDL judges contend that the MDL leadership chosen in various cases is not, as some claim, a "good old boy's club," Alvaré, at 4, but instead is a group of lawyers selected based on merit to handle difficult and important positions. Gluck at 1701–02; *see also* § 7.1. As one MDL judge said, it is no different than a patient trying to find the most skilled physician to perform brain surgery. *Id.* at 1702.

A number of commentators agree that the repeat-player phenomenon provides benefits to plaintiffs. As two commentators note, "[r]epeat-player plaintiffs' lawyers—those who specialize in MDL and aggregate litigation and appear frequently in leadership positions on the plaintiffs' side—can bring experience to rival defendants and their lawyers." Bradt & Rave II at 23. These commentators cite a number of studies confirming that "lawyers who specialize in a particular practice area obtain superior results for their clients than non-specialists." *Id.* They also note that repeat players have "access to capital" and the ability to rely on "economies of scale." *Id.* at 24. And they can use—to the plaintiffs' advantage—"relationships with institutional incumbents," such as judges, defense counsel, and other plaintiffs' lawyers. *Id.*

With respect to concerns about lack of diversity among MDL leadership, there is broad recognition that MDL leadership should be—and can be—more diverse and more representative of plaintiffs as a whole. And while there are no serious legislative or rule proposals for codifying appointment standards, one source urges that, as a matter of "best practices," MDL judges should ensure that leadership appointments "will responsibly and fairly represent all plaintiffs, keeping in mind the benefits of diversity of experience, skills, and backgrounds." MDL Standards at 34–35 (Best Practice 3C).

While much remains to be done to ensure that MDL leadership is more diverse, *see* Alvaré, at 3–10, tangible progress has been made on a number of fronts.

First, those selected to serve as MDL judges are themselves becoming more diverse, just as the federal bench has become more diverse as a result of Obama-era appointments. In 2018, for the first time, white males comprised fewer than half of all MDL judges appointed. Bronstad (Record) at 1. As one commentator has noted, "the current [Panel] appears to be making a concerted effort to expand the gender and racial composition of the pool of MDL transferee judges." Coleman at 651. A recent study supports that assertion. M.S. Williams at 1285 (citing empirical evidence that "the percentage of non-white and female transferee judges chosen by the Panel has increased over time"). By increasing the diversity of judges handling MDLs, there is reason for optimism that leadership appointments will likewise become more diverse.

Second, there is evidence that the number of women on MDL leadership committees has been increasing. In 2018, 35 percent of MDL leadership positions went to female attorneys (versus 21 percent in 2017 and even lower numbers in prior years). Bronstad (Record) at 1. The trend is encouraging.

The situation for minority attorneys is not as promising. For 2018, only six of 190 leadership positions were given to minority lawyers, male or female. Bronstad (Record) at 1.

Third, a number of MDL judges are focusing heavily on increasing diversity in MDL leadership appointments. For instance, in *In re Ethicon, Inc., Power Morcellator Products Liability Litigation*, MDL No. 2652, 2015 WL 7303527 (D. Kan. Nov. 19, 2015), an MDL judge appointed "the first female-majority plaintiffs' steering committee." Bronstad (First) at 1. In the *Volkswagen "Clean Diesel"* MDL, a nationally recognized female lawyer was appointed as sole lead plaintiffs' attorney in one of the most high-profile MDLs in history. *In re Volkswagen "Clean Diesel" Mktg., Sales Practices, & Prods. Liab. Litig.*, No. 3:15-md-02672-CRB (Doc. 1084) (N.D. Cal. Jan. 21, 2016).

Fourth, in addition to focusing on ethnic and gender diversity, a number of MDL judges are focusing on ensuring that leadership appointments reflect a broad array of viewpoints and interests. For instance, in the *Opiate Litigation* MDL, the MDL judge initially rejected a proposed leadership slate consisting entirely of attorneys representing government entities. The MDL judge ordered that attorneys representing hospitals and third-party payors be added to the proposed leadership slate, and they were. Only then did the MDL judge approve the appointments. *In re Nat'l Prescription Opiate Litig.*, No. 1:17-md-02804-DAP (Doc. 37) (N.D. Ohio Jan. 4, 2018).

Similarly, in the *Ashley Madison Data Breach* MDL, the court modified a proposed leadership structure, adding several attorneys to "ensure that the [diverse] interests of all plaintiffs [are] fully represented." *In re Ashley Madison Consumer Data Sec. Breach Litig.*, No. 4:15-md-02669-JAR (Doc. 87), at 1 (E.D. Mo. Feb. 5, 2016). The court "reviewed the various requests for appointment submitted by plaintiffs' counsel" and concluded that the "interim class counsel structure" proposed by one group of counsel, "with some modification, best meets the needs of all Plaintiffs." *Id.*

And in *In re Genetically Modified Rice Litigation*, the MDL judge augmented the proposed leadership to ensure that interests of various types of plaintiffs were represented. No. 4:06-md-01811-CDP (Doc. 182) (E.D. Mo. Apr. 18, 2007) (appointing leadership counsel). The MDL involved suits by thousands of rice farmers and others in the rice business claiming that defendant's genetically modified rice tainted the U.S. supply of rice. After hearing argument from counsel about various proposed leadership structures, the judge determined that one proposal, "with some modification, best [met] the needs of all plaintiffs." *Id.* at 1. The judge modified the proposal by adding two lawyers to the Executive Committee: one who represented "a large number of Mississippi farmers who are expected to be plaintiffs or who are likely to be members of any class that may be certified," and one who represented "a number of farmer and non-farmer plaintiffs who would prefer to have their cases litigated individually and in state court." *Id.* at 2. These modifications, the judge noted, would "ensure that the interests of similarly situated plaintiffs or potential plaintiffs will also be considered." *Id.*

Fifth, although some argue that recoveries by plaintiffs are inadequate in a number of MDL cases, *see* subsection A, a counterargument is that some recent MDL settlements have involved substantial compensation to plaintiffs—in some instances in amounts equivalent to the full value of their injuries. For instance, in *In re Volkswagen "Clean Diesel" Marketing, Sales Practices, & Products Liability Litigation,* the Ninth Circuit observed that, under the class settlement, "[m]ost class members' compensation—buybacks, fixes, or lease terminations *plus* some cash—is as much as, perhaps more than, they could expect to receive in a successful suit litigated to judgment." 895 F.3d 597, 610 (9th Cir. 2018).

Those who criticize recoveries in MDL cases might argue in response that the troublesome cases are not the classwide settlements governed by Rule 23. Rather, the cases of concern are the MDLs involving only non-class claims, particularly drug and medical device cases. Here too, however, those disagreeing with that position would cite non-class MDL settlements in which plaintiffs received substantial compensation, such as *Vioxx*. *See* Issacharoff at 219 ("[M]ost . . . criticisms [of the *Vioxx* settlement] have faded in light of the overwhelmingly positive response by plaintiffs (who collectively had not recovered a cent prior to the settlement) to the terms of the offer.").

Some academics have criticized specific non-class MDL settlements as deficient, but MDL plaintiffs' attorneys have disputed a number of those contentions. For instance, one article describes claims by a scholar that the settlements in the *Propulsid* MDL, No. 00-MD-1355 (E.D. La.), were deficient and that "only a handful of plaintiffs actually recovered[.]" Frankel at 1. However, according to one of the lead plaintiffs' attorneys in the case, the scholar's criticism "does not tell the whole story" in that "[Johnson & Johnson] spent 'many millions' to settle thousands of cases in state court before the MDL settlement." *Id.*

Finally, in criticizing MDL, it is relevant to ask whether there is a better alternative. One commentator, in assessing non-class MDL settlements, argues that "the realit[y] of large-scale products liability litigation . . . is that these suits are very likely to end in some kind of aggregate settlement even if they are remanded." Bone at 123. Given this reality, he argues that "judicial supervision in an MDL has a better chance of producing a good settlement" than a process lacking such supervision. *Id.* at 126.

§ 17.7 EXPANDING AUTHORITY OF MDL JUDGES TO REVIEW AND APPROVE NON-CLASS SETTLEMENTS AND ATTORNEYS' FEES

As noted (§§ 10.2, 11.2), MDL judges have no formal authority to review non-class settlements or awards of attorneys' fees in non-class MDLs. Some MDL judges have found authority to do so by relying on the quasi-class action concept, but many have not taken that approach (*see* § 10.2). As a result, many

MDL settlements and attorneys' fee payments in MDLs lack the supervision or approval of the MDL judge.

Some commentators have argued that MDL judges should be given explicit authority to review non-class settlements in an MDL. One commentator urges that the MDL statute be amended to "[p]rovid[e] a statutory basis for judicial supervision and control of non-class MDL proceedings," and that doing so "would eliminate the need for recourse to fictional doctrines such as the quasi-class action, or the need to rely on inherent judicial power." Mullenix (Litigation) at 166. That commentator suggests an amendment to "make clear that non-class aggregate settlements are . . . subject to Rule 23 requirements." *Id. Accord, e.g.*, Saack at 879 ("[T]he MDL statute should be updated to require courts to consider the adequacy (conflicts of interest) of court appointed attorneys, and the fairness of any global settlements reached."); *see also* Burch (Mass Tort Deals) at 132 (questioning validity of reliance on inherent judicial authority).

There are at least two possible counterarguments. First, there is no "one size fits all" solution for non-class MDLs, and the more flexible quasi-class action approach is better suited to the MDL process. Second, many of the requirements governing class actions, such as numerosity and notice, are not readily transferable to non-class MDLs.

Additionally, some commentators argue that MDL judges do not need formal authority to review settlements, but instead can efficiently use their positions to offer nonbinding assessments of proposed settlements. *See* Bradt & Rave I at 1306–07 ("In overseeing and managing [the MDL] process, the judge should also develop a base of information that she can ultimately use to assess the settlement and send a signal to claimants about its fairness.").

§ 17.8 STATUTORY CHANGES TO INCREASE FEDERAL/STATE COORDINATION OF CASES

As noted (*see* § 1.1), under current law, only federal cases can be transferred to an MDL judge. The judge must rely on informal mechanisms to coordinate with state courts that have overlapping cases. This is a serious limitation. The purpose of MDL is to create efficiencies in discovery and rulings on motions, as well as to provide a vehicle for one judge to facilitate a broad settlement. Those goals are much more difficult if many of the relevant cases are before numerous state court judges.

Various proposals have been offered to bring state cases within the umbrella of federal MDLs. Perhaps the most elaborate and widely publicized proposal was made by the American Law Institute's *Complex Litigation Project* (1994). That proposal would allow removal from state court to federal court of a case not qualifying for diversity jurisdiction when: (1) the case arises from the same transaction or occurrence (or series of transactions or occurrences) as a case in federal court; and (2) the cases share a common factual or legal question. A proposed "Complex Litigation Panel" (modeled after the Judicial Panel on Multidistrict Litigation) would decide whether to allow removal, and also whether the removed case should be consolidated with the case or cases already pending in federal court.

Under the ALI proposal, the Complex Litigation Panel would have exclusive jurisdiction to remove transactionally related cases. The parties would not be permitted to remove the cases unilaterally. Removal by the Complex Litigation Panel could be initiated on the motion of any party to a state proceeding or on certification by a state judge before whom one of the actions was pending. The Panel would then decide whether removal was appropriate. The ALI proposal requires only minimal diversity—*i.e.*, any two adverse parties that are citizens of different states—making removal relatively easy to accomplish. A similar proposal was put forward by a federal judge and his co-authors in 1995. *See* Schwarzer, Hirsch & Sussman at 1552–64.

The ALI and other similar proposals generated substantial controversy, which included federalism concerns and concerns about the workload impacts on the federal courts. As one commentator noted, a "concern, when complex-litigation reforms would consolidate state-law cases in federal court, is with the intrusion on federalist values, not to mention any net addition to federal court caseloads." Rowe at 359.

Subsequent developments may well have pushed many of the cases that the 1994 ALI proposal was addressing into federal court in any event. *See* Bradt & Rave III at 1256–58, 1294–1300 (observing that the Class Action Fairness Act of 2005 and (more recently) the Supreme Court's decision in *Bristol-Myers Squibb v. Superior Court*, 137 S. Ct. 1773 (2017), have moved many mass tort cases from state to federal courts).

The ALI proposal and others like it have not received serious attention in Congress. Likewise, there is no indication that judges, attorneys, and scholars with expertise in MDLs are in favor of adopting a statute to add state cases to federal MDL proceedings. Neither the House legislation (H.R. 985) nor the LCJ proposals focus on this issue. And the materials published by the Rules Subcommittee give no indication that the Subcommittee is looking into this issue.

* * *

The bottom line is that most of the proposals summarized in this Chapter have little chance of being adopted, and there are forceful arguments against many of them. But the various proposals are intriguing and worth discussing, in part because the discussion is ultimately about the benefits and drawbacks of the MDL process itself.

APPENDIX A

28 U.S. CODE § 1407

(a) When civil actions involving one or more common questions of fact are pending in different districts, such actions may be transferred to any district for coordinated or consolidated pretrial proceedings. Such transfers shall be made by the judicial panel on multidistrict litigation authorized by this section upon its determination that transfers for such proceedings will be for the convenience of parties and witnesses and will promote the just and efficient conduct of such actions. Each action so transferred shall be remanded by the panel at or before the conclusion of such pretrial proceedings to the district from which it was transferred unless it shall have been previously terminated: Provided, however, That the panel may separate any claim, cross-claim, counter-claim, or third-party claim and remand any of such claims before the remainder of the action is remanded.

(b) Such coordinated or consolidated pretrial proceedings shall be conducted by a judge or judges to whom such actions are assigned by the judicial panel on multidistrict litigation. For this purpose, upon request of the panel, a circuit judge or a district judge may be designated and assigned temporarily for service in the transferee district by the Chief Justice of the United States or the chief judge of the circuit, as may be required, in accordance with the provisions of chapter 13 of this title. With the consent of the transferee district court, such actions may be assigned by the panel to a judge or judges of such district. The judge or judges to whom such actions are assigned, the members of the judicial panel on multidistrict litigation, and other circuit and district judges designated when needed by the panel may exercise the powers of a district judge in any district for the purpose of conducting pretrial depositions in such coordinated or consolidated pretrial proceedings.

(c) Proceedings for the transfer of an action under this section may be initiated by—

(i) the judicial panel on multidistrict litigation upon its own initiative, or

(ii) motion filed with the panel by a party in any action in which transfer for coordinated or consolidated pretrial proceedings under this section may be appropriate. A copy of such motion shall be filed in the district court in which the moving party's action is pending.

The panel shall give notice to the parties in all actions in which transfers for coordinated or consolidated pretrial proceedings are contemplated, and such notice shall specify the time and place of any hearing to determine whether such transfer shall be made. Orders of the panel to set a hearing and other orders of the panel issued prior to the order either directing or denying transfer shall be filed in the office of the clerk of the district court in which a transfer hearing is to be or has been held. The panel's order of transfer shall be based upon a record of such hearing at which material evidence may be offered by any party to an action pending in any district that would be affected by the proceedings under this section, and shall be supported by findings of fact and conclusions of law based upon such record. Orders of transfer and such other orders as the panel may make thereafter shall be filed in the office of the clerk of the district court of the transferee district and shall be effective when thus filed. The clerk of the transferee district court shall forthwith transmit a certified copy of the panel's order to transfer to the clerk of the district court from which the action is being transferred. An order denying transfer shall be filed in each district wherein there is a case pending in which the motion for transfer has been made.

(d) The judicial panel on multidistrict litigation shall consist of seven circuit and district judges designated from time to time by the Chief Justice of the United States, no two of whom shall be from the same circuit. The concurrence of four members shall be necessary to any action by the panel.

(e) No proceedings for review of any order of the panel may be permitted except by extraordinary writ pursuant to the provisions of title 28, section 1651, United States Code. Petitions for an extraordinary writ to review an order of the panel to set a transfer hearing and other orders of the panel issued prior to the order either directing or denying transfer shall be filed only in the court of appeals having jurisdiction over the district in which a hearing is to be or has been held. Petitions for an extraordinary writ to review an order to transfer or orders subsequent to transfer shall be filed only in the court of appeals having jurisdiction over the transferee district. There shall be no appeal or review of an order of the panel denying a motion to transfer for consolidated or coordinated proceedings.

(f) The panel may prescribe rules for the conduct of its business not inconsistent with Acts of Congress and the Federal Rules of Civil Procedure.

(g) Nothing in this section shall apply to any action in which the United States is a complainant arising under the antitrust laws. "Antitrust laws" as used herein include those acts referred to in the Act of October 15, 1914, as amended (38 Stat. 730; 15 U.S.C. 12), and also include the Act of June 19, 1936 (49 Stat. 1526; 15 U.S.C. 13, 13a, and 13b) and the Act of September 26, 1914, as added March 21, 1938 (52 Stat. 116, 117; 15 U.S.C. 56); but shall not include section 4A of the Act of October 15, 1914, as added July 7, 1955 (69 Stat. 282; 15 U.S.C. 15a).

(h) Notwithstanding the provisions of section 1404 or subsection (f) of this section, the judicial panel on multidistrict litigation may consolidate and transfer with or without the consent of the parties, for both pretrial purposes and for trial, any action brought under section 4C of the Clayton Act.

(Added Pub. L. 90–296, § 1, Apr. 29, 1968, 82 Stat. 109; amended Pub. L. 94–435, title III, § 303, Sept. 30, 1976, 90 Stat. 1396.)

APPENDIX B

RULES OF PROCEDURE OF THE JUDICIAL PANEL ON MULTIDISTRICT LITIGATION

(Effective October 4, 2010; amended July 6, 2011; minor housekeeping amendment, October 4, 2016)

I. RULES FOR MULTIDISTRICT LITIGATION UNDER 28 U.S.C. § 1407

The United States Judicial Panel on Multidistrict Litigation promulgates these Rules pursuant to its authority under 28 U.S.C. § 1407(f).

RULE 1.1. DEFINITIONS

(a) "Panel" means the members of the United States Judicial Panel on Multidistrict Litigation appointed by the Chief Justice of the United States pursuant to 28 U.S.C. § 1407.

(b) "Chair" means the Chair of the Panel appointed by the Chief Justice of the United States pursuant to Section 1407, or the member of the Panel properly designated to act as Chair.

(c) "Clerk of the Panel" means the official that the Panel appoints to that position. The Clerk of the Panel shall perform such duties that the Panel or the Panel Executive delegates.

(d) "Electronic Case Filing (ECF)" refers to the Panel's automated system that receives and stores documents filed in electronic form. All attorneys filing pleadings with the Panel must do so using ECF. All pro se individuals are non-ECF users, unless the Panel orders otherwise.

(e) "MDL" means a multidistrict litigation docket which the Panel is either considering or has created by transferring cases to a transferee district for coordinated or consolidated pretrial proceedings pursuant to Section 1407.

(f) "Panel Executive" means the official appointed to act as the Panel's Chief Executive and Legal Officer. The Panel Executive may appoint, with the approval of the Panel, necessary deputies, clerical assistants and other employees to perform or assist in the performance of the duties of the Panel Executive. The Panel Executive, with the approval of the Panel, may make such delegations of authority as are necessary for the Panel's efficient operation.

(g) "Pleadings" means all papers, motions, responses, or replies of any kind filed with the Panel, including exhibits attached thereto, as well as all orders and notices that the Panel issues.

(h) "Tag-along action" refers to a civil action pending in a district court which involves common questions of fact with either (1) actions on a pending motion to transfer to create an MDL or (2) actions previously transferred to an existing MDL, and which the Panel would consider transferring under Section 1407.

(i) "Transferee district" is the federal district court to which the Panel transfers an action pursuant to Section 1407, for inclusion in an MDL.

(j) "Transferor district" is the federal district court where an action was pending prior to its transfer pursuant to Section 1407, for inclusion in an MDL, and where the Panel may remand that action at or before the conclusion of pretrial proceedings.

RULE 2.1. RULES AND PRACTICE

(a) Customary Practice. The Panel's customary practice shall govern, unless otherwise fixed by statute or these Rules.

(b) Failure to Comply with Rules. When a pleading does not comply with these Rules, the Clerk of the Panel may advise counsel of the deficiencies and set a date for full compliance. If counsel does not fully comply within the established time, the Clerk of the Panel shall file the non-complying pleading, but the Chair may thereafter order it stricken.

(c) Admission to Practice before the Panel. Every member in good standing of the Bar of any district court of the United States is entitled to practice before the Panel, provided, however, that he or she has established and maintains a CM/ECF account with any United States federal court. Any attorney of record in any action transferred under Section 1407 may continue to represent his or her client in any district court of the United States to which such action is transferred. Parties are not required to obtain local counsel.

(d) Pendency of Motion or Conditional Order. The pendency of a motion, order to show cause, conditional transfer order or conditional remand order before the Panel pursuant to 28 U.S.C. § 1407 does not affect or suspend orders and pretrial proceedings in any pending federal district court action and does not limit the pretrial jurisdiction of that court. An order to transfer or remand pursuant to 28 U.S.C. § 1407 shall be effective only upon its filing with the clerk of the transferee district court.

(e) Reassignment. If for any reason the transferee judge is unable to continue those responsibilities, the Panel shall make the reassignment of a new transferee judge.

RULE 3.1. ELECTRONIC RECORDS AND FILES; COPY FEES

(a) Electronic Record. Effective October 4, 2010, the official Panel record shall be the electronic file maintained on the Panel's servers. This record includes, but is not limited to, Panel pleadings, documents filed in paper and then scanned and made part of the electronic record, and Panel orders and notices filed. The official record also includes any documents or exhibits that may be impractical to scan. These documents and exhibits shall be kept in the Panel offices.

(b) Maintaining Records. Records and files generated prior to October 4, 2010, may be (i) maintained at the Panel offices, (ii) temporarily or permanently removed to such places at such times as the Clerk of the Panel or the Chair shall direct, or (iii) transferred whenever appropriate to the Federal Records Center.

(c) Fees. The Clerk of the Panel may charge fees for duplicating records and files, as prescribed by the Judicial Conference of the United States.

RULE 3.2. ECF USERS: FILING REQUIREMENTS

(a) Form of Pleadings. This Rule applies to pleadings that ECF users file with the Panel.

(i) Each pleading shall bear the heading "Before the United States Judicial Panel on Multidistrict Litigation," the identification "MDL No.___" and the descriptive title designated by the Panel. If the Panel has not yet designated a title, counsel shall use an appropriate description.

(ii) The final page of each pleading shall contain the name, address, telephone number, fax number and email address of the attorney or party designated to receive service of pleadings in the case, and the name of each party represented.

(iii) Each brief submitted with a motion and any response to it shall not exceed 20 pages, exclusive of exhibits. Each reply shall not exceed 10 pages and shall address arguments raised in the response(s). Absent exceptional circumstances and those set forth in Rule 6.1(d), the Panel will not grant motions to exceed page limits.

(iv) Each pleading shall be typed in size 12 point font (for both text and footnotes), double spaced (text only), in a letter size document (8 1/2 × 11 inch) with sequentially numbered pages.

(v) Each exhibit shall be separately numbered and clearly identified.

(vi) Proposed Panel orders shall not be submitted.

(b) Place of Filing. Counsel shall sign and verify all pleadings electronically in accordance with these Rules and the Panel's Administrative Policies and Procedures for Electronic Case Filing found at www.jpml.uscourts.gov. A pleading filed electronically constitutes a written document for the purpose of these Rules and the Federal Rules of Civil Procedure and is deemed the electronically signed original thereof. All pleadings, except by pro se litigants, shall conform with this Rule beginning on October 4, 2010.

(i) Pleadings shall not be transmitted directly to any Panel member.

(c) Attorney Registration. Only attorneys identified, or to be identified, pursuant to Rule 4.1, shall file pleadings. Each of these attorneys must register as a Panel CM/ECF user through www.jpml.uscourts.gov. Registration/possession of a CM/ECF account with any United States federal court shall be deemed consent to receive electronic service of all Panel orders and notices as well as electronic service of pleadings from other parties before the Panel.

(d) Courtesy Copy of Specified Pleadings. Counsel shall serve the Clerk of the Panel, for delivery within 1 business day of filing, with a courtesy paper copy of any of the following pleadings: (i) a motion to transfer and its supporting brief; (ii) a response to a show cause order; (iii) a motion to vacate a conditional transfer order or a conditional remand order; and (iv) any response, reply, supplemental information or interested party response related to the pleadings listed in (i), (ii) and (iii). No courtesy copies of any other pleadings are required. Courtesy copies of pleadings totaling 10 pages or less (including any attachments) may be faxed to the Panel. The courtesy copy shall include all exhibits, shall be clearly marked "Courtesy Copy-Do Not File," shall contain the CM/ECF pleading number (if known), and shall be mailed or delivered to:

Clerk of the Panel
United States Judicial Panel
on Multidistrict Litigation
Thurgood Marshall Federal Judiciary Building
One Columbus Circle, NE,
Room G-255, North Lobby
Washington, DC 20544-0005

(e) Privacy Protections. The privacy protections contained in Rule 5.2 of the Federal Rules of Civil Procedure shall apply to all Panel filings.

RULE 3.3. NON-ECF USERS: FILING REQUIREMENTS

(a) Definition of Non-ECF Users. Non-ECF users are all pro se individuals, unless the Panel orders otherwise. This Rule shall apply to all motions, responses and replies that non-ECF users file with the Panel.

(b) Form of Pleadings. Unless otherwise set forth in this Rule, the provisions of Rule 3.2 shall apply to non-ECF users.

(i) Each pleading shall be flat and unfolded; plainly written or typed in size 12 point font (for both text and footnotes), double spaced (text only), and printed single-sided on letter size (8 1/2 × 11 inch) white paper with sequentially numbered pages; and fastened at the top-left corner without side binding or front or back covers.

(ii) Each exhibit shall be separately numbered and clearly identified. Any exhibits exceeding a cumulative total of 50 pages shall be bound separately.

(c) Place of Filing. File an original and one copy of all pleadings with the Clerk of the Panel by mailing or delivering to:

Clerk of the Panel
United States Judicial Panel
on Multidistrict Litigation
Thurgood Marshall Federal Judiciary Building
One Columbus Circle, NE,
Room G-255, North Lobby
Washington, DC 20544-0005

(i) Pleadings not exceeding a total of 10 pages, including exhibits, may be faxed to the Panel office.

(ii) The Clerk of the Panel shall endorse the date for filing on all pleadings submitted for filing.

RULE 4.1. SERVICE OF PLEADINGS

(a) Proof of Service. The Panel's notice of electronic filing shall constitute service of pleadings. Registration/possession by counsel of a CM/ECF account with any United States federal court shall be deemed consent to receive electronic service of all pleadings. All pleadings shall contain a proof of service on all other parties in all involved actions. The proof of service shall indicate the name and manner of service. If a party is not represented by counsel, the proof of service shall indicate the name of the party and the party's last known address. The proof of service shall indicate why any person named as a party in a constituent complaint was not served with the Section 1407 pleading.

(b) Service Upon Transferor Court. The proof of service pertaining to motions for a transfer or remand pursuant to 28 U.S.C. § 1407 shall certify that counsel has transmitted a copy of the motion for filing to the clerk of each district court where an affected action is pending.

(c) Notice of Appearance. Within 14 days after the issuance of a (i) notice of filing of a motion to initiate transfer under Rule 6.2, (ii) notice of filed opposition to a CTO under Rule 7.1, (iii) a show cause order under Rules 8.1, (iv) notice of filed opposition to a CRO under Rule 10.2, or (v) notice of filing of a motion to remand under Rule 10.3, each party or designated attorney as required hereinafter shall file a Notice of Appearance notifying the Clerk of the Panel of the name, address and email address of the attorney designated to file and receive service of all pleadings. Each party shall designate only one attorney. Any party not represented by counsel shall be served by mailing such pleadings to the party's last known address. Except in extraordinary circumstances, the Panel will not grant requests for an extension of time to file the Notice of Appearance.

(d) Liaison Counsel. If the transferee district court appoints liaison counsel, this Rule shall be satisfied by serving each party in each affected action and all liaison counsel. Liaison counsel shall receive copies of all Panel orders concerning their particular litigation and shall be responsible for distribution to the parties for whom he or she serves as liaison counsel.

RULE 5.1. CORPORATE DISCLOSURE STATEMENT

(a) Requirements. A nongovernmental corporate party must file a disclosure statement that: (1) identifies any parent corporation and any publicly held corporation owning 10 percent or more of its stock; or (2) states that there is no such corporation.

(b) Deadline. A party shall file the corporate disclosure statement within 14 days after issuance of a notice of the filing of a motion to transfer or remand, an order to show cause, or a motion to vacate a conditional transfer order or a conditional remand order.

(c) Updating. Each party must update its corporate disclosure statement to reflect any change in the information therein (i) until the matter before the Panel is decided, and (ii) within 14 days after issuance of a notice of the filing of any subsequent motion to transfer or remand, order to show cause, or motion to vacate a conditional transfer order or a conditional remand order in that docket.

RULE 6.1. MOTION PRACTICE

(a) Application. This Rule governs all motions requesting Panel action generally. More specific provisions may apply to motions to transfer (Rule 6.2), miscellaneous motions (Rule 6.3), conditional transfer orders (Rule 7.1), show cause orders (Rule 8.1), conditional remand orders (Rule 10.2) and motions to remand (Rule 10.3).

(b) Form of Motions. All motions shall briefly describe the action or relief sought and shall include:

- (i) a brief which concisely states the background of the litigation and movant's factual and legal contentions;
- (ii) a numbered schedule providing
  - (A) the complete name of each action involved, listing the full name of each party included as such on the district court's docket sheet, not shortened by the use of references such as "et al." or "etc.";
  - (B) the district court and division where each action is pending;
  - (C) the civil action number of each action; and

(D) the name of the judge assigned each action, if known;

(iii) a proof of service providing

(A) a service list listing the full name of each party included on the district court's docket sheet and the complaint, including opt-in plaintiffs not listed on the docket sheet; and

(B) in actions where there are 25 or more plaintiffs listed on the docket sheet, list the first named plaintiff with the reference "et al." if all the plaintiffs are represented by the same attorney(s);

(iv) a copy of all complaints and docket sheets for all actions listed on the Schedule; and

(v) exhibits, if any, identified by number or letter and a descriptive title.

(c) Responses and Joinders. Any other party may file a response within 21 days after filing of a motion. Failure to respond to a motion shall be treated as that party's acquiescence to it. A joinder in a motion shall not add any action to that motion.

(d) Replies. The movant may file a reply within 7 days after the lapse of the time period for filing a response. Where a movant is replying to more than one response in opposition, the movant may file a consolidated reply with a limit of 20 pages.

(e) Alteration of Time Periods. The Clerk of the Panel has the discretion to shorten or enlarge the time periods set forth in this Rule as necessary.

(f) Notification of Developments. Counsel shall promptly notify the Clerk of the Panel of any development that would partially or completely moot any Panel matter.

RULE 6.2. MOTIONS TO TRANSFER FOR COORDINATED OR CONSOLIDATED PRETRIAL PROCEEDINGS

(a) Initiation of Transfer. A party to an action may initiate proceedings to transfer under Section 1407 by filing a motion in accordance with these Rules. A copy of the motion shall be filed in each district court where the motion affects a pending action.

(b) Notice of Filing of Motion to Transfer. Upon receipt of a motion, the Clerk of the Panel shall issue a "Notice of Filing of Motion to Transfer" to the service list recipients. The Notice shall contain the following: the filing date of the motion, caption, MDL docket number, briefing schedule and pertinent Panel policies. After a motion is filed, the Clerk of the Panel shall consider any other pleading to be a response unless the pleading adds an action. The Clerk of the Panel may designate such a pleading as a motion, and distribute a briefing schedule applicable to all or some of the parties, as appropriate.

(c) Notice of Appearance. Within 14 days of issuance of a "Notice of the Filing of a Motion to Transfer," each party or designated attorney shall file a Notice of Appearance in accordance with Rule 4.1(c).

(d) Notice of Potential Tag-along Actions. Any party or counsel in a new group of actions under consideration for transfer under Section 1407 shall promptly notify the Clerk of the Panel of any potential tag-along actions in which that party is also named or in which that counsel appears.

(e) Interested Party Responses. Any party or counsel in one or more potential tag-along actions as well as amicus curiae may file a response to a pending motion to transfer. Such a pleading shall be deemed an Interested Party Response.

(f) Amendment to a Motion. Before amending a motion to transfer, a party shall first contact the Clerk of the Panel to ascertain whether such amendment is feasible and permissible considering the Panel's hearing schedule. Any such amendment shall be entitled "Amendment to Motion for Transfer," and shall clearly and specifically identify and describe the nature of the amendment.

(i) Where the amended motion includes new civil actions, the amending party shall file a "Schedule of Additional Actions" and a revised Proof of Service.

(ii) The Proof of Service shall state (A) that all new counsel have been served with a copy of the amendment and all previously-filed motion papers, and (B) that all counsel previously served with the original motion have been served with a copy of the amendment.

(iii) The Clerk of the Panel may designate the amendment with a different denomination (*e.g.*, a notice of potential tag-along action(s)) and treatment.

(g) Oral Argument. The Panel shall schedule oral arguments as needed and as set forth in Rule 11.1.

RULE 6.3. MOTIONS FOR MISCELLANEOUS RELIEF

(a) Definition. Motions for miscellaneous relief include, but are not limited to, requests for extensions of time, exemption from ECF requirements, page limit extensions, or expedited consideration of any motion.

(b) Panel Action. The Panel, through the Clerk, may act upon any motion for miscellaneous relief, at any time, without waiting for a response. A motion for extension of time to file a pleading or perform an act under these Rules must state specifically the revised date sought and must be filed before the deadline for filing the pleading or performing the act. Any party aggrieved by the Clerk of the Panel's action may file objections for consideration. Absent exceptional circumstances, the Panel will not grant any extensions of time to file a notice of opposition to either a conditional transfer order or a conditional remand order.

RULE 7.1. CONDITIONAL TRANSFER ORDERS (CTO) FOR TAG-ALONG ACTIONS

(a) Notice of Potential Tag-along Actions. Any party or counsel in actions previously transferred under Section 1407 shall promptly notify the Clerk of the Panel of any potential tag-along actions in which that party is also named or in which that counsel appears. The Panel has several options: (i) filing a CTO under Rule 7.1, (ii) filing a show cause order under Rule 8.1, or (iii) declining to act (Rule 7.1(b)(i)).

(b) Initiation of CTO. Upon learning of the pendency of a potential tag-along action, the Clerk of the Panel may enter a conditional order transferring that action to the previously designated transferee district court for the reasons expressed in the Panel's previous opinions and orders. The Clerk of the Panel shall serve this order on each party to the litigation but shall not send the order to the clerk of the transferee district court until 7 days after its entry.

(i) If the Clerk of the Panel determines that a potential tag-along action is not appropriate for inclusion in an MDL proceeding and does not enter a CTO, an involved party may move for its transfer pursuant to Rule 6.1.

(c) Notice of Opposition to CTO. Any party opposing the transfer shall file a notice of opposition with the Clerk of the Panel within the 7-day period. In such event, the Clerk of the Panel shall not transmit the transfer order to the clerk of the transferee district court, but shall notify the parties of the briefing schedule.

(d) Failure to Respond. Failure to respond to a CTO shall be treated as that party's acquiescence to it.

(e) Notice of Appearance. Within 14 days after the issuance of a "Notice of Filed Opposition" to a CTO, each opposing party or designated attorney shall file a Notice of Appearance in accordance with Rule 4.1(c).

(f) Motion to Vacate CTO. Within 14 days of the filing of its notice of opposition, the party opposing transfer shall file a motion to vacate the CTO and brief in support thereof. The Clerk of the Panel shall set the motion for the next appropriate hearing session. Failure to file and serve a motion and brief shall be treated as withdrawal of the opposition, and the Clerk of the Panel shall forthwith transmit the order to the clerk of the transferee district court.

(g) Notification of Developments. Parties to an action subject to a CTO shall notify the Clerk of the Panel if that action is no longer pending in its transferor district court.

(h) Effective Date of CTO. CTOs are effective when filed with the clerk of the transferee district court.

RULE 7.2. MISCELLANEOUS PROVISIONS CONCERNING TAG-ALONG ACTIONS

(a) Potential Tag-alongs in Transferee Court. Potential tag-along actions filed in the transferee district do not require Panel action. A party should request assignment of such actions to the Section

1407 transferee judge in accordance with applicable local rules.

(b) Failure to Serve. Failure to serve one or more of the defendants in a potential tag-along action with the complaint and summons as required by Rule 4 of the Federal Rules of Civil Procedure does not preclude transfer of such action under Section 1407. Such failure, however, may constitute grounds for denying the proposed transfer where prejudice can be shown. The failure of the Clerk of the Panel to serve a CTO on all plaintiffs or defendants or their counsel may constitute grounds for the Clerk to reinstate the CTO or for the aggrieved party to seek § 1407(c) remand.

RULE 8.1. SHOW CAUSE ORDERS

(a) Entry of Show Cause Order. When transfer of multidistrict litigation is being considered on the initiative of the Panel pursuant to 28 U.S.C. § 1407(c)(i), the Clerk of the Panel may enter an order directing the parties to show cause why a certain civil action or actions should not be transferred for coordinated or consolidated pretrial proceedings. Any party shall also promptly notify the Clerk of the Panel whenever they learn of any other federal district court actions which are similar to those which the show cause order encompasses.

(b) Notice of Appearance. Within 14 days of the issuance of an order to show cause, each party or designated attorney shall file a Notice of Appearance in accordance with Rule 4.1(c).

(c) Responses. Unless otherwise provided by order, any party may file a response within 21 days of the filing of the show cause order. Failure to respond to a show cause order shall be treated as that party's acquiescence to the Panel action.

(d) Replies. Within 7 days after the lapse of the time period for filing a response, any party may file a reply.

(e) Notification of Developments. Counsel shall promptly notify the Clerk of the Panel of any development that would partially or completely moot any matter subject to a show cause order.

RULE 9.1. TRANSFER OF FILES; NOTIFICATION REQUIREMENTS

(a) Notice to Transferee Court Clerk. The Clerk of the Panel, via a notice of electronic filing, will notify the clerk of the transferee district whenever a Panel transfer order should be filed in the transferee district court. Upon receipt of an electronically certified copy of a Panel transfer order from the clerk of the transferee district, the clerk of the transferor district shall transmit the record of each transferred action to the transferee district and then, unless Rule 9.1(b) applies, close the transferred action in the transferor district.

(b) Retention of Claims. If the transfer order provides for the separation and simultaneous remand of any claim, cross-claim, counterclaim, or third-party claim, the clerk of the transferor district shall retain jurisdiction over any such claim and shall not close the action.

(c) Notice to Clerk of Panel. The clerk of the transferee district shall promptly provide the Clerk of the Panel with the civil action numbers assigned to all transferred actions and the identity of liaison counsel, if or when designated. The clerk of the transferee district shall also promptly notify the Clerk of the Panel of any dispositive ruling that terminates a transferred action.

RULE 10.1. TERMINATION AND REMAND

(a) Termination. Where the transferee district court terminates an action by valid order, including but not limited to summary judgment, judgment of dismissal and judgment upon stipulation, the transferee district court clerk shall transmit a copy of that order to the Clerk of the Panel. The terminated action shall not be remanded to the transferor court and the transferee court shall retain the original files and records unless the transferee judge or the Panel directs otherwise.

(b) Initiation of Remand. Typically, the transferee judge recommends remand of an action, or a part of it, to the transferor court at any time by filing a suggestion of remand with the Panel. However, the Panel may remand an action or any separable claim, cross-claim, counterclaim or third-party claim within it, upon

(i) the transferee court's suggestion of remand,

(ii) the Panel's own initiative by entry of an order to show cause, a conditional remand order or other appropriate order, or

(iii) motion of any party.

RULE 10.2. CONDITIONAL REMAND ORDERS (CRO)

(a) Entering a CRO. Upon the suggestion of the transferee judge or the Panel's own initiative, the Clerk of the Panel shall enter a conditional order remanding the action or actions to the transferor district court. The Clerk of the Panel shall serve this order on each party to the litigation but shall not send the order to the clerk of the transferee district court for 7 days from the entry thereof.

(i) The Panel may, on its own initiative, also enter an order that the parties show cause why a matter should not be remanded. Rule 8.1 applies to responses and replies with respect to such a show cause order.

(b) Notice of Opposition. Any party opposing the CRO shall file a notice of opposition with the Clerk of the Panel within the 7-day period. In such event, the Clerk of the Panel shall not transmit the remand order to the clerk of the transferee district court and shall notify the parties of the briefing schedule.

(c) Failure to Respond. Failure to respond to a CRO shall be treated as that party's acquiescence to it.

(d) Notice of Appearance. Within 14 days after the issuance of a "Notice of Filed Opposition" to a CRO, each opposing party or designated attorney shall file a Notice of Appearance in accordance with Rule 4.1(c).

(e) Motion to Vacate CRO. Within 14 days of the filing of its notice of opposition, the party opposing remand shall file a motion to vacate the CRO and brief in support thereof. The Clerk of the Panel shall set the motion for the next appropriate Panel hearing session. Failure to file and serve a motion and brief shall be treated as a withdrawal of the opposition and the Clerk of the Panel shall forthwith transmit the order to the clerk of the transferee district court.

(f) Effective Date of CRO. CROs are not effective until filed with the clerk of the transferee district court.

RULE 10.3. MOTION TO REMAND

(a) Requirements of the Motion. If the Clerk of the Panel does not enter a CRO, a party may file a motion to remand to the transferor court pursuant to these Rules. Because the Panel is reluctant to order a remand absent the suggestion of the transferee judge, the motion must include:

(i) An affidavit reciting whether the movant has requested a suggestion of remand and the judge's response, whether the parties have completed common discovery and other pretrial proceedings, and whether the parties have complied with all transferee court orders.

(ii) A copy of the transferee district court's final pretrial order, if entered.

(b) Filing Copy of Motion. Counsel shall file a copy of the motion to remand in the affected transferee district court.

(c) Notice of Appearance. Within 14 days of the issuance of a "Notice of Filing" of a motion to remand, each party or designated attorney shall file a Notice of Appearance in accordance with Rule 4.1(c).

RULE 10.4. TRANSFER OF FILES ON REMAND

(a) Designating the Record. Upon receipt of an order to remand from the Clerk of the Panel, the parties shall furnish forthwith to the transferee district clerk a stipulation or designation of the contents of the record or part thereof to be remanded.

(b) Transfer of Files. Upon receipt of an order to remand from the Clerk of the Panel, the transferee district shall transmit to the clerk of the transferor district the following concerning each remanded action:

(i) a copy of the individual docket sheet for each action remanded;

(ii) a copy of the master docket sheet, if applicable;

(iii) the entire file for each action remanded, as originally received from the transferor district and augmented as set out in this Rule;

(iv) a copy of the final pretrial order, if applicable; and

(v) a "record on remand" as designated by the parties in accordance with 10.4(a).

RULE 11.1. HEARING SESSIONS AND ORAL ARGUMENT

(a) Schedule. The Panel shall schedule sessions for oral argument and consideration of other matters as desirable or necessary. The Chair shall determine the time, place and agenda for each hearing session. The Clerk of the Panel shall give appropriate notice to counsel for all parties. The Panel may continue its consideration of any scheduled matters.

(b) Oral Argument Statement. Any party affected by a motion may file a separate statement setting forth reasons why oral argument should, or need not, be heard. Such statements shall be captioned "Reasons Why Oral Argument Should [Need Not] Be Heard" and shall be limited to 2 pages.

(i) The parties affected by a motion to transfer may agree to waive oral argument. The Panel will take this into consideration in determining the need for oral argument.

(c) Hearing Session. The Panel shall not consider transfer or remand of any action pending in a federal district court when any party timely opposes such transfer or remand without first holding a hearing session for the presentation of oral argument. The Panel may dispense with oral argument if it determines that:

(i) the dispositive issue(s) have been authoritatively decided; or

(ii) the facts and legal arguments are adequately presented and oral argument would not significantly aid the decisional process.

Unless otherwise ordered, the Panel shall consider all other matters, such as a motion for reconsideration, upon the basis of the pleadings.

(d) Notification of Oral Argument. The Panel shall promptly notify counsel of those matters in which oral argument is scheduled, as well as those matters that the Panel will consider on the pleadings. The Clerk of the Panel shall require counsel to file and serve notice of their intent to either make or waive oral argument. Failure to do so shall be deemed a waiver of oral argument. If counsel does not attend oral argument, the matter shall not be rescheduled and that party's position shall be treated as submitted for decision on the basis of the pleadings filed.

(i) Absent Panel approval and for good cause shown, only those parties to actions who have filed a motion or written response to a motion or order shall be permitted to present oral argument.

(ii) The Panel will not receive oral testimony except upon notice, motion and an order expressly providing for it.

(e) Duty to Confer. Counsel in an action set for oral argument shall confer separately prior to that argument for the purpose of organizing their arguments and selecting representatives to present all views without duplication. Oral argument is a means for counsel to emphasize the key points of their arguments, and to update the Panel on any events since the conclusion of briefing.

(f) Time Limit for Oral Argument. Barring exceptional circumstances, the Panel shall allot a maximum of 20 minutes for oral argument in each matter. The time shall be divided among those with varying viewpoints. Counsel for the moving party or parties shall generally be heard first.

RULES 12–15: [RESERVED]

II. RULES FOR MULTICIRCUIT PETITIONS FOR REVIEW

UNDER 28 U.S.C. § 2112(A)(3)

OMITTED

APPENDIX C

CASE STUDY APPENDIX

An MDL case that has achieved wide publicity is the *Volkswagen "Clean Diesel"* litigation. This litigation started with hundreds of lawsuits against Volkswagen (VW) throughout the United States for the fraudulent sale and marketing of approximately 500,000 diesel vehicles (years 2009–2015). VW allegedly installed defeat devices in those vehicles, which enabled the vehicles to pass emissions tests, even though the vehicles were polluting at up to 40 times the legal limit. The cases were transferred by the MDL Panel to the Northern District of California. Ultimately, the parties reached classwide settlements that were approved by the MDL judge. Numerous orders were issued during the course of the MDL, first by the MDL panel (consolidating the cases for pretrial purposes), and then by the MDL judge. The following is a list of the key orders from the docket, the issues that they address, and where to find them online.

Because (as in many MDLs), the VW settlements were also class action settlements, the court issued the typical orders under Rule 23(e) (*e.g.*, approving the content of class notice and a multimedia notice campaign), appointed and required periodic reports from a settlement administrator, and approved attorneys' fees and costs under Rule 23(h).

Selection of the Transferee Court. In the *VW* case, the MDL Panel determined that consolidation for pre-trial purposes was appropriate and designated the district court and judge. *In re Volkswagen "Clean Diesel" Mktg., Sales Practices, and Prods. Liab. Litig.*, 148 F. Supp. 3d 1367 (J.P.M.L. 2015) (appointing Judge Charles Breyer of the Northern District of California).

Scheduling Initial Case Management Conference and Establishing Website. In its first pretrial order, the MDL court set a date and agenda for an initial case management conference for all actions. Pretrial Order No. 1, *In re Volkswagen "Clean Diesel" MDL*, No. 15-MD-2672-CRB (JSC) (Doc. 336) (N.D. Cal. Dec. 9, 2015) at 1–2. The court also established a case website, to include "dates and times of upcoming proceedings, along with significant court orders and other documents." *Id.* at 4. All of the orders listed in this appendix are available at the website, http://www.cand.uscourts.gov/crb/vwmdl.

Appointment of Lead Counsel and Steering Committees. A major task for the MDL judge is the appointment of lead counsel and members of the plaintiffs' steering committee ("PSC"). Those attorneys have primary responsibility for representing plaintiffs' interests in the MDL. In the *VW* case, the court appointed lead counsel, along with 21 lawyers from firms across the country to serve on the PSC. *See* Pretrial Order No. 2: Applications for Appointment of Plaintiffs' Lead Counsel and Steering Committee Members, *In re Volkswagen "Clean Diesel" MDL*, No. 15-MD-2672-CRB (JSC) (Doc. 336) (N.D. Cal. Dec. 22, 2015); Pretrial Order No. 7: Order Appointing Plaintiffs' Lead Counsel,

Plaintiffs' Steering Committee, and Government Coordinating Counsel, *In re Volkswagen "Clean Diesel" MDL*, No. 15-MD-2672-CRB (JSC) (Doc. 1084) (N.D. Cal. Jan. 21, 2016).

Common Benefit Work. In MDL proceedings, payment for the plaintiffs' lead counsel and steering committee comes out of a "common benefit fund." The MDL judge issued an order establishing a protocol for common benefit work and expenses. *See* Pretrial Order No. 11: Protocol for Common Benefit Work and Expenses, *In re Volkswagen "Clean Diesel" MDL*, No. 15-MD-2672-CRB (JSC) (Doc. 1254) (N.D. Cal. Feb. 25, 2016).

Initial Case Management. Initial case management orders provide the groundwork for various stages of an MDL. The MDL judge issued an initial case management order in the *VW* case. *See* Pretrial Order No. 8: Initial Case Management, *In re Volkswagen "Clean Diesel" MDL*, No. 15-MD-2672-CRB (JSC) (Doc. 1087) (N.D. Cal. Jan. 22, 2016).

Discovery Orders. Discovery orders set out the protocol for both plaintiffs' and defense counsel, such as the requirement that defense counsel serve all discovery requests on plaintiffs' lead counsel. For the *VW* discovery order, *see* Pretrial Order No. 9: Discovery Schedule, *In re Volkswagen "Clean Diesel" MDL*, No. 15-MD-2672-CRB (JSC) (Doc. 1252) (N.D. Cal. Feb. 25, 2016).

Preservation of Documents. It is frequently necessary to ensure that key documents, particularly electronically stored information ("ESI"), are preserved. For the *VW* preservation order, *see* Pretrial Order No. 15: Order Regarding the Preservation of Documents and Electronically stored Information, *In re Volkswagen "Clean Diesel" MDL*, No. 15-MD-2672-CRB (JSC) (Doc. 1379) (N.D. Cal. Mar. 24, 2016).

Appointment of Special Settlement Master. In some MDL proceedings, the judge may decide to appoint a "Special Settlement Master" to facilitate settlement discussions. In the *VW* MDL, the MDL judge appointed a special master for settlement purposes. *See* Pretrial Order No. 6: Order Appointing Robert S. Mueller III as Settlement Master, *In re Volkswagen "Clean Diesel" MDL*, No. 15-MD-2672-CRB (JSC) (Doc. 973) (N.D. Cal. Jan. 19, 2016).

Granting Approval of the Settlement. Settling an MDL is often a lengthy, multi-step process. In the *VW* litigation, a proposed settlement was preliminarily approved in July of 2016. It applied to the 2.0-liter class of plaintiffs (*i.e.*, those plaintiffs who purchased 2.0-liter vehicles from VW). *See* Amended Order Granting Preliminary Approval of Settlement, *In re Volkswagen "Clean Diesel" MDL*, No. 15-MD-2672-CRB (JSC) (N.D. Cal. July 29, 2016), Docket No. 1698. In October 2016, after full briefing, consideration of objections, and a fairness hearing, the MDL judge entered an order granting final approval of the settlement. *See* Order Granting Final Approval of the 2.0-Liter TDI Consumer and Reseller Dealership Class Action Settlement, *In re Volkswagen "Clean Diesel" MDL*, No. 15-MD-2672-CRB (JSC) (Doc. 2102) (N.D. Cal. Oct. 25, 2016).

There was also a separate settlement involving 3.0-liter vehicles. *See* Order Granting Preliminary Approval of the Consumer and Reseller Dealership 3.0-Liter Class Action Settlement, No. 15-MD-2672-CRB (Doc. 2919) (N.D. Cal. Feb. 16, 2017); Order Granting Final Approval of the Consumer and Reseller Dealership 3.0-Liter Class Action Settlement, No. 15-MD-2672-CRB (Doc. 3229) (N.D. Cal. May 17, 2018).

Appeal of Attorneys' Fees. The fee award in VW was appealed to the Ninth Circuit. *See In re Volkswagen "Clean Diesel" MDL*, 914 F.3d 623 (9th Cir. 2019). The MDL judge awarded $175 million in attorneys' fees and costs to class counsel for common-benefit work, while denying 244 fee applications from non-class counsel. Non-class counsel appealed the denial of fees to the Ninth Circuit, which affirmed the district court. The appellate court found that "the district court did not abuse its discretion when it determined that the efforts of non-Class Counsel for which they sought fees did not benefit the class such that they would be entitled to compensation." *Id.* at 642. Although non-class counsel "worked diligently and presumably competently for their clients," the court of appeals found "no indication that any of these efforts actually benefited the class[.]" *Id.* at 645. The U.S. Supreme Court denied certiorari on October 7, 2019. *Nagel Rice, LLP v. Volkswagen Group of America, Inc.,* No. 18-1503, ___ S. Ct. ___, 2019 WL 4923470 (Oct. 7, 2019).

APPENDIX D

TABLE OF SECONDARY SOURCES

[2018 Calendar Statistics] United States Judicial Panel on Multidistrict Litigation, Calendar Year Statistics: January Through December 2018, https://www.jpml.uscourts.gov/sites/jpml/files/JPML_Calendar_Year_Statistics-2018.pdf, 16, 19

[2018 Fiscal Year Statistics] United States Judicial Panel on Multidistrict Litigation, Statistical Analysis of Multidistrict Litigation Under 28 U.S.C. § 1407, Fiscal Year 2018, https://www.jpml.uscourts.gov/sites/jpml/files/JPML_Statistical_Analysis_of_Multidistrict_Litigation-FY-2018.pdf, 12

[Advisory Committee April 2018 Agenda Book] Advisory Committee on Civil Rules, Civil Rules Agenda Book, April 10, 2018, https://www.uscourts.gov/sites/default/files/2018-04-civil-rules-agenda-book.pdf, 367

[Advisory Committee April 2019 Agenda Book] Advisory Committee on Civil Rules, Civil Rules Agenda Book, April 2–3, 2019, https://www.uscourts.gov/sites/default/files/2019-04_civil_rules_agenda_book.pdf, 354

[Alvaré] Dana Alvaré, Vying for Lead in the "Boys' Club": Understanding the Gender Gap in Multidistrict Litigation Leadership Appointments (2017), 371, 373

American Law Institute, Complex Litigation Project (1994), 379

[Baker] Lynn A. Baker, Mass Torts and the Pursuit of Ethical Finality, 85 Fordham L. Rev. 1943 (2017), 260

[Beisner, Miller & Rubin] John Beisner, Jessica Miller & Gary Rubin, Selling Lawsuits, Buying Trouble: Third-Party Litigation Funding in the United States, U.S. Chamber Inst. for Legal Reform (2009), *available at* https://www.instituteforlegalreform.com/uploads/sites/1/thirdpartylitigationfinancing.pdf, 183

[Beisner & Schwartz] John H. Beisner & Jordan M. Schwartz, U.S. Chamber Institute for Legal Reform, MDL Imbalance: Why Defendants Need Timely Access to Interlocutory Review (Apr. 2019), *available at* https://www.instituteforlegalreform.com/uploads/sites/1/MDL-Defendent-Interlocutory-Review-Timely-Access.pdf, 313

[Bellwether Guide] Melissa J. Whitney, Bellwether Trials in MDL Proceedings: A Guide for Transferee Judges (Fed. Judicial Ctr), *available at* https://www.fjc.gov/content/338847/bellwether-trials-mdl-proceedings-guide-transferee-judges, 224, 226–231

[Berenson] Alex Berenson, Merck Agrees to Settle Vioxx Suits for $4.85 Billion, N.Y. Times, Nov. 9, 2007, 238

[Bock] Jordan F. Bock, Note, All Disputes Must Be Brought Here: Atlantic Marine and the Future of Multidistrict Litigation, 106 Cal. L. Rev. 1657 (2018), 129

[Bone] Robert G. Bone, Settlement and the "Good" Judge, 38 Rev. Litig. 101 (forthcoming 2019), 377

[Bradt (Fordham)] Andrew D. Bradt, The Looming Battle for Control of Multidistrict Litigation in Historical Perspective, 87 Fordham L. Rev. 87 (2018), 3

[Bradt (Notre Dame)] Andrew D. Bradt, The Shortest Distance: Direct Filing and Choice of Law in Multidistrict Litigation, 88 Notre Dame L. Rev. 759 (2012), 165–167, 292–293

[Bradt (Penn.)] Andrew D. Bradt, "A Radical Proposal": The Multidistrict Litigation Act of 1968, 165 U. Pa. L. Rev. 831 (2017), 5, 9–12

[Bradt (William & Mary)] Andrew D. Bradt, The Long Arm of Multidistrict Litigation, 59 Wm. & Mary L. Rev. 1165 (2017), 70, 306–307

[Bradt & Clopton] Andrew D. Bradt & Zachary D. Clopton, MDL v. Trump: The Puzzle of Public Law in Multidistrict Litigation, 112 Nw. U.L. Rev. Online 85 (2018), 7

[Bradt & Rave I] Andrew D. Bradt & D. Theodore Rave, The Information-Forcing Role of the Judge in Multidistrict Litigation, 105 Calif. L. Rev. 1259 (2017), 260, 379

[Bradt & Rave II] Andrew D. Bradt & D. Theodore Rave, It's Good to Have the "Haves" on Your Side: A Defense of Repeat Players in Multidistrict Litigation, 108 Geo. L. Rev. ___ (forthcoming 2019), 178, 366, 372

[Cox & Walker] Brandon Cox & Charissa Walker, Your Case Has Been Remanded by the MDL Court—Now What?, Law360, Feb. 9, 2018, *available at* https://www.tuckerellis.com/webfiles/Your%20Case%20Has%20Been%20Remanded%20By%20The%20MDL%20Court%20%20Now%20What.pdf, 333

[DeGaris] Annesley H. DeGaris, An Introduction to Multidistrict Litigation: Practice and Procedure, 77 Ala. Law. 180 (2016), 48–49, 331

[Devine] Brian Devine, Letter to Committee on Rules of Practice and Procedure, June 25, 2019, *available at* https://www.uscourts.gov/sites/default/files/19-cv-p-suggestion_devine_0.pdf, 313, 353, 359

[Dodge] Jaime Dodge, Facilitative Judging: Organizational Design in Mass-Multidistrict Litigation, 64 Emory L. J. 329 (2014), 174, 176, 182, 338

[Dodson] Scott Dodson, Plaintiff Personal Jurisdiction and Venue Transfer, 117 Mich. L. Rev. 1463 (2019), 297, 305, 307

[Engstrom] Nora Freeman Engstrom, Missing the Forest for the Trees: The Lessons of Lone Pine, 129 Yale L.J. __ (forthcoming 2019), 205

[Erichson (Vanderbilt)] Howard M. Erichson, Response, What MDL and Class Actions Have in Common, 70 Vand. L. Rev. En Banc 29 (2017), 256

[Erichson & Zipursky] Howard M. Erichson & Benjamin C. Zipursky, Consent Versus Closure, 96 Cornell L. Rev. 265 (2011), 259, 263

[Fallon] Eldon E. Fallon, Common Benefit Fees in Multidistrict Litigation, 74 La. L. Rev. 371 (2014), 29, 49, 173, 180–181, 266–268

[Fallon, Grabill & Wynne] Eldon E. Fallon, Jeremy T. Grabill, & Robert Pitard Wynne, Bellwether Trials in Multidistrict Litigation, 82 Tul. L. Rev. 2323 (2008), 224–227, 231, 233, 235–240

[Fed. Civil Caseload] Federal Civil Caseload is Now Majority MDL, https://docs.wixstatic.com/ugd/6c49d6_a6ee7cca9e3749878bf0c650d2c19e67.pdf, 12

[Frankel] Alison Frankel, A handful of plaintiffs' lawyers dominates MDL litigation. Is that a problem?, Reuters, Apr. 27, 2017, https://www.reuters.com/article/otc-mdl-idUSKBN17T33G, 377

[Gluck] Abbe R. Gluck, Unorthodox Civil Procedure: Modern Multidistrict Litigation's Place in the Textbook Understandings of Civil Procedure, 165 U. Pa. L. Rev. 1669 (2017), 4–6, 19, 132, 165, 177, 198, 206, 217–218, 220–221, 225, 321, 339, 353, 371–372

[Hanks] Hon. George C. Hanks, Jr., Searching from Within: The Role of Magistrate Judges in Federal Multi-District Litigation, 8 Fed. Cts. L. Rev. 35 (2015), 217–218, 339

[Hellerstein, Henderson & Twerski] Alvin K. Hellerstein, James A. Henderson, Jr. & Aaron D. Twerski, Managerial Judging: The 9/11 Responders' Tort Litigation, 98 Cornell L. Rev. 127 (2012), 228

[Hensler] Deborah R. Hensler, Third-Party Financing of Class Action Litigation in the United

[Hodges Interview] Interview with Wm. Terrell Hodges, Chair of Judicial Panel Sees Role as Gatekeeper, The Third Branch, Nov. 2005, *available at* https://www.jpml.uscourts.gov/sites/jpml/files/The%20Third%20Branch%20-%20November-2005-Hodges%20Interview.pdf, 86

[Issacharoff] Samuel Issacharoff, Private Claims, Aggregate Rights, 2008 Sup. Ct. Rev. 183 (2008), 376

[Klonoff (Class Action Nutshell)] Robert H. Klonoff, Class Actions and Other Multi-Party Litigation in a Nutshell (5th ed. 2017), 32, 35–36, 252–253, 255

[Klonoff (Wash. U.)], The Decline of Class Actions, 90 Wash. U. L. Rev. 729 (2013), 29

[Lahav] Alexandra D. Lahav, A Primer on Bellwether Trials, 37 Rev. Litig. 185 (2018), 224, 227, 229, 235

[LCJ Proposals] Lawyers for Civil Justice, MDL Practices and the Need for FRCP Amendments: Proposals for Discussion with the MDL/TPLF Subcommittee of the Advisory Committee on Civil Rules (2018), *available at* https://www.lfcj.com/uploads/1/1/2/0/112061707/lcj_memo_-_mdl__tplf_proposals_for_discussion_9-14-18__004_.pdf, 357, 362–364, 366–368, 381

[LCJ, Rules 4 MDLs], https://www.rules4mdls.com/copy-of-new-data-on-products-liabil, 12

[Lee, Borden, Williams & Scott] Emery G. Lee III, Catherine R. Borden, Margaret S. Williams, and Kevin M. Scott, Multidistrict Centralization: An Empirical Examination, 12 J. Empirical Legal Stud. 211 (2015), 16

[Manual] Manual for Complex Litigation, Fourth, (Fed. Judicial Center 2004), *available at* https://www.uscourts.gov/sites/default/files/mcl4.pdf, 7–8, 38, 88, 95, 168, 171, 179, 186, 189, 207, 228, 243, 260, 325–326, 330–331, 333, 337–340

[Marcus (Tulane)] Richard L. Marcus, Cure-All for an Era of Dispersed Litigation? Toward A Maximalist Use of the Multidistrict Litigation Panel's Transfer Power, 82 Tul. L. Rev. 2245 (2008), 5, 91, 145

[Marcus (Yale)] Richard L. Marcus, Conflicts Among Circuits and Transfers Within the Federal Judicial System, 93 Yale L.J. 677 (1984), 288

[MDL Overview] Law360, To Transfer or Not to Transfer: An MDL Overview (Jan. 30, 2012), 43

[MDL Standards] MDL Standards and Best Practices for Large and Mass Tort MDLS, Duke Law School Ctr. for Judicial Studies (2014), *available at* https://law.duke.edu/sites/default/files/centers/judicialstudies/MDL_Standards_and_Best_Practices_2014-REVISED.pdf, 5, 15, 174, 176–189, 201, 205, 207–208, 220, 228, 230–232, 243, 251, 266, 272–273, 277, 325, 331–333, 338–341, 372

[MDL Statistics Report, July 16, 2019] MDL Statistics Report—Distribution of Pending MDL Dockets by District, July 16, 2019, *available at* https://www.jpml.uscourts.gov/sites/jpml/files/Pending_MDL_Dockets_By_Actions_Pending-July-16-2019.pdf, 15–16, 133

[A. Miller] Arthur R. Miller, Simplified Pleading, Meaningful Days in Court, and Trials on the Merits:

Reflections on the Deformation of Federal Procedure, 88 N.Y.U. L. Rev. 286 (2013), 11

[Mueller] Christopher B. Mueller, Taking a Second Look at MDL Product Liability Settlements: Somebody Needs To Do It, 65 U. Kan. L. Rev. 531 (2017), 174, 176

[Mullenix (Emory)] Linda S. Mullenix, Ending Class Actions As We Know Them: Rethinking the American Class Action, 64 Emory L.J. 399 (2014), 13

[Mullenix (Litigation)] Linda S. Mullenix, Policing MDL Non-Class Settlements: Empowering Judges Through the All Writs Act, 37 Rev. Litig. 129 (2018), 258, 378

[Nelson] Zach Nelson, Personal Jurisdiction Problems in Multidistrict Litigation (manuscript on file at Lewis & Clark Law School), 307

[Pollis] Andrew S. Pollis, The Need for Non-Discretionary Interlocutory Appellate Review in Multidistrict Litigation, 79 Fordham L. Rev. 1643 (2011), 358

[Rave] D. Theodore Rave, Closure Provisions in MDL Settlements, 85 Fordham L. Rev. 2175 (2017), 246–247

[Rensberger] Jeffrey L. Rensberger, The Metasplit: The Law Applied After Transfer in Federal Question Cases, 2018 Wis. L. Rev. 847 (2018), 286–290, 292

[Rhodes] Blake M. Rhodes, Comment, The Judicial Panel on Multidistrict Litigation: Time for Rethinking, 140 U. Pa. L. Rev. 711 (1991), 117

[Richards] Daniel A. Richards, Note, An Analysis of the Judicial Panel on Multidistrict Litigation's Selection of Transferee District and Judge, 78 Fordham L. Rev. 311 (2009), 114, 116–117, 121–123, 126, 137

[Rothman] Alan Rothman, And Now a Word From The Panel: 4 MDL Lessons at 40, Mondaq.com, July 29, 2019, http://www.mondaq.com/unitedstates/x/830948/trials+appeals+compensation/And+Now+A+Word+From+The+Panel+4+MDL+Lessons+At+40, 16

[Rothstein Pocket Guide] Barbara J. Rothstein & Catherine R. Borden, Federal Judicial Center, Judicial Panel on Multidistrict Litigation, Managing Multidistrict Litigation in Products Liability Cases, A Pocket Guide for Transferee Judges (2011), *available at* https://www.fjc.gov/sites/default/files/2012/MDLGdePL.pdf, 179, 200–201, 207–208, 220–221, 226

[Rowe] Thomas D. Rowe, Jurisdictional and Transfer Proposals for Complex Litigation, 10 Rev. Litig. 325 (1991), 380

[Rubenstein (Attorney Fee Digest)] William B. Rubenstein, On What a "Common Benefit Fee" Is, Is Not, and Should Be, 3 Class Action Attorney Fee Digest 87 (2009), 276

[Rubenstein (Newberg)] William B. Rubenstein, 4 Newberg On Class Actions (5th Ed. 2018), 229, 234

[Saack] Amy L. Saack, Note, Global Settlements in Non-Class Mass Torts, 21 Lewis & Clark L. Rev. 847 (2017), 243, 246, 257, 263, 378

[Savage] Zachary B. Savage, Note, Scaling Up: Implementing Issue Preclusion in Mass Tort Litigation Through Bellwether Trials, 88 N.Y.U. L. Rev. 439 (2013), 233–234

[Schwarzer, Hirsch & Sussman] William W. Schwarzer, Alan Hirsch & Edward Sussman, Judicial Federalism: A Proposal to Amend the Multidistrict Litigation Statute to Permit Discovery Coordination of Large-Scale Litigation Pending in State and Federal Courts, 73 Tex. L. Rev. 1529 (1995), 380

[Sekula] Thomas Sekula, Note, Selective Settlement and the Integrity of the Bellwether Process, 97 Tex. L. Rev. 859 (2018), 366

[Sherman (Louisiana)] Edward F. Sherman, When Remand Is Appropriate in Multidistrict Litigation, 75 La. L. Rev. 455 (2014), 230, 232

[Sherman (Tulane)] Edward F. Sherman, The MDL Model for Resolving Complex Litigation if a Class Action is Not Possible, 82 Tul. L. Rev. 2205 (2008), 238, 251, 335–336, 341–342

[Silver (Fordham)] Charles Silver, The Responsibilities of Lead Lawyers and Judges in Multidistrict Litigation, 79 Fordham L. Rev. 1985 (2011), 182, 186

[Silver & Miller] Charles Silver & Geoffrey P. Miller, The Quasi-Class Action Method of Managing Multi-

District Litigations: Problems and a Proposal, 63 Vand. L. Rev. 107 (2010), 180

[Smith] Douglas G. Smith, Resolution of Common Questions in MDL Proceedings, 66 Kan. L. Rev. 219 (2017), 201, 205, 211–212, 216

[Tighe] Patrick A. Tighe, Committee on Rules of Prac. and Proc., Survey of Federal and State Disclosure Rules Regarding Litig. Funding (Feb. 7, 2018), *in* Advisory Committee on Civil Rules, Civil Rules Agenda Book, April 10, 2018, http://www.uscourts.gov/sites/default/files/2018-04-civil-rules-agenda-book.pdf, 369

[Vance Speech] Judge Sarah S. Vance, JPML Chair, Remarks at the Duke Law Mass Tort MDL Program for Judicial Conference Committees (Oct. 8, 2015), *reprinted in* Advisory Committee on Civil Rules Agenda Book at 179, *available at* https://www.uscourts.gov/sites/default/files/2018-04-civil-rules-agenda-book.pdf (last visited June 9, 2019), 5, 13–14, 68, 70

[Varner] Chilton Davis Varner, The Beginning of MDL Consolidation: Should Cases Be Aggregated and Where?, 37 Rev. Litig. 227 (2018), 48

[Wee] Melissa Wee, TC Heartland v. Kraft and the Resurrection of the Place of Incorporation or "Regular and Established Place of Business" Test for Patent Venue, 33 Berkeley Tech. L.J. 981 (2018), 63

[Willging & Lee] Thomas E. Willging & Emery G. Lee III, From Class Actions to Multidistrict

Consolidations: Aggregate Mass-Tort Litigation After Ortiz, 58 Kan. L. Rev. 775 (2010), 14, 19, 29

[M.S. Williams] Margaret S. Williams, The Effect of Multidistrict Litigation on the Federal Judiciary over the Past 50 Years, 53 Ga. L. Rev. 1245 (forthcoming 2019), 12–19, 107, 114, 126, 133, 136, 139, 373

[Williams & George] Margaret S. Williams & Tracey E. George, Who Will Manage Complex Civil Litigation? The Decision to Transfer and Consolidate Multidistrict Litigation, 10 J. Empirical Legal Stud. 424 (2013), 3, 10, 19, 39, 42–43, 70, 111, 113–118, 125–128, 133, 136–137, 139

[Wright & Miller, et al.] Charles Alan Wright et al., Procedure Before the Multidistrict Panel, 15 Fed. Prac. & Proc. Juris. § 3865 (4th ed.), 165–166

MDL Court Websites:

[*Ashley Madison* MDL website] https://www.moed.uscourts.gov/mdl/415-md-02669-jar, 220

[*Deepwater Horizon* MDL website] http://www.laed.uscourts.gov/OilSpill/OilSpill.htm, 193

[N.D. Ill. MDL links] https://www.ilnd.uscourts.gov/mdl.aspx, 220

[*VW "Clean Diesel"* MDL website] https://www.cand.uscourts.gov/crb/vwmdl, 220

INDEX

References are to Pages
